America's Last Wild Horses

Books by Hope Ryden:

1970 *America's Last Wild Horses*

1972 *Mustangs: A Return to the Wild*

1975 *God's Dog*

1981 *Bobcat Year*

1989 *Lily Pond*

1999 *Wild Horses I Have Known*

America's
Last Wild Horses

The Classic Study of the Mustangs—
Their Pivotal Role in the History of the West,
Their Return to the Wild, and the
Ongoing Efforts to Preserve Them

Hope Ryden

Photographs by Hope Ryden

The Lyons Press
Guilford, Connecticut
An imprint of The Globe Pequot Press

In Loving Memory of My Mother and My Father

Portions of Chapter 34 first appeared in the October 1977 issue of *Defenders: The Magazine of Defenders of Wildlife.*

Copyright © 1970, 1978, 1990, and 1999 by Hope Ryden

Update copyright © 1999 by Hope Ryden

First Lyons Press paperback edition, 1999, 2005

New introduction copyright © 2005 by Hope Ryden

The Lyons Press is an imprint of The Globe Pequot Press.

10 9 8 7 6 5 4 3 2 1

Printed in the United States of America

ISBN 1-59228-873-1

The Library of Congress has previously cataloged an earlier (paperback) edition as follows:

Ryden, Hope.
    America's last wild horses / Hope Ryden. —Rev. and updated.
        p. cm.
    Includes bibliographical references and index.
    ISBN 1-55821-976-5
    1. Wild horses—West (U.S.) I. Title.
SF360.3.U6R92   1990
599.72'5—dc20

90-46337
CIP

Contents

America's Last Wild Horses

The More Things Change,
the More They . . .

I've come to the conclusion that horses are unlucky creatures, and wild horses are ill fated. As lovely as they are—their wide-set eyes taking in panoramic views of their rugged habitats; their lithe necks embellished with thick manes (so useful to toss!); their radiant, athletic bodies shiny with color—still, they are denigrated and abused, dismissed as trespassers on our public lands, and time and time again, have needed rescuing from the ill will directed toward them, animals that provide human beings with neither sport nor profit.

This book is a salute to wild horses and tells their story. It also chronicles the many impediments to the way of their survival, the latest of which is unfolding, even as I write. So I shall ignore chronology and place this update not at the end, but ahead of the beginning, because it needs your attention.

It is more than discomfiting to learn that, now, after all the tribulations that America's wild horses have somehow survived over their four-century-long sojourn in the West, they are once again in trouble. This time they are up against the legalization of their slaughter.

How has such a thing happened?

Not surprisingly the answer is: by the political maneuvering of a clever opportunist.

Late into the night, in November of 2004, a rider was tacked on to the U.S. 2005 Appropriations Bill by Montana's Senator Conrad Burns—a former horse and cattle auctioneer. Nobody debated Burns's attachment, because the weary legislators present were not made aware of its existence. Moreover, they were anxious to vote and go home. And so his amendment slipped through and, in so doing, gutted the very essence of the Wild Free-Roaming Horse and Burro Act of 1971 and opened the way for wild horses to be sent to slaughter.

Why did Burns do this?

I can only presume that he expected his action would be applauded by his constituency, a large percentage of whom are stockmen. After all, the removal of so-called worthless horses from public lands could free up cheap grazing permits for the privately owned cattle herds that share the wild horses' habitats. For every horse that the Bureau of Land Management (BLM) eliminates from the public domain, a cow and a calf can replace it at the ridiculously low cost of $1.79 a month to the rancher. (When it comes to grass consumption, as measured by the bureau's managers, one horse, whatever its size, counts as a cow and a calf.)

Burns's stealthy mischief that night did not remain a secret for long. When horse lovers and humane organizations got wind of it, they were outraged and expressed their anger in letters to Congress and newspapers. The response of legislators was heartening. Congressman Nick Rahall and Representative Ed Whitfield drew up HR 297, a bill which, should it gain hearings and an affirmative vote, would restore the 1971 Wild Free-Roaming Horse and Burro Act to its original no-kill intent, for the language in the original act, unequivocally, states:

> *In no event shall horse remains or any part thereof be sold for any consideration, directly or indirectly (Section 4/d)*

And again:

> *Any person who . . . processes or permits to be processed into products the remains of a wild free roaming horse or burro will be subject to a fine up to $2,000 and/or imprisonment up to one year (Section 8/4)*

I am well acquainted with this language. Together with the late Velma Johnson (familiarly known as Wild Horse Annie) and the late Joan Blue of the American Horse Protection Association, I had conferred with Congressman Walter Baring during the drafting of the legislation. But now, thirty-four years later, our carefully chosen words no longer shielded wild horses from the brutality of the abattoir. Senator Burns had found a way to circumvent them.

In the Senate, too, Robert C. Byrd of Virginia (known to many as the "Father of the Senate") introduced S576 to restore the prohibition on the commercial sale of wild, free-roaming horses and burros. But several months passed and no action was taken in either chamber to move these bills. With war in Iraq and Social Security issues and judicial nominations dominating the congressional agendas, wild horses were not of paramount concern.

Then, in late April, the carnage began. News that six wild horses had been slaughtered at a Belgian-owned plant in DeKalb, Illinois, brought the issue back to life. As e-mails from saddened wild horse lovers grew too numerous for me to answer, the Associated Press reported thirty-five additional mustangs had met the same fate. This revelation was followed by a report from two agricultural inspectors who, during a routine check of the DeKalb plant, observed the delivery of another truckload of mustangs, sixteen in number.

Whatever negative views that many BLM field personnel frequently reveal in regard to wild horses, no one in the bureau's Washington office was happy about these developments. For one thing, it was bad press for an agency that had been charged by Congress with the management of the wild horse herds. And so the BLM scrambled to rescue the latest sixteen animals in line to have their throats slit. A hasty call to Ford Motor Company's Mustang Division brought $19,000, money enough to buy back the doomed horses and pay for their upkeep until the BLM could pick them up.

But trafficking in wild horses did not stop. When word that thirty-six more mustangs were passing through Nebraska en route to the same Illinois slaughtering plant, the BLM acted swiftly and intercepted the rig, diverting it to one of its mustang holding facilities in the Midwest. Salvaging mustangs had, suddenly, become a high priority issue at the BLM. But how much longer could it intervene in slaughter that had become legal?

Meanwhile, the Burns amendment was sabotaging the bureau's Wild Horse Adoption Program, which, until now, had served as a benign method of disposing of horses that had been "excessed" from the wild. It worked this way:

For a nominal fee, screened individuals could "adopt" a wild horse, but would not be given title to it for one year. By that time, it was assumed, the adopter would have invested so much care and money in the animal that no profit could be made from its sale to a slaughterhouse. Thus the program not only promoted compliance with the law, which prohibited commerce in wild horse parts, it also attracted self-selected people, whose interest in owning a wild horse was genuine.

The Burns amendment changed all that by mandating the sale of all corralled horses older than ten, as well as all younger horses that have not been selected for adoption after being looked over three times. It even goes so far as to declare that "any excess animal sold under this provision shall no longer be a wild free-roaming or burro for purposes of this Act."

So what did this do to the adoption program ?

Who now would bother with the rigamarole involved in adopting, when any number of passed-over horses have been made available for immediate purchase? For a fifty- or hundred-dollar bill, anyone can walk away with a three-time reject and do what he pleases with it. Moreover, in corrals packed with wild horses, who on earth is checking teeth to determine the animals' ages? And surely no records will be kept on how many times any one of the horses has been passed over.

Where now are the safeguards to protect the animals, to guarantee them humane outcomes? The horses currently being held are up for grabs, all twenty thousand of them.

And why on earth were so many gathered in the first place? In the history of the wild horse and burro program, never have the holding facilities teemed with so many wild horses. What could the bureau be thinking?

The mess that the BLM has created by gathering twenty thousand horses, certainly, must have played into Senator Burns's desire to legalize their sale. The sorrow of it all is that the adoption program had worked well and would have continued to do so, had a reasonable number of animals been removed from the range. I know this from letters I receive from ecstatic people who describe the animals they adopted and trained as "super intelligent," "gorgeous," "loveable," "humorous," "wonderful," "magical."

One has to wonder if the BLM was de facto complicit in what Burns wrought by rounding up more horses than the adoption program could absorb, thus inviting the senator's self-serving final solution to the matter.

And what of the mustangs left in the wild? How are they faring after their numbers have been so decimated? If the bureau's figures are correct, only 37,000 are out there, scattered in isolated populations across nine states. Some herds have lost so many members there is reason to fear they may no longer be viable and will die out. Yet the bureau plans to further reduce numbers by 9,800.

It is worth noting that such drastic culling will reduce the wild horse population to fewer animals than existed in 1971, when Congress saw fit to protect them.[1] It was certainly not the intention of Congress to manage them at such a perilous level.

By contrast, livestock use of the public domain has increased dramatically. Although range managers at the Bureau of Land Management could not tell me how many head of cattle, sheep, and goats graze on our public domain, by comparing the disproportionate number of AUMs (animal units per month) the bureau allots to livestock as compared to wild horses, I made a shocking discovery: privately owned herds consume sixty-nine times more forage than wild horses. Clearly, livestock numbers and the impact of livestock on the public domain greatly exceed that of wild horses. Yet it is the wild horse that is singled out as a threat to watersheds and to the environmental health of the public lands, an allegation unsupported by actual data.

The rationale that the BLM gives for such drastic removals is that the wild horses are posing a threat to watersheds and to the environmental health of the public lands, an allegation the agency is unable to support with actual data. On the contrary, what environmental analysis it has carried out shows that cattle, not wild horses, are the culprits.

In any case, it is not as though the BLM lacks funding to upgrade any wild horse habitats that need it. In its 2005 budget, Congress provided the bureau with $39 million for the wild horse and burro program. Unfortunately, almost all of this is being spent on roundups and the upkeep of doomed horses, languishing in crowded corrals.

So what now can be done for all the wretched and dispirited captives in BLM custody?

I propose that the BLM truck them back to the herds from which they were plucked. They will be of real value there. Once they have reintegrated with their former bands, they will survive perfectly well on their own at no cost to taxpayers. That is what wild horses do—survive on their own. That is what distinguishes mustangs from their domesticated cousins. That is what makes them so interesting to folks who like to catch sight of them.

I know this from my own experience and also through the letters I receive from ecstatic people who have been privileged to sight wild horses at a watering hole or who observed two stallions sparring or who watched a new mother introduce her new foal to her harem sisters.

Yet at this writing, thousands of imprisoned horses are headed for a gruesome death. My only hope is that the public will care enough about them to demand that Congress hold hearings to repeal Burns's destructive amendment.

It must not end as it is. We can do better.

[1] Although at the time of the passage of the wild horse and burro act, the bureau stated that the wild horse population stood at 17,000, that figure was suspect, as it had been touted, unchanged, for five years. So in 1982, at the request of Congress, a panel of top scientists, appointed by the National Science Foundation, developed data on wild horse population dynamics and, by means of retrogression, determined that in 1971 the horse herds had to have numbered at least 35,000.

1. The Controversial Horses

It is not surprising that when I set out on the track of wild horses, guided by scant information, vague locations, and uncertain horse counts, residents near wild-horse habitats frequently were reluctant to help me, and whenever I inquired about the local horse bands, I received discreetly polite but ambiguous answers:

"Yes, there are horses back in those hills," people would admit vaguely.

But when I asked to go back and see them, I was told it would be impossible.

"The horses are too smart," they would explain. "They'll move ahead as you approach. You'll never get close enough to see them."

And so I began to wonder: Are there really horses back in those hills? Or are these people trying to get rid of me? For Westerners who live near wild-horse habitats had good reason for being suspicious of strangers who came around asking questions. It often happened that, following the appearance of such a stranger, nearby canyons and mountaintops no longer rang with the whinnies and nickertalk of wild horses, and a familiar black, white, or buckskin stallion that habitually posed on the rimrocks and ledges overhanging a little Western town was never seen again.

Profiteers, who sold meat to dog-food canneries or mink farms, combed the West for wild horses and flushed herds from remote hideaways, gathering them in one-day roundups for shipment to rendering factories—the polite name for slaughterhouses. Usually, these roundups were conducted as profitably and, as a consequence, as inhumanely as possible. Many horses were shot, blinded, trampled, and impaled in the process.

But in time, when local people no longer suspected me of being an agent for a meat packer, the day would arrive when someone would say, "You really want to see those horses? . . . Okay, I'll take you." And off we would go in a four-wheel-drive car into the hills.

That was how I became acquainted with the existence, the behavior, and the history of many of the wild-horse bands that live in ten of our Western states.

In 1967, the Bureau of Land Management estimated that seventeen thousand wild horses were inhabiting the public domain, and they guessed that a few thousand more probably lived on Indian-reservation lands. A century earlier, however, wild horses numbered in the millions, and their decline was not occurring at a steady rate, but was accelerating. Though the wild horse could still be preserved, immediate attention, knowledge, and legislation would be required to save it.

At that time the wild horse was not protected by any existing wildlife law, Because it was classified as a *feral* animal (meaning a domestic stray), all laws that apply to *wild* animals—such as deer, moose, antelope, and even rabbits—did not apply to it. Therefore, in a sense, it was open season on wild horses twelve months of every year, and a hunting license was not required to shoot, gather, trap, or torment them. However, since the wild horse was not a target animal (it is neither meat for the table, nor is its head a trophy to be mounted and hung over a mantelpiece), it held little interest for sportsmen, who often work to conserve game animals. Who then was stalking the wild horse, and why should its existence have been so imperiled?

Probably no animal in North America is so controversial as the wild horse, nor does any creature have so many and such diverse enemies. Whether or not these enemies are justified in their negative attitude toward the wild horse will be examined in depth. For the moment, however, a few of these enemies and their motives can be briefly mentioned:

The wild horse has been the scapegoat for stockmen, who blamed it for the deterioration of the range.

The wild horse has been victimized by certain sportsmen's associations that wanted it removed from its secluded retreats so that those habitats could be stocked with target animals.

The wild horse has been the prey of profiteers who chased and corraled it and sold it to dog-food canneries or fur raisers.

But more insidious than any of these tangible enemies, the wild horse has been the object of widespread prejudice, which is most difficult to combat because its origin is forgotten.

Perhaps the only way to understand all this is to examine the role of the Plains horse during the four centuries that it inhabited Indian Territory in the West. Though its role was often positive (it helped Lewis and Clark, the early trappers, the infant cattle industry, the Republic of Texas, and untold numbers of pioneers and early ranchers), it also became an impediment to the aims of the first settlements. For it was the Plains horse, more than any other single asset, that enabled the Indians to perpetuate their nomadic hunting style of life at the expense of a farming culture being imported to the West by the whites. And though the struggle between these two cultures has long been resolved, the Indians having been broken and corralled, many of their ponies never submitted to internment. And some of the descendants of those that escaped still live wild and free, defiant of fences, and resistant to man's domination.

The derogatory term "Cayuse" by which a wildhorse is frequently labeled provides the essential clue to its unpopularity. "Cayuse" was the name of a now-extinct Indian tribe, once renowned for the great number of horses they possessed. Today, all horses that bear a resemblance to any Indian stock are still referred to as Cayuse horses. And most wild horses are Cayuses.

Perhaps these living reminders of an almost obliterated Indian culture are despised because they not only continue to enjoy a free-roaming existence in the wilderness, but haunt the American conscience as well. Bands that have managed to elude their persecutors are wary, careful to avoid any encounter with men, so it was not surprising that in 1967 when I set out to track them, local people who loved the horses guarded their secret whereabouts.

Once I earned their trust, however, I learned that wild-horse enthusiasts recognize and know about each other. Wyoming wild-horse lovers told me whom to contact to find horses in Nevada, and once I had been accepted and trusted in one area, I was invariably directed to another person or source who could help me locate horses elsewhere, whether in a distant state or the remote past.

2. The Question of Origin

Though I have loved horses all of my life, the wild horse captivated my affection and seized my interest in a new way. I was fascinated by him. Where had he come from?

The wild horse in America has a romantic history that dates back nearly four centuries. His domestic ancestors carried the Conquistadors through an unexplored territory, transformed the Indians' style of life, and gave inspiration to such artists as Remington and Russell. The Age of Exploration might better have been called the Age of the Spanish Horse, for without this particular type of horse, the New World would have remained almost impenetrable. But perhaps the most interesting thing that this horse ever did in America he did for himself when he took his freedom.

The wild horse of the West is not indigenous to America, he is a transplant. But like so many transplants, including the English sparrow, the Chinese pheasant, and man, the wild horse flourished in America.

Columbus carried the first domestic horses to the New World, transporting breeding stock to the West Indies on his second voyage. By the middle of the nineteenth century, the number that had taken their freedom and were grazing in undisturbed peace in the unsettled Western Territories has been variously estimated between five and seven million. A more conservative opinion by J. Frank Dobie, connoisseur of horses and an authority on Western history, places the number at two million. The horse found America a paradise until the white man began to move westward in the last half of the nineteenth century, claiming all the pasturage for himself and leaving nothing for his ancient friend and onetime servant, the wild horse.

Though no horses were found in North America when the Conquistadors began to penetrate the continent, the environment was not alien to the horse. In fact, it was here that the genus *Equus* in its various ancestral forms had evolved, and the modern horse had been absent from the continent for only a relatively brief eight thousand years when the New World was opened to civilization.

The most ancient ancestor of the horse, the tiny, four-toed creature called *eohipus,** opened its large eyes and gazed on the world some fifty million years ago in an area that is now western United States. Its skeleton has been unearthed from fossil beds near Mount Blanco in the Texas Panhandle, and abundant fossil remains, have been found in rich Eocene beds in the Bighorn Basin in Wyoming, within a few miles of the present habitat of the Pryor Mountain wild horses.

Fossil bones of an *eohippus* of the same prehistoric date have also been found near what is now Suffolk, England, where they were turned up by a bricklayer as long ago as 1838. At that early date, the strange skeletal remains were wrongly classified. The skull looked so unlike that of a modern horse that the connection between the two was not realized, and the rodentlike creature was first named *Hyracotherium* by the British.

Notwithstanding the fact that *eohippus* bones have been found in both England and North America, all modern horses are held to be lineal descendants of the American *eohippus*. In the beginning of the Cenozoic era, that amazing period when mammals came into being on the planet and began to display such diversity of form, the British Isles and North America were attached; both formed part of the supercontinent of Laurasia, which included North America, Greenland, and Europe north of the Alps and as far east as the Himalayas.

During the long period when Laurasia was fragmenting and drifting apart, certain land connections remained which permitted animals to migrate back and forth freely, and it was during this time that *eohippus* arose and simultaneously inhabited both what is now England and Texas.

Later, when the connecting land bridges were severed and European *eohippus* was isolated from its American relatives, it took an evolutionary turn that ended in extinction. The North American *eohippus,* on the other hand, created descendants along quite different lines, models with three toes, two toes, and finally with a single hoof. From *Orohippus* to *Merychippus* to *Hipparion,* these creatures gradually became modified into what we know today as *Equus caballus,* or the horse. Since the fossil remains of the horse at every stage of development—from tiny *eohippus*

---

* Because of general use, the word *eohippus* spelled with a small "e" will be used to designate the ancestor of the horse although Hyracotherium is in fact the accurate scientific name.

to the giant form we are familiar with today—have been found only in what is now western United States, the horse, it must be concluded, is a native of North America.

Yet, paradoxically, when Columbus arrived, horses were not found in the New World. All the modifications and types had become extinct on the North American continent. Fortunately, however, for every horse, burro, pony, mule, and zebra alive in the world today, before *eohippus* and its offspring disappeared from the American landscape, many intrepid members of this diverse family had migrated across the land bridge connecting Alaska and Siberia and entered Asia where they had perpetuated themselves and sired the many present-day variations on the horse theme. That, in brief, is the history of the evolution of the horse that is generally accepted by the scientific world.

The earliest horses had some interesting company in America. Camels and giant mastodons browsed in the same habitats. The sudden and, relatively speaking, recent disappearance of all of these animals has long intrigued archeologists who cannot agree on the reason.

Glaciation would not have affected them seriously in the Pleistocene era, since vast areas were no longer covered by the shrinking polar cap, and the survivors that had already weathered the severe glacial epoch were then enjoying a relatively mild climate. Disappearance of proper forage can likewise be dismissed so far as horses are concerned, for they, more than any other animal, were capable of migrating long distances and, in fact, had done so. Fossil evidence indicates that horses had even traveled as far as the tip of South America shortly after the two continents became joined. The variety of forage available over such a vast area would have sustained a certain number of them whatever famine conditions may have existed regionally. Yet no horses survived in either North or South America. Competition from another grazing animal, such as the American bison, has been suggested as the possible cause for the mysterious demise of the horse, but the prairie grasses were wholly suitable to support vast herds of both horses and bison, as proved by the rapid spread of wild horses across the Western plains after they were reintroduced to North America in the sixteenth century. Early trappers and travelers who visited the unsettled West reported seeing enormous numbers of wild horses and "buffalo"* coexisting, grazing side by side in pastoral harmony much like the zebras and wildebeests in Africa.

Referring to the cluster of herd animals eliminated during this period,

---

* Although the "buffalo" is not a true buffalo but a bison, popular usage necessitates the use of the misnomer. Here too bison will be referred to as buffalo.

archeologist P. S. Martin advances a theory that is widely accepted by the scientific community at the present time. He suggests that the Paleolithic Indians may have had a hand in wiping out the native horses and exterminating the aboriginal camels and mastodons as well. He says, "This extinction was postglacial in time and affected in the main the larger animals. The principal factor isolated as cause is the appearance of man."

Ten thousand years ago when late Pleistocene man entered North America, perhaps by way of the Bering Strait, he rapidly traversed the Western Hemisphere, leaving a trail of stone and bone tools which marked his migration routes even to the tip of South America. A brief two thousand years after the appearance of this man in North America, horses and camels were extinct! Their charred bones, along with hunting and butchering tools, have been unearthed from remains of prehistoric cooking sites found wherever man had wandered, leaving little doubt that these two animals were a part of the diet of the early Indians.

Anthropologists, too, suggest that the pressure of the hunting tribes on edible species, combined perhaps with a virulent disease of epidemic proportions, wiped out the horse and the camel. It seems unlikely that either factor *alone* could have accomplished a task of such magnitude, one that took place simultaneously across two continents. If this theory has validity (and it is the only one that has any significant number of adherents in the scientific community), and man did play a part in the extinction of the native horse in America, such an event would someday be a familiar story.

Whatever the explanation, the fact remains that the horse had been extinct in the Western Hemisphere for eight thousand years when Columbus discovered America, and all our wild horses today are descendants of imported domestic stock that have once again reverted to their natural state.* For this reason most North American ecologists do not regard wild horses as native wildlife, and wild horses, therefore, have not been granted sanctuary in our National Parks, which conserve and protect only indigenous animals or animals that were found here when the white man landed.

This policy of excluding nonindigenous animals from national wildlife preserves was based on a 1963 report to the North American Wildlife Conference by a special advisory committee of eminent scientists appointed by Secretary of the Interior Steward L. Udall. The question examined by this committee was: Which of the various communities of

---

* This view is disputed by one group of people who believe that the horse was not extinct here when Columbus landed and that our wild horses are descendants of the native stock. Their theories and rationales will be discussed later.

animals that had existed during different periods of time should the Parks Service restore, re-create, or maintain within its boundaries. To resolve this confused issue, that had resulted from modern man's manipulation of and interference with the balances of nature, a definitive policy was needed. The biotic associations of animals in North American wilderness areas had undergone a great many successive changes since the West had been opened to civilization.

Among the many thoughtful recommendations made by this distinguished committee, one had an adverse effect on existing bands of wild horses. In the final report a recommendation advised that park officials devote their efforts to the preservation of only those animals observed in North America by the first European explorers. Thus, all imported animals that had gone wild, whether goat, hog, or horse, were to be regarded as "undesirable" and not granted sanctuary in the park systems.

A distinction, however, should have been made between those animals that were true exotics, imports that had never before existed in the New World, and the wild horse which had, in fact, evolved here and, except for a brief absence, had been a part of the ecological design of North America for millions of years.

Moreover, the first view that the white man had of much of the West, particularly in the northernmost regions, did indeed include wild horses. It is well documented that the first white men to visit the Plains in the seventeenth century and the Pacific Northwest in the early nineteenth century found wild horses in these regions. Two centuries earlier, horses lost by the Spaniards far to the south had spread to Oregon Country and the northern Plains. Thus the committee's recommendation that the wilderness areas on Park lands be restored to the conditions first observed by white men, should not in many places have excluded the wild horse.

To the despair of wild-horse enthusiasts, however, the unique history and biological background of the wild horse was not pointed out in the generally excellent report. All feral animals and all animals transplanted to America from other continents have since been regarded as "undesirable" and not granted sanctuary in our National Parks.

One wild-horse enthusiast suggested that, since the committee's recommendation has been interpreted so literally, all human beings other than Indians should be barred from our National Parks. After all, as she points out, the white man did not see a counterpart of himself on the Western landscape when he first arrived.

The classification of horses as nonnative does seem arbitrary, for if the horse is not to be considered native in North America where it actually evolved, where would it be regarded as indigenous? The resolution, as applied to wild horses, seems even more equivocal when one considers that our National Parks were set aside to protect native flora and fauna from the predatory impulses of man. But in the particular case of the horse, the Parks were organized just eight thousand years too late. Man, the transplant, had already entered, and, it seems likely, had already destroyed the native American horse.

3. The Question of Blood

When the horse was finally reintroduced to the land that had originally conceived it, *equus caballus* had become transformed. The native horse had been changed physically by the steppes of Asia, the deserts of Africa, and all the countless complicated civilizations that had imposed special demands on it. But the most radical change that had taken place in him was a psychological one. It had become domesticated.

Yet, almost from the moment the horse entered western America, it began exchanging its domestic condition for the hazards of an independent life. No ordinary horse could have made the transition from total dependency to the perils of life in the wilderness with quite the ease of the superb mounts that were brought to the New World by the Spanish Conquistadors. Unmatched for intelligence, endurance, speed, recovery power, and horse sense, the animals bred in Andalusia and Seville during the sixteenth century were without peers in Europe. Only horses with superior stamina could have survived the oppressive sea-crossings to the New World, crossings that often lasted several months. Throughout these miserable trips, the animals were forced to hang in slings, were fed stale hay, and offered little water to drink. Yet, notwithstanding such a debilitating experience, the Spanish horses, when lowered from their rigs, were said to be able to walk off the ships, be mounted, and break trail while bearing burdens almost one quarter their own weight. Had the British or the French possessed such remarkable animals—horses that, moreover, could penetrate the virgin continent without benefit of special grain, cross untrodden mountains unshod, and survive in desert wasteland with nothing but alkaline water to drink—the history of the Southwest might have been written somewhat differently.

The sixteenth-century Spaniards placed such a high value on these extraordinary animals that Spain was accused by her neighbors of developing a "horse culture." Even her music resounded to the rhythm of hoofbeats as castanets clattered to the step of Spain's wonderful horses. And in the wild horses now living in western America there still remains a strong trace of these venerated sixteenth-century Spanish horses; occasionally, even an apparently pure-blooded Spanish horse can be found. To understand the heredity of today's wild horses, the bloodline of the Spanish horse of the Conquest must be examined and appreciated.

In the year A.D. 711, when the Moors invaded and conquered Spain, they did so on the backs of vigorous mounts, born to survive in the inhospitable deserts of North Africa. These Bedouin horses were small but tough, and their hot blood* and fast reflexes made them well suited for combat.

The Mohammedan invaders, bent on proselytizing for Islam and Allah regarded these desert war-horses as sacred, and treated them accordingly. Though in their attitude toward animals in general the Moors were unsentimental, often brutal, they did not hold these war-horses to be animals at all, but rather trusted allies in holy battle. And though they had no compassion for weak, old, injured, or imperfect horses, abandoning a wounded creature for predators to feed upon, they are reputed to have shown a fit horse more deference than they displayed toward their women, extolling the creature in poetry and song and even bringing it into their tents at night.

The heavy European horses that were being ridden by the medieval Spaniards were, by contrast, large, slow, and sturdy, having been bred to carry the weight of the armor-clad knights of the Middle Ages. The Moors, in their lightweight garb, put no extra strain on their swift and delicate horses. Consequently, they easily outmaneuvered the thick-legged, heavily muscled animals from Europe, and the result was victory for the Moors.

The hot-blooded North African horse that so affected the course of Spain's history could trace its ancestry to a mixture of Arabian and Barb stock. The Barb was itself an offshoot of the Arabian horse, having been developed by the Libyans from that breed at an even earlier date. But severity of life in North Africa had modified the Barb horse and it had lost

* All modern horse breeds are called either hot-bloods, cold-bloods, or warm-bloods. The hot-bloods are swift and temperamental types, descended from the Arab horses. The cold-bloods are larger and more placid than the hot-bloods and were developed in northern Europe during the Middle Ages—the horses of the armored knight, the draft breeds. Warm-bloods are breeds developed through crossing hot-bloods and cold-bloods.

some of its good looks. So the Moors had reintroduced Arabian blood, and the North African war-horse had, as a result, recovered much of its former handsome appearance; the Arabian horse, then as now, was viewed by many as the unparalleled beauty of the equine world. Arabian horsemen, it seems, could not tolerate a drab steed, and bred only animals that possessed beauty, intelligence, courage, and strength in equal amounts.

Recognizing the superiority of their conquerors' horses, the Spaniards immediately set out to breed a smaller horse for themselves. They added a touch of their own breeds—especially the Norse dun horse—to the Arabian-Barb mixture to produce the Jennet, a slightly larger animal, a horse with such distinctive qualities, intelligence, and speed, that for the next eight hundred years Andalusia and Seville were renowned throughout the civilized world for their superior animals.

This was the horse that the first explorers brought with them to the New World, transporting them in such numbers that Spain became alarmed and finally put an embargo on her horses in order to preserve enough for her needs at home. But the shrewd gold-seekers had foreseen this possibility and had already established breeding farms in the newly founded West Indian colonies of Cuba, Puerto Rico, and Santo Domingo, stocking these ranches with the finest stallions and brood mares that had been brought out of Spain. Thus the adventurers were assured a source of mounts for their expeditions across North and South America and into Mexico.

At one critical moment, however, in the great thrust across the continents, the demand for horses exceeded what these breeding farms were able to produce. But Barb horses, which had been part of the original foundation stock, were still available from North Africa. So these were now shipped to the West Indies and Barb blood was once again introduced into the line.

The fresh blend of Barb and Arabian was successful, though occasionally traits of one breed or the other separated, producing foals that strongly reflected either a predominantly Arabian or Barb background. Both types, however, were regarded as equally desirable. Today in the wild-horse bands it is possible to detect Barb characteristics in one animal and qualities distinctively Arabian in the horse running at its side. The Roman nose is thought to be Barb; the slightly dished face, Arabian.

The blend is referred to as an Andaluz mustang. According to the Spanish Mustang Registry, the Andaluz is a small horse by modern standards, with intelligent, quizzical eyes, widely separated by a flat forehead. Its profile is straight, its ears are small, its muzzle gracefully tapered, and its nostrils delicate and slanting. It is high in the withers, long in the shoulder. Its body gives the impression of sturdiness, for it tends to stand with its two very round front legs stiffened under a deep but narrow chest. Due to good musculature, its front legs V up together under its chest (unlike many horses whose legs support them from four distinct points like table legs, as one mustang fan puts it). Its back is short, for it has inherited the spine of an Arabian ancestor whose backbone lacked one vertebra. It comes in all colors.

The wild horses in our Western states still have much in common with their ancestors, but their first cousins, the Jennets in present-day Spain, resemble less closely the prized sixteenth-century animals from which they also have descended. Cunninghame Graham, who had firsthand knowledge of the horses of Spain, and horses of North and South America, described the twentieth-century horse of Spain as "a long-legged, showy animal deficient in both bone and stamina and fitted more for parade than for hard work."

In contrast, when he wrote of the horse of the North American Plains, he said, "Except for size [they] must be identical with those the Conquistadors brought from Spain."

Graham, in his book, *Horses of the Conquest,* goes on to elaborate the ways in which the American wild horse might have become somewhat modified in size and appearance, though not in ability:

"Possibly by reason of being obliged to think and to rely upon themselves, their heads grew larger and their ears, always strained to catch the slightest sound, grew longer and more mobile than those of horses stable-fed and cared for from earliest years. Without doubt, their eye-sight became more acute and their hearing infinitely sharper than that of a stabled horse. Their sense of locality became almost as much to be relied on as a dog's."

Today, though only a few hundred pure-blooded descendants of those sixteenth-century animals ridden by the Conquistadors have been salvaged from the wild and are in captivity in special registries in North and South America, the blood of these rare horses still flows in the veins of wild horses in scattered bands throughout our West. In a great many cases, however, it has been diluted by the blood of other strains, for during the three and a half centuries that have elapsed since the first mustangs found their way to freedom, many domestic horses have heard their cry and joined them—renegades from the United States cavalry, runaways from ranches, and old favorites turned out to pasture. Though the wild strain may often be a mixture, it is interesting that the Spanish horse's traits frequently emerge in animals of as little as one thirty-second Spanish ancestry. The Spanish genes are apparently so persistent that even random matings between two wild horses of obviously mixed ancestry will sometimes produce a colt that confounds observers by appearing to be pure Spanish in all details.

4. Attempts to Recover the Spanish Horse

It was inevitable that sooner or later efforts would be made by horse lovers to locate and capture from the wild bands in the West enough pure-blooded Spanish horses to restore the lost Spanish breed. In 1920, Robert Brislawn of Oshoto, Wyoming, and his brother Ferdinand Brislawn of Gusher, Utah,* began a fifty-year project, conscientiously searching in the wild for animals that appeared to carry untainted Spanish blood for inclusion in what they hoped would become a Spanish Mustang Registry. The difficulty of such a task can be appreciated when one reflects on the fact that the Spanish mustang tends to "absorb" or "mask" the characteristics of other breeds, and mistakes could spoil the pure line that the Brislawns were trying to establish.

Foundation stock was obtained by the two brothers from wild-horse bands ranging in Oklahoma, New Mexico, Montana, and Utah, and from herds of ponies found on a few Indian reservations. The original Indian pony was a Spanish mustang that had been rustled from the long-vanished Spanish settlements in the Southwest. But after the annexation of the Plains region by the United States in 1803, the Indian pony gradually became crossed with American breeds, and by the end of the century bore little resemblance to the horses of the Conquest.

However, some horse-loving Indian tribes did succeed in protecting a few of their fiery small horses from outside contamination. The Cheyennes, in particular, saved some of their "Indian ponies" from the blundering good intentions of the United States Government which, in 1909, planted large draft stallions on reservation lands to help the Indians get bigger animals (size being confused with quality). The Cheyennes outwitted the

*Both these men died in the 1970s.

Government planners by castrating all the donated stallions and thus were able to preserve some of their fine Spanish-blooded horses.

Beginning with the purchase of several of these Cheyenne ponies, together with a few captured wild horses whose conformation, size, color, and disposition corresponded to the characteristics of the horses first found in the West by American frontiersmen in the nineteenth century, the Brislawns began breeding their little herd. Since both brothers, octogenarians when I met them, were born when the West was still young, they could rely to a large extent on their personal knowledge of the original mustang in evaluating the purity of any horse they obtained.

Ultimately, however, all decisions regarding the bloodline of a particular animal could be submitted to a clear test; when an animal died, if its spinal column contained six lumbar vertebrae instead of the five of its North African ancestors, no offspring of that horse could be retained for the planned registry.*

The Spanish Mustang Registry, when it was finally established in 1958 by the Brislawn family, together with Dr. Lawrence Richards of Idaho State College and Robert Racicot of Thompson Falls, Montana, differed from most horse registries in America. For one thing, it was set up as a strictly nonprofit venture. Its stated purpose was to perpetuate the mustang for posterity and to establish a permanent reserve for the animal as a part of the heritage of the people of the United States.

"We are trying to restore a breed, not create one," Robert Brislawn announced. "Blood, pure blood, is what we are after. We are not like other horse breeders and we are not trying to compete against them for show or for ribbons."

Besides being nonprofit, the Spanish Mustang Registry differs from ordinary horse-breeding organizations in yet another way. The animals, however valuable they may be to those who have made such strenuous efforts to locate, capture, and preserve them, are nevertheless permitted to run free and live in a wild state on Brislawn's four-thousand-acre Cayuse ranch near Oshoto, Wyoming. There they can be viewed against a primitive prairie landscape looking very much the way wild horses must have appeared to the first pioneers who crossed the Plains.

Only a few colts are occasionally sold to interested individuals willing to breed the line elsewhere (a precaution against disease or catastrophe

* The bone structures of the three types of Spanish horses differ slightly; the Barb mustang carries only five vertebrae; the Arabian and the Andaluz may carry a small sacral vertebra that is fused to the last lumbar vertebra. See page 31 for diagram.

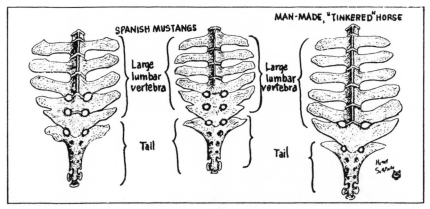

The Barb type has 5 large lumbar vertebrae.

The Andalusian type shows 5½ (or 5 and a piece) large lumbar vertebrae.

Modern breeds of to-day, except the Arabian, have 6 large lumbar vertebrae.

Sketches by Henry Schipman for the *Spanish Mustang News*

on the Cayuse ranch), for the little registry is still very much in its infancy and does not yet have a sufficient number of horses to guarantee its own long-range aim. At the time I visited it only four herds of stallion-dominated harems grazed on the Wyoming prairie reserve that was once homesteaded by Robert Brislawn. Part of this untrammeled prairie was willed by him to the public along with some of the beautiful ponies that still decorate its slopes.

However, despite the perseverance of the supporters of the Spanish Mustang Registry, the Spanish horse by no means can be said to be saved. Although over the years nearly two hundred animals have qualified for and been admitted to the Registry, no such number ever existed at any one time. In 1969 there were on the reserve no more than twenty mares that Brislawn said, "are straight as lodge poles" and only five stallions, "pure as the day the Spaniards landed."

To build up their herd and yet avoid inbreeding, the Registry had to look to the wilderness for additional animals to be added to the reserve. But the extreme caution and discrimination that the Registry exercised in accepting wild caught horses created an unexpected and unfortunate public reaction against the remaining wild horses. Many people concluded that all the true Spanish mustangs had been removed from the wild bands

Prized grulla-colored mare, Little Mex, lives in protected freedom on the Spanish Mustang Reserve near Oshoto, Wyoming.

(ABOVE) *Zebra stripes on Little Mex's legs indicate reversion to more primitive horse coloration.*

(BELOW) *A blue-roan Spanish Mustang, with Barb characteristics, playfully nips a filly.*

and that none existed except those that had been collected by the Bris-lawns. From this false premise, it was a small step to the equally irra-tional conclusion that any horse passed over by the Spanish Mustang Registry must not be worth preserving. Ironically, Brislawn found himself in a paradoxical position of having to defend feral horses of questionable descent from such self-declared purists:

"My aims are different," he wrote in *The Spanish Mustang News*. "Certainly feral horses in Canada and the United States have the colors and characteristics of their Spanish ancestors, proving beyond a doubt that they carry Spanish blood. They run the gamut of colors, including grullos, appaloosas, palominos, blues, war bonnets [Medicine Hats dis-cussed later], all shades of duns, buckskins, roans, and paints. All the common solid colors are found. Roan hairs are present in all the colors. Wild gene patterns such as dorsal stripes cross over the withers and zebra stripes are common characteristics."

Though it became increasingly difficult for the Registry to find suitable animals for their reserve, nevertheless, pure-blooded mustangs, descen-dants of the original Spanish horse, do still exist in the wild and could be found. One young stud, Chico, pictured in this book was taken out of the Utah Bookcliffs in the summer of 1969. Since the wild horse bands were the only source from which the Spanish Mustang Registry could obtain additional stock, it was naturally imperative to that organization that the wild herds receive some measure of protection. But that was not their sole motive in wanting to see the wild horses protected:

"Anyway, we love all horses," Brislawn says. "The feral horses [whether or not they are pure] are, of course, the best; and the reason is that they have not been crossed up as badly as our domestic horses. To obtain the desired beauty and conformation, modern breeders have inbred, crossbred, outbred, and backbred. The mustang does not inbreed any more than any other wild animal unless interfered with by man."

Brislawn, who believed that most of man's recent efforts at "tinkering with horses" resulted only in the breeding down of the animal, was also convinced that nature is a better horse breeder than modern man. From observations of his own semiwild herds, he noted that stallions expel their female offspring from their individual harems when these fillies reach a year of age. Just what mysterious mechanism of nature triggers this reac-tion, preventing the sires from mating with their daughters is unknown. However, when left alone to organize their own social units, the practice of "line breeding" (or father-daughter breeding) commonly employed by

(ABOVE) *Dejected in captivity, this recently corralled wild stud was judged to be pure-blooded by the Spanish Mustang Registry.*

(BELOW) *Robert Brislawn and son, Shane, verify that a deceased Spanish Mustang lacked a final vertebra, indicating his distinguished ancestry.*

Playmates—two Arabian-type colts frolic on the Spanish Mustang Reserve.

professional horse breeders, does not occur among horses. Brislawn adhered to the policy that nature is the better judge and he did not try to arrange special combinations among his own animals, leaving the selection of mares completely up to the individual stallions. Once a mare was accepted by a stud, she was herded into that stallion's harem and is jealously guarded by him from any neighboring stallion that displayed interest in her.

The difference between the efforts made by the Spanish Mustang Registry to recover Spanish mustangs from the wild and similar attempts made by such groups as the American Mustang Association of Phoenix, Arizona, was that the latter improved on the captured feral horses through a breeding program; whereas the efforts of the former were directed solely toward the restoration of a lost breed.

The American Mustang Association also founded their registry on wild-horse stock, but immediately instigated steps to improve the animal, to breed up its size and to standardize the variable appearance of the Barb, the Arabian, and the Andaluz. Toward this end, stallions were imported from Peru* and bred with the best mustang mares that could be located and captured in the Southwest. The efforts of the American Mustang Association resulted in a collection of a few fine horses, all considerably larger than the pure animal recovered from the wildernesses of North America by the Brislawns, but nevertheless retaining much of the style and ability of the Spanish horse. Most of the horses in this Registry measure fifteen hands or over, a hand or two taller than animals admitted to the Spanish Mustang Registry. No claim was made by the American Mustang Association that their stock was "straight Spanish," for their purpose, unlike that of the Brislawns, was not to preserve the little horse of the Conquest, but to develop a superior animal able to compete against the established breeds in the show ring and in the marketplace.

The National Mustang Association, based in Salt Lake City, Utah, had yet another purpose behinds its organization. It was not a *registry* but a club, which enrolled members interested in the sport of "mustanging," or running and capturing wild horses for their own personal use. Its aim was to provide recreation for its members and to educate the public on the conservation needs of the wild horses. Members who took part in mustang roundups, of course, hoped to obtain a Spanish-blooded horse for themselves, and animals captured by individuals were evaluated and graded according to how much Spanish blood they appeared to carry. But

* See Appendix for information on the Spanish Horse Registries in South America.

since these captured horses were then scattered among the membership (which came from fifty states), the Spanish-blooded horse, as a breed, was not particularly perpetuated by this activity. That, however, was not the declared purpose of the National Mustang Association. It was more concerned with the problems of conservation and control of the limited number of mustangs still living in the wilderness, and it hoped to act as a "field crew" to implement any management program that might be enacted in the future.

Insofar as the National Mustang Association's aims were directed toward the conservation of wild horses, it was in accord with the purposes of the International Society for the Protection of Mustangs and Burros* headquartered in Reno, Nevada. This latter organization, however, made no distinction as to breed or past history of the wild horse bands it sought to protect, but worked solely for humane treatment of the remaining animals. Its very effective work will be discussed more fully later. A similar organization in Richmond, British Columbia, was called the Canadian Wild Horse Society.

Conserving wild-horse bands and salvaging a lost breed are two entirely different aims. A wild horse, in its natural state, is an interesting and unique creature; and whether it made its escape from a Spanish cavalier, an Indian warrior, or a white settler, its existence gives equal pleasure to those who catch a glimpse of it walking along the rimrocks or racing across the desert flats. Though the lineage of certain wild horse bands is undeniably an historical asset, the factor of pedigree should not be unduly weighed in determining the public value of any particular band of wild horses. Pure bloodline or not, the pluck and audacity of a wild horse, its hardiness, and ability to survive the droughts and heat of a desert summer and the cruel blizzards of a mountain winter make it deserving of our respect and admiration. Simply by meeting nature's harshest test, the survival of the fittest, the wild horse, whatever its pedigree, has earned the right to be respected as a wild and free creature.

*Now named Wild Horse Organized Assistance, or WHOA.

Wild yearlings at home again on ancestral soil.

5. The Return of the Native

Though the horse had been known to prehistoric ancestors of the American Indians, there existed among them no memory trace of the animal, either in myth, creative design, or legend, and the first recorded reaction of the Indians to the sight of a man riding a horse was one of total and debilitating fear.

No centaur, designed by the Greeks to inspire a sense of reverence and awe, succeeded so effectively in inciting profound emotions as the apparition of mounted Spaniards produced in the hearts of the Indians. They fled in panic when the strange monster proved it could come apart—the man from the horse—and reassemble itself again, without loss of life. They assumed it was a god, and the Spaniards exploited their credulity, sustaining it with acts of cruelty and murder on horseback.

When the Indians began to realize their mistake, they were naturally anxious to acquaint their fellow tribesmen with the true nature of the phenomenon, and horses were stolen and dissected around Indian campfires as experimental proof of the animal's mortality.

Whenever it was possible, the horses that bore the Spaniards to Mexico, to the Southwest, and to the Mississippi River were selected with the utmost care, for the survival of these animals was a life and death matter to the cavaliers. Cortés plainly stated that he valued the life of one horse above the lives of twenty men.

The first horses in 8,000 years to set their hoofs on the mainland of the North American continent were brought from Spanish breeding stock in the West Indies by Cortés, when, on his first voyage to Mexico in 1519, he sailed along the Yucatán coast and discovered the Aztec civilization. Bernal Diaz, a horse-fancying member of that expedition, kept a diary of the event in which he describes in detail the sixteen horses that shared the adventure. He wrote:

"And the horses were divided up among the ships and loaded; mangers erected and a store of maize and hay put aboard. Captain Cortés had a dark chestnut stallion that died when we reached San Juan Ulúa. . . . Moron, a settler of Bayamo, had a pinto with white stockings on his forefeet well reined. . . . Diego de Ordás had a barren gray mare, a pacer who therefore seldom ran. . . . Ortez, the musician, and Bartolomé Garciá, who had gold mines, had a black horse called El Arriero and he was one of the best horses taken in the fleet. . . . Sixteen horses were brought plus one foal to the brown mare owned by Sedeña, a settler of Havana."

When Diaz, at the age of eighty, reflected on this momentous expedition, undertaken with such meager provisions and so few horses, he wrote: "In these days there were no horses to be got or Negroes either, except at a great price, and that was why we embarked with no more horses for there were hardly any to be had."

So important were these few available animals to the success and safety of the party that Cortés did not permit their owners to ride them, but assigned the horses to men who were better equestrians. Thus, El Arriero, the excellent stallion jointly owned by Ortez, the musician, and Bartolomé Garciá, who had gold mines, was assigned to Alonso de Avila, and poor Ortez and Garciá were forced to proceed on foot, for as Diaz bluntly puts it, "Neither of them could ride."

El Arriero apparently was a versatile horse. At one critical moment, he enacted a role devised for him by Cortés and succeeded in intimidating a group of Indians. Cortés, uneasy about the intentions of some Indians who were lurking about, instructed one of his men to lead a mare "in heat" past the tree where El Arriero was tied. As the mare moved slowly into range, the stallion began to act up and created such an exhibition of ferocity, snorting, stamping his feet and neighing, that the Indians became frightened.

Cortés reassured the Indians that they had nothing to fear, and indicated that he would talk to the excited horse and instruct him not to hurt them. He then ambled over to the stallion, which was already showing signs of settling down after the mare had passed, and whispered in the animal's ear. The Indians watched in amazement as the mighty horse grew docile and nudged Cortés affectionately.

When Cortés' own chestnut stallion was killed near San Juan Ulúa, the

Spanish leader was quick to appropriate El Arriero for himself and rode him for the remainder of the expedition. One wonders if poor Ortez, the musician, and Garciá, who had gold mines, ever suspected, as they trudged through the dense jungle, that they might have been invited to come along on this adventure because they could supply such a horse as El Arriero.

Just as today rockets have made the United States into a leading world power, and just as ships were the weapon with which Great Britain won her world empire, so, in the sixteenth century, the horse delivered the New World to Spain. Legions of Indians were no match for the mounted Spaniards. In one conflict alone eight hundred Indians were reported killed by the steel-tipped lances of the invaders. Though the Spaniards and their horses sustained many wounds, the majority of both survived. When Cortés departed from Mexico for Seville with his four ships heavily weighted with treasures (a golden cache of bells, jewels, earrings, and nose ornaments, "books such as the Indians use," a golden calendar in the shape of four interlocking wheels, feather ornaments mounted in jewels, and four fantastically attired Totanacs*), space was nevertheless found on the loot-laden ships for the surviving horses; only one was left behind. It was the foal of the brown mare who had escaped, gone wild, and was last seen running with a herd of deer. The little colt, the first foal on North American soil since the mysterious disappearance of the horses eight thousand years earlier, significantly had taken his freedom.

Other explorers who hacked their way into the interior lost horses to Indian arrows, sickness, and even to their own desperate need for food. Every expedition seems to have set out well stocked with animals—magnificent mounts, mules for pack, and even a certain number of pigs for food—but after months of hardship, war, and illness, the men who survived frequently came wandering back on foot, telling horrendous stories of watching their last horse being burned alive by Indians, or of jettisoning the wretched creature from a getaway raft while under attack. Though the horse was the key to Spain's conquest of Mexico and her successful penetration to the Mississippi and the Southwest, the horse can also be regarded as a true martyr to that cause.

Obviously, the foal of the brown mare did not beget the wild-horse bands that later populated the West. Poetry and legend name six surviving animals of De Soto's expedition to the Mississippi as the sires of the great herds that eventually swept across the plains. However, in view of the pitiful condition of the six when they were finally abandoned to their fate

* Members of a Mexican tribe.

along the mosquito-infested banks of the river—and bearing in mind the fierceness of the Southern Indians, who slaughtered explorers' horses for vengeance, food, and sport—it is unlikely that any were able to "fling off their iron and cut the green" as Mark Van Doren's poem, "The Distant Runners," picturesquely suggests. Though the poem expresses a fine feeling about the true nature of wild horses and should not be faulted for a literal waywardness, historians have been quick to point out that no wild horses have ever been recorded in this area of the lower Mississippi, nor is it probable that those six wretched animals were able to travel the five- or six-hundred-mile distance to the Plains states where in the late seventeenth century wild horses were reported by Frenchmen.

In 1541, while De Soto's horses were enduring to the end, along the banks of the Mississippi, Coronado's party was pushing across the baking deserts of the Southwest mounted on the backs of similar stock. It was the dream of "golden cities," such as those found by Cortés and Pizarro, that had lured both De Soto and Coronado to explore America's interior in the first place. Seduced by Indian "fantastic tales" about a mythical kingdom of Quivera, Coronado assembled fifteen hundred animals and two hundred and fifty men and trekked across Mexico into what is now Arizona, where he turned northeast and traveled as far as present-day Kansas.

There, instead of riches, Coronado discovered the Plains Indians, backward foot hunters whose way of life differed little from that of their aboriginal ancestors. Unlike the Eastern and Northern Indians, who practiced agriculture and who lived in permanent or semipermanent villages, the Plains Indians were nomadic, packing their tents and bundles on cross-poles strapped to dogs (later called *travois* by the French), and dragging their meager possessions from one campsite to another in pursuit of the elusive buffalo. Moving camp and hunting occupied them almost totally.

The Conquistadors, frustrated by a dawning awareness that their quest was a vain one, tortured these backward Indians for not revealing the locations of their fabulous cities. Though it must have occurred to the crazed explorers that such simple, horseless people had seen less of the continent than had they themselves, they nevertheless murdered men, women, and children in retaliation for the years that had been sacrificed in a fruitless search.

Ironically, it was these simple Plains Indians who, after being initiated into the use of the horse, so expanded their culture that they, above all Indian tribes, were best able to resist the relentless encroachment of the white man across the continent. But in the beginning they were no match for the Spaniards, who enslaved them and treated them brutally. Naturally, they reacted in kind. Chiefs, who had at first been friendly and even served as guides, began to attack and burn the white man's camps. To impede the progress of the explorers, braves relieved them of horses, thus setting large numbers of the invaders on an equal footing with the Indians, in the most literal sense of the word.

Though some of these stolen horses may have been released in remote places to become the nucleus of wild bands, many were simply tortured by the curious Indians, who could not decide at first what use to make of them—whether to eat them, worship them, or ride them.

Such expeditions as those of De Soto and Coronado lasted too short a time, however, for the Indians to learn from them how to ride and care for horses and thus adopt the animal into their culture. By the same token, it was not until horses had passed into the hands of the Indians that the animals had their first real opportunity to escape man's domination and to roam the Plains on a large scale. For the Indians were careless herders, and when they weren't actually making war astride a horse, or galloping after buffalo herds, they left their "ponies" to shift for themselves on the open range. Needless to say, every stallion worthy of the name wasted no time organizing a band of mares and making his escape.

The Indians' best lesson in the use of horses did not come for two generations after Coronado failed to find Quivera. Around 1600, Juan de Oñate took up the search for the mythical kingdom, though he approached the problem not as an explorer but as an empire builder. Together with a few hundred men and a multitude of livestock—goats, sheep, horses, and oxen—he moved into New Mexico and settled near the present city of Santa Fe, where his large flocks of domestic animals overgrazed and eventually turned the grass-covered mesa into a desert.

For the next eighty years these settlers defended their animals from the raiding Apaches, who were pleased to discover that domestic horses, unlike wild buffalo, would allow themselves to be driven to the Indian camps and villages where they could be conveniently slaughtered. At first the Indians took horses only for food, but in time the Apaches, the Utes, and the Navajos, having observed the methods by which the Spaniards trained and handled domestic animals, began to acquire not only horses but horsemanship as well.

When at last the American Indians concluded that horses were for riding, they became as skilled as the finest horsemen the world has seen. Without benefit of bridle or saddle, clinging to braids made in the horse's mane and supported by a bare heel dug into the animal's back, an Indian could not only ride astride a horse, but in battle, could slip to one side, thus utilizing the animal as a shield as well as a mount.

The isolated little Santa Fe colony, finding itself at the mercy of these horse-fancying Indians, turned for help to the Pueblo Indian, the most advanced tribes in the Great Basin, and tried to win their friendship. Franciscan priests were even brought to Santa Fe to minister to the Pueblo's spiritual needs and, in exchange for being Christianized, these tribes were expected to fend off the fierce Apaches for the Spaniards.

But the half-converted Pueblo tribes soon grew weary of their indebtedness to the white man for saving their souls, and in 1680 they joined the other Basin Indians in routing the entire settlement. The attack came suddenly, and the settlers in their haste to depart for Mexico left most of their horses and livestock behind. Possibly some of these animals became wild, but most were probably taken by the Indians, who had already begun to demonstrate that passion for horses for which they were to become so noted.

When the refugees stopped running, they were near El Paso on the Rio Grande River. Here they staked out land, built new ranches, and requested replacement horses and livestock from the Spanish government in Mexico. The records indicate that thousands of horses and brood mares were sent to them.

But the new settlement on the Rio Grande fared no better from the Indians than had the Santa Fe colony. Although a royal decree prohibited Indians from riding horses, frequent reiteration of this order indicates that it was probably unenforceable throughout Mexico. In any case the Indian tribes in the north of New Spain could not be intimidated by royal decrees. Apaches and Comanches, by this time excellent horsemen, carried out raids as far south as Chihuahua and Sonoro.

Nor could the horse itself be contained any longer. So many were scattered in the confusion of the perpetual rustling that stray horses sighted by the Spaniards were dubbed "mestenos" (belonging to the *mesta,* a Spanish word referring to stock growers). In time, this word became mustang, the name by which we still call our wild horses.

One authority, Cunninghame Graham, disagrees with this explanation of the etymology of the word. He believes "mustang" is derived from *monstrenco,* meaning "roving, rough, wild." Though this theory is not the generally accepted one, it would better account for the hard "g" sound that Texans and Californians added to the word.

Regardless of how the wild mustang got its name, it is certain that by 1680 it had gained its freedom. Large numbers had slipped through the careless hands of their new masters, the Indians, inexperienced in animal husbandry and reckless with the providential supply of Spanish ranch animals from which they could always replenish their losses.

6. The Horse Transforms the Plains Indians

The wild horse owes its present-day existence to the readiness with which the Plains Indians adopted the strange animal that obeyed like a dog and carried the white man across the far-flung hunting grounds.

Had the Indians failed to recognize the superiority of horse power over the labor of their dogs in packing and dragging their belongings from camp to camp, and had they not, moreover, been flexible enough to alter their style of hunting and of making war so as to make use of this "gift from the white man," it is doubtful that many horses would have found their way to freedom. But when the Indians began in earnest to take horses from the Spanish settlements along the Rio Grande, passing them from tribe to tribe until every warrior, brave, and chief from the Mexican border to Saskatchewan was the proud possessor of horses, the wild-horse bands began to spread like a grass fire across the Plains.

The period from 1640 to 1880 has been called by anthropologists the period of the Indian horse culture. During this time, wild-horse bands multiplied without interference from an advancing frontier of white settlers and, consequently, their numbers rapidly increased. The swelling bands of wild mustangs frequently lured mares away from the Indians' loosely guarded stock, yet the Indians seldom drew on the wild bands for replacements. They preferred horses already broken and, as trained animals bearing Spanish brands were readily available through the Apaches, the Comanches, the Pawnees, and the Osages, who acted as horse brokers to the Northern tribes, the wild bands were seldom tapped.

Since the Northern tribes themselves had no direct contact with the remote Mexican ranchers who provided them with stock, it is not surprising that they should refuse to believe that the horse was a "gift from the white man," and to assume that it was native. For generations before the Northern tribes saw a white man, they had possessed horses and they knew the wild bands on the Plains.

As time passed, even the Basin tribes of the Southwest began to forget how they had been introduced to horses and they, too, came to believe the animal was indigenous to their desert. I talked with a Paiute chief in Yerington, Nevada, an old man, who recalled the stories of horses told to him by his grandfather; he vehemently insisted that the Indians had always had horses, saying: "Far back as I heard they were here. I heard people say they came from the Spaniards. The white people say that. But the Indians say the horses was here. They are our horses. That's all I heard. I've heard as far back as I can remember from the old folks who used to talk about them. 'The real Indian pony is the little, short, chunky one . . . low to the ground,' they told me, 'short and chunky, the real Indian pony. There's a lot of them never was broke and running all over,' they told me, 'here, there, and in Smith Valley, and all around.' "

It is little wonder that the Indians could not credit the white man with bringing them the horse. When Marquette journeyed west of the Mississippi in 1673, the first Indians who greeted him were already mounted. Eleven years later another Frenchman, Henri Du Tisne, visited the northern Plains and editor P. Margry quotes him as having written: "It is called Emissourita and it is well peopled. There are even villages of savages which use horses to go to war and to carry away the carcasses of cattle [buffalo] which they kill."

So completely did the Plains Indians assimilate the horse into their culture that the animal even began to play an important part in their myths. By the late 1700's the Blackfeet had populated their vision of heaven with horses, women, and buffalo, in that order.

One present-day wild-horse expert, Kent Gregersen, a founder of the National Mustang Association, believes the Paiute Indians are correct in their belief that the horse "was always here."

The Indians, he thinks, may have coexisted with the wild horse without attempting to tame it or ride it. Historians who feel that the Indians had never seen a horse merely because the tribes expressed terror at the sight of the mounted Conquistadors may not have understood that it was men riding horses which caused the Indians' alarm.

"You can't make me believe the Indians would think of riding a buffalo or a bull elk either, until they had seen someone else do it," Gregersen said.

As for the absence of fossil remains dating from more recent years, Gregersen calls this negative evidence which proves nothing except that such bones have not yet been unearthed.

Dr. Richard Tedford of the American Museum of Natural History Department of Paleontology listened to this argument regarding bone finds and agreed at least with the logic of it. He commented: "It's impossible to say that he is wrong, though in view of the fact that no bones have turned up, it would seem unlikely that any will. But we've been wrong before."

Though horse bones that appear to be as young as 100 years B.C. have been found, scientists have rejected these datings as unreliable. Apparently the geological context in which these late fossil remains were discovered (near St. Petersburg, Florida) is not clear.

The latest accepted date for the extinction of the horse in North America is 7,756 B.P. (before the present), plus or minus 370 years; this is based on carbon-dated bones from White Water Draw, Arizona. Abundant fossil remains of greater antiquity have been found, and it is safe to conclude that horses inhabited this continent in profuse numbers until eight thousand years ago and did not become abundant again until they were reintroduced by the Spaniards.

Scientists and historians have, of course, reversed themselves on many matters when new evidence has suggested that their previous ideas were incorrect, and if Mr. Gregersen ever proves that they have been wrong in their conclusions regarding the "native" horse, the effect will be far-reaching. Wild horses will then have to be regarded as "native wildlife," entitled to whatever protection our indigenous American animals enjoy. They might even be admitted to the wildlife sanctuaries in our National Parks.

Whether or not it can ever be proven that the native horse still existed in North America when the Spaniards landed, clearly the animals had never been domesticated by the American Indians before that point in history, and the effect of the use of horses on the lives of the nomadic Plains tribes was revolutionary.

In the pre-Columbian evolution of various Indian cultures in North America, those tribes that had learned to practice agriculture were the most advanced; the nomads were the most backward. Quite logically, the stability and the food surplus created through farming gave the agricultural tribes the leisure and security necessary to create art and to amass nonutilitarian wealth. Hunting tribes, by contrast, struggled the year round just to obtain enough food to eat.

When Coronado first met the Plains tribes, they were the most primitive of all the North American Indians, roving foot-hunters, who stalked buffalo in much the same way that their aboriginal ancestors had once hunted mammoth. Covering themselves with animal skins and creeping on all fours, hunters stole up on herds of grazing antelope and buffalo and waited hours for a chance to throw their arrowheads at unsuspecting beasts.

In sharp contrast to these primitive people were the Aztecs, the Toltecs, and the Mayans of Mexico, whose horticultural practices were highly sophisticated and even included floating gardens, irrigation, and the use of fertilizer. On an intermediate level, but far surpassing the buffalo hunters, were the Eastern Indians—the Iroquois and the Shawnees—who planted maize and squash and lived in semipermanent villages. And in the Southwest, the adobe-building Pueblo Indians had also learned to plant, and consequently they, too, had sufficient leisure to acquire skills in weaving and the making of pottery. Even those tribes that had not yet adopted agriculture but were "collectors," gathering wild produce such as berries, roots, seeds, and fish, were a great deal more advanced than the poor, nomadic buffalo hunters of the Plains.

Life, to these hunting tribes, was mere subsistence, and they were always on the move. The erratic herds of buffalo appeared and disappeared unpredictably, and camp was constantly being pulled up, packed, dragged, and pitched. Little time was left to make the fancy footgear and the elaborate costumes essential to ceremonial dances. Little energy was left to take an enemy's scalp and send his soul to serve the victor's departed ancestors in the Great Beyond. Excessive possessions were merely a burden to the nomads, whose dogs could not drag more than the essential teepees, blankets, and tools.

But the acquisition of the horse so extended the hunter's speed, mobility, and endurance that hunting became a sport. First-rate horses, trained to follow whichever beast was singled out for slaughter, permitted the riders to charge into stampeding herds. The Indian hunters, riding in their peculiar headlong fashion, no longer regarded their work as a long game of patience, but now responded to the challenge of the hunt with enthusiasm, seldom returning to the encampment without food.

If the buffalo herd left the region of the camp, the tribe simply loaded their belongings on the horses, tied the little children to saddles, mounted, and moved as far as fifty miles in one day, or until they located another herd. Children and old people no longer retarded the tribe's progress. The inferior size and strength of dogs no longer limited the amount of possessions that could be carried; larger teepees and nonutilitarian belongings could be packed by horses with no strain.

Soon after the acquisition of the horse, the Plains tribes began to acquire material tastes and possessions. Leisure and all that it signified also became a property of the new Horse Culture enjoyed by the Western Indians. Since a village of one hundred people could survive on twelve thousand pounds of meat a month, six hunters need kill only two or three buffalo apiece for all the people to be fed. With the help of horses this task became relatively simple, and the hunters had additional time in which to become warlike and to acquire material wealth.

The horse so changed the Plains Indians' way of life and gave their backward hunting culture such an upward swing that certain of the more advanced agricultural tribes eventually abandoned their crops and their village life and joined the Horse Indians in buffalo country. This conversion of horticultural tribes to nomadism created a population explosion in the High Plains where the buffalo, the object of all these hunters, were so numerous. The movement to the Plains proceeded both from the east, where the Indians were feeling the pressure of the advancing white settlers, and from the western High Plateau country, where "collecting" Indians from the Columbia River, the Nez Percé, proudly mounted their spotted Appaloosas and headed east to hunt.

Tribes that had never before met now exchanged ideas, objects, and arrows. Horse raiding created conflicts, and conflicts developed into full-scale wars. Even within the Plains, a general southward movement began toward the diffusion point of the rustled horses, the Apaches being pushed farther south by the more powerful Comanches.

Though the period was one of great chaos, stability itself was no longer an asset and, in fact, had become a handicap. Planting tribes found their fields surrounded by mobile Horse Indians, who attacked them and took their produce. From the east, the white frontier was advancing as unremittingly as an ocean tide. Tribes without horses were at the mercy of whites on one side and the Horse Indians on the other. An early account of the situation, written by a trapper, describes the disparity between the primitive Sioux, who already possessed horses, and the gardening Cheyenne, who at the time did not.

Tabeau's Narrative reads: "The Sioux, always wandering, left little for capture to the enemy who often knew not where to find them, and the Cheyennes [who were] settled there, every day were exposed, in spite of their superior courage, to some particular catastrophe. To lessen the disparity more, they abandoned agriculture and their hearths and became a nomadic people."

Like all innovations, the adoption of the horse by the Plains Indians had disruptive effects. But the little Spanish horse was only beginning to play its role in history.

7. *Indian War-Horses*

With the acquisition of horses, the Plains tribes gained in leisure, mobility, and militancy. Horses had an unsettling effect on tribal boundaries and friendships. Formerly, combat had been circumscribed by the distance the invading warriors could advance or retreat on foot. Now, mounted on horses, tribes plundered remote neighbors and vanished with their booty. Indians without horses were at a serious disadvantage. One chief described to David Thompson, an early trapper and chronicler of the Northwest, the plight of his tribe, the Ojibwas, after the nearby Dakotas had become horsemen:

"While they keep to the plains we are no match for them; for we being footmen, they could get to windward of us and set fire to the grass; when we marched for the woods, they would be there before us, dismount and, under cover, fire on us. . . . Until we have horses like them, we must keep to the woods and leave the plains to them."

When these forest-dwelling Ojibwas acquired horses, they did indeed quit the woods and moved to the Plains, leaving their more advanced "collecting" way of life for the more simple culture of the roving hunters.

At the same time, the Cree, pressured by a steadily advancing white frontier, tried to seize territory belonging to the Blackfeet, who were living on the grassy lower slopes of the northern Rockies. Though the Cree possessed firearms, they had no horses, and the Blackfeet, without guns but mounted, were able to defeat the invaders and hold on to their own lands.

A Piegan chief described to David Thompson a similar situation between his tribe, equipped with rifles, in a battle against an enemy of horsemen, armed only with bows and arrows:

"But this time we had more guns and iron-headed arrows than before, but our enemies, the Snake Indians, and their allies had missitutin [Big

Dogs, meaning horses] on which they rode, swift as the deer, on which they dashed at the Piegans and with their stone puk-amoggan knocked them on the head. . . . This news we did not well comprehend and it alarmed us, for we had no idea of horses and could not make out what they were. . . . We were anxious to see a horse of which we had heard so much. At last we heard that one was killed by an arrow shot in his belly. Numbers of us went to see him, and we all admired him. He put us in mind of a stag that had lost his horns, and we did not know what name to give him. But he was a slave to man like the dog which carried our things. He was named Big Dog."

So expert did the Indian become at attacking from horseback that almost every artist and writer of the West depicts him in this posture. And so frequently have we been exposed to this version of the American Indian that it is sometimes hard to realize that not all Indians were Horse Indians, and that, in fact, even the Horse Indians possessed horses for only a comparatively short time.

To the Plains Indian, war on the backs of horses was more than a necessary and honorable part of life—it became a mystique. All the theatrics of preparing for battle, the paint, the dance, and the feathers were elaborated to include the horse, and the ceremonial aspects of heading off to war astride feathered, painted, prancing horses added a richness and excitement to the event that delighted the ritual-loving Indians. The young Indian males spent hours painting their faces in preparation for the pre-battle parade. They also painted their horses with bright vermillion stripes across their foreheads, necks, and withers. Feathers were braided into their tails, and bells and "medicine ornaments" (eagle claws, herbs, any object thought to have magical properties) were strung along their bridles. The mounted braves wore buffalo robes or scarlet blankets draped across their shoulders and carried goose-feather fans to shield themselves from the sun. Arms, necks, and shoulders glittered with beads and ornaments. Spare horses pranced beside each rider. These were the real hunters or war-horses that would actually carry their riders into the stampeding herd of buffalo or charge the enemy in battle. But until that moment they were kept fresh, and the Indians used parade horses for the preliminary ceremonies.

For this purpose gaudy pintos that added color to the visual spectacles were preferred. Though the spots of the pinto horses may have been good camouflage, being less visible at a distance than an all-dark or all-light animal, it was not exclusively for this reason that the Indians liked parti-colored ponies; it was also for the flamboyant effect they created. Though the Plains Indians did not understand the principles of selective breeding, they accomplished the same end by trading off animals that did not conform to their tastes. Thus, in time, each tribe acquired herds that bred their preferred colors or types.

A special mystique surrounded a particular type of pinto developed by the Plains Indians and known by them as the Medicine Hat horse. The white people called this animal a War Bonnet because a special bonnetlike marking covered its head and ears and a dark shield "protected" its chest. Only braves who had proven themselves were allowed to mount a horse so marked, and a Comanche warrior who rode a Medicine Hat into battle considered himself to be invincible.

This vaunted war-horse was, of course, simply a color phase of the Spanish mustang; the Indians had no access to other breeds as yet. But beneath its peculiar spots flowed blood that was particularly wild and hot. The link of "bonnet" and "mettle" apparently bred true, for the Cheyenne, the Sioux, the Blackfeet, and the Comanches all desired these sacred pintos and possessed them in numbers by the 1860's when the Plains Indians made their most forceful stand in battles against the whites. Charles Russell, the great documentary artist of the West, immortalized the Medicine Hat war-horse in two paintings titled: "When Sioux and Blackfeet Meet" and "Redskin Raiders."

All the Indian ponies, however, regardless of markings seemed able to outmaneuver the larger "blooded horses" ridden by the U.S. cavalry. the Army, it seemed, often picked its mounts as much for conformity of appearance as for ability or stamina. Bays, fifteen hands or over, were preferred for military parade, so bays went to war. This preference by the whites for a horse of a certain color was, of course, psychologically no different from the Indians' partiality for pintos, Medicine Hats, and Appaloosas, though objectively speaking, the Indian horse, regardless of how it was marked, seemed a better war-horse.

Chief Bobby Yellowtail of the Crow tribe repeated to me what he had personally been told many years ago by fellow tribesmen (long since deceased) who had acted as scouts for Custer. These scouts described the horses of the fated Seventh Cavalry as follows:

"Those Kentucky Thoroughbreds were all grain fed and curried, but they had a heck of a time. Those 'wonderful' horses they had brought up here all the way from Fort Abraham Lincoln were already spent when they got here. They had gotten into bad weather, so they just grained them and kept on using them."

When I asked Chief Yellowtail about the horses used by the Indian warriors, I was told a different story:

"They were called by the white men 'old Indian Cayuses.' That was a kind of an impolite name for an inferior breed of horses. But we developed those kind of horses that could catch up with the buffalo and run right into the herd. It takes a real horse to do that! And he was a prince of a horse, and the Indians called him 'his buffalo-catcher.' Now that's the kind of horse we developed. He could go clear down to the Nebraska country and come back. No oats! No hay! Live off of what he could pick up on the road. No shoes! Live on sagebrush . . . whatever he could find. We had a superior horse, although he had no pedigree. His pedigree was Indian Cayuse."

Because the Medicine Hat color phase of the Spanish mustang played such a dramatic role in the history of the West, Robert Brislawn particularly wanted to locate and capture this type of pinto from the wild bands for his reserve. One day he was notified by some Navajo Indians at Santo Domingo Pueblo that a young Medicine Hat stallion had been brought in from the wild. Immediately he went to see the horse to determine if it was indeed a Spanish-blooded horse that possessed typical Medicine Hat markings. The moment he laid eyes on the animal he realized it was the one he had been searching for. Brislawn named him San Domingo.

San Domingo, whose bonnet and shield are red roan floral (or roseate mottling) is presently living on the Brislawn Cayuse Ranch and possesses a harem of seven mares. Of his many offspring, he has thus far sired five Medicine Hat fillies; an earlier male offspring was sold to Canada. Since a wild stallion will not permit one of his own fillies to remain in his herd after she has matured, and since Brislawn does not try to tamper with the natural herding and breeding behavior of his semiwild horses, San Domingo will obviously not be crossed with one of his Medicine Hat daughters. Still, another stallion could emerge from one of San Domingo's solid-colored offspring. Brislawn, who is patiently waiting for the sacred pinto to appear, says, "The genes are in the herd now. It's only a question of when that stud colt will turn up again."

The six Medicine Hats now in the Registry are of different colors: red, black, blue, purple, and tan, but all roanish. All have black or striped hoofs (the Indians thought white hoofs too brittle, for they did not shoe their horses; at most they merely tacked pieces of green buffalo hide to their feet).

After visiting the Spanish Mustang Refuge in northeastern Wyoming

*His harem threatened, a rare Medicine Hat stallion
senses and then routs an intruder* (SEE FOLLOWING PAGES).
*The bonnet and shield markings on this type of Spanish Mustang
were believed to be magical by the Cheyenne Indians.*

and getting acquainted with the Medicine Hats, I can well understand why the Cheyenne believed these horses to have mystic powers. San Domingo, who seemed to be totally aware of himself at all times, was charged with personality. He was also the most discriminating of the four stallions on the Cayuse Ranch in his choice of mares. Apparently he was quite satisfied with his collection of seven females and was not interested in adding any of Brislawn's newly acquired fillies to his harem; he even fought them off his territory. (Komawi, a black stallion of more relaxed tastes, accepted the females that San Domingo rejected.) Yet no stallion was more possessive of his band of females than was this Medicine Hat. It was not a good idea to approach San Domingo on horseback, even when riding a gelding. San Domingo met all comers, rearing and raring for a fight like the good war-horse that he was.

One day, while tracking wild horses near Yerington, Nevada, I unexpectedly came upon two mares, a gray and a bay, grazing on a slight landrise in the desert. The bay mare spotted me first, raised her head, and then, as is frequently the habit of wild horses, took two or three challenging steps toward me before sounding the alarm. At the mare's signal, eight horses rose up from the slight land depression behind her, and in a swirl of dust, wheeled off into the desert.

I got the quick impression that one of the horses in the fleeing band was a rare Medicine Hat pinto, and though my main concern was to get photographs, I took my eye from the viewfinder for one instant to see if I could verify this. But the horses were moving so swiftly I had to resume shooting immediately or lose my pictures. Later however, when I examined the not-too-successful photographs, the animal in question did indeed appear to bear the typical markings of a Medicine Hat pinto.

A few such Medicine Hats may well still exist in the back hills and canyons where the wild bands have sought their last refuge, but Brislawn's chance of recovering them becomes less likely every day that the wild horse lives outside of any legal protection.

8. The Scattering of the Horses

The horse gave the Spaniards the ability to penetrate the wilderness; the Spaniards gave the Indian the horse; and the Indian inadvertently gave the horse freedom. This circle of gifts so interlocks that it is impossible to understand the impact of one without knowledge of the other two.

Though the Spanish horse had unquestionably given the Conquistador the edge in his early conquests, it was the same remarkable horse that, in the hands of the Indian, prevented the Spaniards from successfully colonizing the Southwest. With their horses, the Indians were able to drive the settlers back into what is now Mexico and to retain the whole of the West for themselves for another two centuries.

The biggest boon to the wild-horse population was the "there are plenty more where these came from" attitude of the Comanche Indians. With the supply of trained animals so available to them from the Spanish *ranchos* along the Rio Grande, the Comanches saw little reason to take horses from the wild bands, or even to recapture those that escaped. Instead, they perfected the art of horse stealing.

The more unobtrusively a horse theft could be accomplished, the more status an Indian acquired for his feat, and a brave who could sneak into a ranch in the dead of night, quietly round up all the horses, silently release them from a locked and guarded compound, and stealthily drive them in the direction of his camp without provoking so much as a whinny or a nicker, was admired as much for his expertise in horse handling as for being a clever thief. Of course, more violent seizures were resorted to if the animals could not be procured by such subtle art.

Of all the horse thieves in the southern Plains, the Comanches were the most aggressive, as well as being the most powerful warriors and the most successful defenders of their territory. They hurled the lesser tribes back against the creeping white frontier on the east and held the Spaniards to the Rio Grande on the south. Whatever cruelties they had once endured at the hands of the mounted Conquistadors, they now repaid in kind to the Spanish *rancheros*. In fact, the Comanches' lust for the settlers' horses made life along the border extremely perilous.

If the ranchers' horses were in short supply, or if the size or color of the animals displeased the raiders, women and children were carried off instead. Needless to say, the Spaniards relinquished their horses without retaliation, and the Mexican Government kept an endless parade of replacement animals marching northward to the ransacked ranches. So much horse rustling occurred and with such regularity that well-worn trails led from Texas into the border states* of Mexico and on down into Durango, Cacatecas, and San Luis Potosi. The Comanches bragged that the only reason they allowed the Spaniards to remain in these regions was to raise horses for them.

Though the Spanish Government tried in every way to negotiate peace with the Comanches, its efforts failed. The Indians would settle for nothing less than all the horses in Mexico, and the Government's attempts to bribe the chiefs into keeping the peace only resulted in teaching the Indians the extortion game. The raiders began extracting gifts from individual ranchers, but did not refrain from taking their horses on another day.

Horses were, in every sense of the word, a form of money to the Comanches, who exchanged them for such rare items as white buffalo skins and exotic furs more accessible to the Northern tribes. They also sought guns and powder from the first white trappers and traders beginning to find their way into the Southwest.

These Frenchmen from Arkansas and traders from the United States, who had penetrated as far as New Mexico on what was to become known as the Santa Fe Trail, were viewed as friends by the Comanches and as useful outlets for their stolen booty. The Spaniards foolishly refused to trade with these merchants, thus strengthening the Comanches in the role of middleman. As a result of Mexico's self-imposed trade restrictions, the

---

* Until Mexico declared her independence from Spain in 1821, all the territory embracing what is now Texas, New Mexico, Arizona, and California was claimed by Spain. Much of it was unsettled, occupied by fierce Comanche and Apache tribes. Though scattered haciendas existed above the Nuecos and Rio Grande, for the most part these rivers marked the boundaries below which the Horse Indians of the Southwest held the hated Spaniards.

French and the Americans encouraged their Indian friends to steal whatever items they needed from the established ranches to the south and were thereby instrumental in promoting the hostility that steadily escalated between the Comanches and the Spaniards. Finally, out of desperation, the Mexican Government put a bounty on Indian scalps, and the hatred between the two peoples hardened beyond repair.

After 1821, the new government in Mexico was anxious to remedy this ancient vendetta and to colonize her vast and unsettled northern reaches, so a liberal colonization policy was instituted. Since the Indians in the region tolerated Americans over the Spanish-speaking people, isolated Anglo settlements sprang up in the Southwest. These were serviced, not by Mexico, but by the United States. Millions of dollars' worth of goods were carried across dangerous Indian Territory on the Santa Fe Trail yearly. The caravans were not altogether safe from Indian attack, though the Comanches were pleased to trade fresh horses stolen from Mexico for trinkets and guns.

The result of all of this horse raiding and trading was the dispersion of the wild-horse bands across a wide area, and as animals were passed northward from tribe to tribe, many slipped out of the hands of their new and inexperienced masters. Two main horse-trading routes extended along either side of the Rockies from Mexico to Saskatchewan: On the east, the powerful Comanches passed horses to the Pawnees who, in turn, passed them on to the Dakotas (Sioux), and so they proceeded from one Buffalo Tribe to the next. Along the western route, the desert Paiutes brought horses to the Shoshoni who passed them to the Crows, who held an annual horse fair on the upper Missouri River in Montana and traded them to the Piegans, Blackfeet, Mandans, and other Northern tribes. Business was good at the horse fair, for attrition was high due to the poor care and hard use the animals endured. What's more, the Indians could never seem to own enough horses to satisfy them, and their camps were surrounded by horses of every size, shape, and color.

A description of such an Indian camp with its flock of horses is given in *Travels in North America* . . . , by Charles Murray, who, out of a spirit of adventure, went west to try to locate and join the wandering Pawnees during the summer of 1834. After searching for weeks for a sign of the tribe, he suddenly came upon them encamped by a river and describes the scene as follows:

"As far as the eye could see were scattered herds of horses, watched by urchins whose whole dress and equipment [in summer] was the slight bow and arrow, with which they exercised their infant archery upon the heads of the taller flowers or upon any luckless blackbird perched near them. Here and there might be seen some gay young warrior ambling along the heights, his painted form partially exposed to view as his bright scarlet blanket waved in the breeze, while his small fretful horse was scarcely to be recognized under the variety of trappings with which the vanity of the rider had tricked him out; near him might be seen another naked savage without a saddle, and his only bridle a thong around the horse's head, galloping at full speed and waving in his extended right hand a 'laryette' with which he was chasing some refractory mule or runaway steed."

It might be mentioned here that as early as 1521 Bishop Sebastian Ramirez de Fuenleal, a benevolent Governor of New Spain, sent a request to the King for three hundred jennies to be given to the Indians. No such number were ever delivered, but in 1531 twelve jennies and three jacks were shipped from Spain to Mexico. Offspring of some of these burros were later brought to the Oñante settlement in Santa Fe, and from this stock proceeded the feral burro population whose descendants can still be found in the Southwest, especially in the Grand Canyon area. The inter-breeding of these burros with the Spanish mustangs produced the sterile mules which the Indians valued for their high intelligence and stamina. But since the mule is a hybrid and seldom can reproduce itself, there are, of course, no bands of feral mules in the West. However, the wild burros and the Spanish mustangs still occasionally crossbreed, and single mules are sometimes seen running with the bands.

One white mule, the leader of a band of horses in southern Nevada, was seen on the desert for a period of fifty-five years. When the old white mule was finally found dead in 1965, it was discovered that old-age had not killed her; she had died from a bullet. A wild mule, like a wild horse, is classified a feral animal with all that such implies.

"The naked urchins" mentioned by Murray were not only given the responsibility of guarding the tribe's stock from outside raiders, they were also instructed to make off with any stranger's horse if given an opportunity, and they proudly wore the number of horses they had succeeded in stealing marked on their shirts or arms.

But horse stealing was no child's game. It was a dangerous business and, for the most part, raids were carried out by the most intrepid warriors. The risks that were taken to acquire a few extra steeds, and the violent skir-mishes that resulted, seemed sheer folly to the United States Government which, in the early nineteenth century, tried to put a stop to the constant strife on the Plains. Among the devices employed by Washington was a stipulation that only those tribes that did not send out parties to steal horses from other tribes would receive the annuities promised to them for ceded lands taken by the United States. Just what the justice of this arrangement was it is difficult to understand. In any case, the Indians simply agreed to the stipulation and proceeded to ignore it. Washington was far away, and near at hand were strange tribes that had invaded the prairies to hunt and to steal horses. The Plains Indians were compelled to make reprisals. Charles Murray, in *Travels in North America* . . ., expresses the philosophy of the Indians on the matter:

"The Indian notions of reprisals are very cosmopolitan; if thirty horses are stolen from them and they cannot discover the thieves, they consider themselves perfectly justified in stealing thirty from the first party or tribe that may offer the opportunity."

One of the most brazen methods of horse stealing practiced by the Pawnees and their neighbors involved entering a strange camp shortly after dark, when the light of the evening campfires illumined only small patches of ground in front of the various lodges and tents, and when the majority of the inhabitants were still awake and milling about. As the thieves roamed through the darkened camp unnoticed, passing as members of the tribe, they surreptitiously and systematically cut the lariats that staked the special Buffalo Runners and war-horses before the tents of their respective owners. Unaware that they were no longer tethered, the horses remained quietly in their places while the raiders did their work. When a sufficient number had been freed, the thieves let out a mighty whoop and leaped on the back of the nearest horse. At the sudden noise, all the horses bolted, and the raiders drove the panicked animals out of the camp and into the dark of night. During such a mad scramble many no doubt escaped from their abductors and took refuge with the wild bands.

In order to maintain what the Indians considered to be a "status-sized" herd, it was imperative to take such risks, and though a certain amount of legitimate horse trading continued between the tribes, raiding was the more expedient means of obtaining replacements. For even the most lowly tribesmen felt compelled to own at least two or three horses; braves and lesser chiefs possessed from eight to twelve, but a great chief could not maintain his prestige with fewer than thirty.

Though at this time horses in the West were overwhelmingly of one type, those which were captured from the wild bands had already begun to acquire a slightly altered appearance, a special look that distinguished them from related horses that had never tasted freedom. Murray, in the previously mentioned *Travels* . . ., describes such an animal, chosen by the Great Pawnee Chief to ride in a ceremony preliminary to an important hunt: "The chief rode a light dun* or a cream-colored steed, whose long mane and frontlock, wild fiery eye and light active form, showed it to be a child of the wilderness. . . ."

The riding accouterment of this particular chief was already two centuries old and must have once belonged to a caballero of the seventeenth century. The reins were decorated with gilt stars, chains, and buckles, and the curved bit was long enough to break the horse's jaw should the animal be so unwise as to strain against it.

The Great Pawnee Chief was said to "favor his wild horse," though the Pawnees are not believed to have practiced much horse running and generally left the wild bands in peace. An indication of the size of the unchecked wild-horse population in Pawnee territory (present-day Nebraska) is suggested by Murray's account of a wild-horse stampede through camp:

"As the galloping mass drew nigh, our horses began to snort and prick their ears, then to tremble; and when it burst upon us they became completely ungovernable from terror. All broke loose and joined their affrightened companions except my mare which struggled with the fury of a wild beast, and I only retained her by using all my strength and, at last, throwing her on her side. On went the maddened troop, trampling in their headlong speed over skins, dried meat, etc. and throwing down some of the smaller tents. They were soon lost in the darkness of the night and in the wilds of the prairies and nothing more was heard of them save the distant yelping of the curs who continued their ineffectual pursuit."

Thus Murray, one of the first white men to sojourn among the Indians of the Plains, gives evidence of the extensiveness of the wild-horse population in the West prior to the arrival of white settlers. The number of horses that had already lived and died in unchallenged freedom since the Plains Indians had first become "horsed" one hundred and fifty years earlier, can only be guessed. Left to their own devices, winter and summer, generations of colts had been foaled that had never known the halter and were as wild as young deer.

---

* The wild horses were apparently already beginning to take on the dun or faded-earth coloration common to them today. Dun horses range from a light sand color to a deeper shade of rich loam (the mouse duns). Many dun horses wear a subtle stripe along their spines and finger marks around their legs. This muted pattern breaks up the total form of the animal, thus serving as protective coloration.

9. Explorers Use Indian Ponies

The search for a northern water route by which adventurous mariners could sail from the Atlantic to the Pacific, and thence to the Orient, had been pursued with extraordinary zeal for more than three centuries after the discovery of America. When it finally became evident that no practical passage existed, American explorers began to center their efforts on finding a land route that would bring them to the shores of the Pacific and the "Oregon Country." In this difficult and hazardous undertaking, Indian ponies of Spanish origin were destined to play a significant role.

The region that had captured the imagination of America was the Pacific Northwest; the intermediate Plains area was passed over for another half-century. But only one year after the Louisiana Purchase, Meriwether Lewis and William Clark were pushing their way across the northern latitudes on a course that was long and arduous, but later proved to be the best of the few possible routes to the Pacific Ocean.

Commencing their historic journey in St. Louis in 1804, they took their keelboats and canoes up the Missouri River, navigating through the present day states of Missouri, Kansas, Nebraska, South Dakota, North Dakota and Montana. For the rest of the distance, which required crossing one massive mountain impasse after another, the explorers needed horses. Fortunately, they were able to obtain some from the Shoshoni Indians, who happily traded their excess ponies for guns, cloth, metal utensils, and other such goods of the white man. The party thus was able to continue journeying on the backs of thirty Indian ponies, some of which bore Spanish brands! As the explorers progressed Westward, these mounts were traded for fresh stock from other horsed tribes.

The first explorers in the Northwest were wise in leaving their American domestic horses at home. It is extremely doubtful that stable-fed animals could have survived the difficult climb over snow-capped mountains, where forage was scarce, or been able to long endure on the baking deserts where water was either alkaline or nonexistent. Since no feed was packed for the horses, they often traveled for days without nourishment. The horse of the Indian possessed an acquired fortitude to make such a journey.

So, mounted on Spanish-blooded Indian ponies, Lewis and Clark struggled onward, gradually conquering one mountain system after another as they searched for the "hypothetical" river whose course, they postulated, would carry them downstream to the Pacific Ocean. As events turned out, the river they chose to follow—the Columbia—did indeed empty into the sea, and so the long-sought overland route to the Pacific Ocean was at last discovered.

The epoch-making journey of Lewis and Clark immediately stimulated interest among speculators and commercial fur companies, who quickly outfitted expeditions to cross the newly blazed trail for the purpose of exploiting the rich resources of the Oregon country.

The ambitious men who organized or signed on to these expeditions assembled in the frontier town of St. Louis, where the Missouri River flows into the Mississippi. Here, before setting off on their one-thousand-mile river trip, they loaded their keelboats with the kind of merchandise the Indians most desired—knives, kettles, cloth, and guns—to trade for horses for the land legs of their journey.

Following the course blazed by Lewis and Clark, they disembarked in North Dakota in the territory of the Mandan and the Arikara Indians where thousands of horses, representing the worldly wealth of these Indian nations, surrounded the Tartarlike encampments. Tents were decorated with gorgeous colors and gaily painted; mounted warriors trotted or galloped among the teepees.

The Mandans and the Arikaras welcomed these first Americans to appear in their territory, and willingly traded horses with them for firearms. In fact, so enthusiastically did the Indians negotiate for knives and gunpowder that their herds of ponies soon became depleted. To remedy this, parties of Mandans and Arikaras set off on horse-stealing raids with renewed vigor. Obviously, the situation did not make for peaceful conditions on the Plains.

But the Plains Indians were philosophical about such matters. Their pragmatic viewpoint is amusingly recorded by Washington Irving, who documented the account of the Astoria Expedition of 1811 as told to him by Lewis Hunt, leader of the first commercial expedition to follow the track of Lewis and Clark. Here is how Irving describes negotiations between Hunt and the Arikaras over horses:

"Mr. Hunt then spoke, declaring the object of his journey to the Great Salt Lake beyond the mountains [first stage], and that he should want horses for that purpose, for which he was ready to trade, having plenty of goods. . . . The left-handed chieftain, in reply, promised friendship and aid to the newcomers and welcomed them to his village. He added that they had not the number of horses to spare that Mr. Hunt required, and expressed a doubt whether they should be able to part with any. Upon this, another chieftain, called Gray-Eyes, made a speech, and declared that they could readily supply Mr. Hunt with all the horses he might want, since, if they had not enough in the village, they could easily steal more. This honest expedient immediately removed the main difficulty."

The Crows of Wyoming, whose territory was contiguous to that of the Mandans and Arikaras, became the obvious victims of this illicit traffic in horses. However, the Crows were a formidable enemy, besides having a natural bent for "commerce" themselves. They in turn seized horses from the Shoshonis, a downtrodden tribe living in the desert region of Idaho, and herded the stolen stock eastward to the Mandan market, no doubt scattering a good many to the wild in the process. Here the clever Crows got in on the bonanza and obtained guns and trinkets for themselves, as well as a surplus of these highly prized possessions to trade with more remote neighbors.

These remote neighbors were not Plains Indians like the Mandans, Arikaras, or Crows, but lived in mountainous, desert, or plateau regions, and their cultures and attitudes differed greatly from those of the Horse Indians of the Plains. Nevertheless, nearly all of these tribes were horsed and were reported to be so by Lewis and Clark, who had obtained additional mounts from them along the course of their journey. Now the expeditions that followed expected to do the same. But the Indians of the Northern Rockies and beyond were not always in agreement with this idea, and often it was the Indian who obtained the white man's horses instead of parting with his own, leaving the whites stranded.

The most dangerous and warlike people to be met with in the Northwest region were the Blackfoot Indians, who not only plundered and bullied all the Indian nations of the Northern Rockies, but also attacked nearly every party of whites that attempted to cross their mountains. The object of their belligerence was always the same—horses! Riding a horse through Black-foot territory was much like carrying a goat through a tiger-infested jungle; it was an invitation to be attacked. The Blackfeet, who did not welcome the whites into their country in any case, were savage fighters, and explor-ing parties were fortunate if these Indians merely rustled their horses, leaving the expedition stranded and starving, but alive.

An account of such a catastrophe is given by John Stuart, who was in charge of the Astoria Expedition on its return trip. One day, while peace-fully encamped on a mountain meadow where their horses were quietly grazing, Stuart's party was startled by the yells and whoops of Indians, who literally seemed to materialize out of the air. Instantly the party's panicked horses began to scatter—"nothing short of broken necks could stop them"—and as their owners watched helplessly, the screaming animals were driven scuttling down the rocky ledge.

Thus stranded amid mountain chains and ridges extending like a choppy sea as far as the eye could see, the men had no choice but to try to walk out of the treacherous range, carrying all of their belongings on their backs. As they struggled onward, growing weaker with each passing day—for without horses they couldn't hunt enough "to keep their bones together"— the men began to despair. Some flung themselves on the ground and begged to be left behind; one crazed and starving individual suggested the drawing of lots for one to die that the others might live.

And so, two thousand miles from home and without a single packhorse to help them over the snowy heights, the party's only hope for survival lay in reaching an encampment of friendly Indians willing to provide them with horses. That they did, and lived to tell their story, speaks eloquently for the courage of these early trailblazers as well as for the compassion of certain Indian tribes who furnished them with the animals they needed.

It is even more revealing of the importance of horses in the opening of the Northwest. For without the help of the Western Indians' little Spanish horse, the first explorers seeking a land route to the Pacific, and all those who immediately succeeded them, would neither have found nor been able to follow the route to the Northwest.

10. Explorers Lose Horses

The Northwestern tribes differed widely in their reaction to the bearded strangers who, footsore and bedraggled, staggered into their villages asking for horses. Some saw their chance to bargain and to obtain large quantities of knives and gunpowder in exchange for the poorest animal in their herds. On the other hand, the reluctance with which certain Indians traded away their horses may not have stemmed from mercenary motives at all, but might have had a deeper underlying cause.

No white man could ever quite understand the peculiar relationship that existed between the Indian and his horse. Though a brave or warrior might possess a vast herd of superfluous ponies, he would nevertheless risk his life to recover a single stolen animal. And though his family might be on the verge of starvation, he would oftentimes refuse to part with one horse to obtain the food needed. Despite all of this, however, he treated his horses abominably.

Around 1816 the youthful adventurer, Ross Cox, recorded the following observations in his *Columbia River* journal:

"They [the Indians] are hard taskmasters; and the hair-rope bridles, with the padded deerskin saddles, which they use, lacerate the mouths and backs of the unfortunate animals in such a manner as to render them at times objects of commiseration. . . . In summer they [the horses] have no shelter from the heat, in winter no retreat from the cold, and their only provender throughout the year is the wild loose grass of the prairies, which in the latter season is generally covered with snow, and in the former is brown and arid, from the intense heat of the sun."

Yet, despite the hardness of their lives, the Indian ponies seemed to display the same strange attachment for their riders that the Indians felt for their mounts. Washington Irving, in *Astoria,* marvels at the way the animals performed for their masters:

"It is said that the horses of the prairies readily distinguish an Indian from a white man by the smell, and give preference to the former. Yet the Indians in general are hard riders and, however they may value their horses, treat them with great roughness and neglect. Occasionally, the Cheyenne joined the hunters in pursuit of buffalo and elk and, when in the ardour of the chase, spared neither themselves nor their steeds, scouring the prairies at full speed, and plunging down precipices and frightening ravines that threatened the necks of both horse and horsemen. The Indian's steed, well trained to the chase, seems as mad as the rider and pursues the game as eagerly as if it were his natural prey, on the flesh of which he was to banquet."

There can be no doubt that a strong bond existed between the Indian and his horse, which made it extremely difficult for the red man to part with even his poorest animal. Consequently, in many instances, Indians refused to trade their horses to the assorted parties of traders and trappers who followed on the heels of Lewis and Clark. Moreover, some of these visitors to the Northwest may have been somewhat misled by Captain Clark's exaggerated report of the region in the *History of the Expedition* . . . , stressing the ease and convenience with which horse replacements could be obtained along the route:

"An elegant horse may be purchased of the natives for a few beads or paltry trinkets, which in the United States would not cost more than one or two dollars. The abundance and cheapness of horses will be extremely advantageous to those who may hereafter attempt the fur-trade to the East Indies by way of the Columbia River and the Pacific Ocean."

That such was not the complete picture is suggested by an entry in Lewis' diary:

"After unloading and arranging the camp, we went to the Skilloot village where we found Captain Clark. He had not been able to procure more than four horses, for which he was obliged to finally double the price of these formerly purchased from the Shoshonees and the first tribe of Flatheads. These, however, we hoped might be sufficient, with the aid of the small canoes, to convey our baggage as far as the villages near Muscleshell Rapid, where horses are cheaper and more abundant, and where we may probably exchange the canoes for as many horses as we want. The Skilloots have a number of horses, but they are unwilling to part with them, though at last we laid out three parcels of merchandise, for each of which they promised to bring us a horse in the morning."

The strange change of heart on the part of these Columbia River tribes, and their sudden reluctance to trade more horses to Lewis and Clark may have been a result of the Indian's reaction to the explorer's practice of eating horses that were too exhausted to be of any further service. Such a possibility is at least implicit in Clark's description of the dietary habits of the Coppanish (Nez Percé).

"The otter is a favorite food [of the Coppanish], though much inferior, at least in our estimation to the dog, which they will not eat. The horse is seldom eaten and never except when absolute necessity compels them, as the only alternative to dying of hunger. This fastidiousness does not proceed so much from any dislike of the food, as from an attachment to the animal itself, for many of them will eat heartily of the horse-beef which we give them."

The poorest tribe of the region, the desert-dwelling Shoshoni, would starve before eating a horse.

To Indians who had never raised livestock for food, the two animals that lived with them, the horse and the dog, were regarded as being on a higher level than the wild game. Though fifteen horses might be killed in a sacred ceremony and buried with an important warrior, slaughtering a horse for food was apparently out of the question.

On the Astoria Expedition, in 1811, Lewis Hunt did procure from the Sciatago tribe a horse with which to feed his emaciated party, but afterward the Sciatagos refused to let the men enter their huts.

Meanwhile the wild-horse population had rapidly exploded across the Plains. For, as the area surrounding an Indian camp inevitably became overgrazed, horses would move off—stallions sensibly herding their harems of mares to better pastures—and the Indians, in order to maintain "respectable numbers of horses," would immediately seek from other tribes replacements for these missing animals. Thus the cycle would continue, the Indians unwittingly feeding the wild herds with fresh stock.

One strange incident illustrates the extreme value that the Indians placed on the possession of horses, even to the point of sacrificing their own tribesmen for the sake of owning a few extra steeds.

A party of Arikaras on a horse-stealing expedition to Crow territory in Wyoming suddenly encountered a detachment of white explorers from the Bonneville expedition. The Americans had just turned their horses loose to graze when they were approached by three Arikara warriors who began to make conversation with them. While the three scouts distracted the whites, other Arikara warriors stole around the grazing horses and drove them off.

When the Bonneville party discovered the trick, they immediately seized the three dissemblers and held them as hostages, shouting to the horse thieves to release their animals or their fellow tribesmen would be burned on a pyre.

At first the Arikaras seemed undecided what to do. They released a single horse. After a time, seeing that the hostages were not to be set free, a second horse was released. When no more horses seemed to be forthcoming, the whites decided to dramatize their threat and they began to build a roaring fire.

At this point, the hostages became frightened and cried out to their fellow warriors, imploring them to give up the stolen horses. But the Arikaras were too passionately attached to horses to listen to their pleas and, "with many a parting word and lamentable howling," they abandoned the hostages to the flames.

Such incidents naturally resulted in more violence, for in view of the Indians, revenge need not be taken on the same party that had wronged them; the murder of any member of the guilty man's "tribe" would suffice to equal the score. Such Indian attacks were always "unprovoked," springing "from the barbarian's innate love of cruelty," according to the whites, who had some difficulty relating their own previous actions to the reactions of the Indians.

Horses were the major cause of Indian conflict during this period. Ironically, during the violent skirmishes that were fought over them, many horses slipped from the hands of both Indian and white man. A number of the explorers' animals were also lost through their own carelessness, the Indians' larcenous habits merely providing the white men with a convenient face-saving alibi.

Since none of the half-broken male horses purchased from the Indians were gelded, it was obviously necessary to guard these animals constantly, for the whinny of a mare, whether wild or belonging to an Indian herd, would lure them off. Besides, horses that had been recently purchased did not like to leave their home range and, if given the opportunity, would break loose and "return to the barn," so to speak.

The following excerpts from the Lewis and Clark journal, *History of the Expedition* . . . , give some indication of the difficulties that the men had with "straying horses":

"April 24 . . . We began early to look for our horses, but they were not collected before one o'clock.

"April 27 . . . Sunday . . . We were detained until nine o'clock before a horse which broke loose in the night could be recovered.

"April 29 . . . The horses having strayed to some distance, we could not collect them in time to reach any fit place to camp, if we began our journey, as night would overtake us before we came to water.

"April 30 . . . Although we had hobbled and secured our new purchases, we found some difficulty in collecting all our horses."

By July, the party no longer blamed themselves for the loss of any horses; instead they charged the Indians with luring away any stock that was missing:

"July 7 . . . In the morning our horses were so much scattered that although we sent out hunters in every direction to range the country for six or eight miles, nine of them could not be recovered. They were the most valuable of all our horses and so much attached to some of their companions [referring to other horses] that it was difficult to separate them in the daytime. We therefore presumed that they must have been stolen by some roving Indians."

Later that month, a Sergeant Pryor and two other men were detached from the expedition and entrusted with the duty of leading the horses to the confluence of the Yellowstone and the Bighorn rivers in Montana, where the party planned to rendezvous for the return journey to the United States. The horses in Pryor's custody were of extreme importance to the expedition, for much of the remaining trip would be made by water and the men planned to trade these horses to the Mandans for enough corn and beans to sustain them until they reached St. Louis.

On August 8, 1806, Sergeant Pryor camped on the creek, which now forms a boundary of the Crow Indian Reservation in the Pryor Mountain range. This region is a few miles from the habitat of the Pryor Mountain wild-horse bands (the animals marked by the Bureau of Land Management for roundup and auction). Here, in the mountains that now bear his name, Pryor lost all of his horses.

Captain Clark's journal reproduced in the *History of the Expedition* . . . , details Pryor's explanation:

"A shower of rain fell, and the creek swelled so suddenly that several horses, which had straggled across the dry bed of the creek were obliged to swim back. They [the three men] now determined to form their camp and the next morning were astonished at not being able to find a single horse.

They immediately examined the neighborhood and soon finding the track of the Indians who had stolen the horses, pursued them for five miles where the fugitives divided into two parties. They now followed the largest party five miles further, till they lost all hope of overtaking the Indians."

Though Captain Clark obviously accepted Pryor's account of what happened, the possibility remains that the horses simply may have been lost through Pryor's carelessness. They were particularly slippery and high-spirited animals, and two weeks earlier Pryor had come very close to losing them when the detachment encountered a herd of buffalo. Captain Clark records Pryor's explanation of that incident as follows:

"The horses [riderless], trained by the Indians to hunt, immediately set off in pursuit of them [the buffaloes] and surrounded the herd with as much skill as their riders could have done. At last, he [Pryor] was obliged to send one horseman forward to drive all the buffalo from the route."

It is easy to see how such horses were later turned into cow ponies. It is also easy to see how such horses might make a successful break for freedom during the night while Pryor's three-man detachment slept. If rather than being stolen by Indians the horses led by Sergeant Pryor did indeed take their freedom, the wild horses that inhabit the Pryor Mountains today might conceivably date back to August 8, 1806, when the first white man to cross that range lost a string of high-spirited animals.

On the other hand, there may well have been wild horses in the region even before Sergeant Pryor documented the range. Written records do not give rise to regions, peoples, or horses, all of which somehow have managed to exist through unrecorded ages, even without the written notations of man.

11. Explorers Capture Wild Horses

A map of the territory of the eighteenth-century Horse Indian tribes might also serve as a map of the wild-horse habitats, for it was only where conditions were suitable for horses to survive without any special care or fodder that the Indians possessed them. Since the horse did not feel at home in a heavily wooded area, the forest-dwelling Indians who adopted them moved out of the woods and on to the western Plains, where large numbers of animals escaped at the earliest opportunity.

Tribes living in the Great Basin west of the Rockies, however, had no difficulty maintaining herds of horses even in that dry and barren wasteland. The North African blood of the Spanish horse permitted it to survive and even thrive in the desert. So the Utes, the Navajos, and the Apaches were not forced to migrate to the grasslands, but could remain rooted in the desert, using their mounts primarily for war and to make occasional hunting forays into buffalo country.

Today, most of the surviving wild horses live in the desert states and are descended from stock kept by these Great Basin tribes. According to a Bureau of Land Management survey, nearly half the wild horses estimated to be on public lands, are found in the desert state of Nevada; the lush Plains, though preferred by the horses, have been too much exploited and appropriated by the white man for many wild animals of any kind to have survived there. The few scattered horse bands that do persist in the Plains states live for the most part on ranges too rugged to support livestock. (Cows lack the sure-footedness of the mustangs.)

This was not always the case. The natural tendency of the wild ones was to drift to where grass was most abundant, and stallions led their harems to those green pastures where the buffalo, along with the wolves that preyed upon them, had held such a long tenure.

Only when their stock became unexpectedly depleted by war, raiding, or disease, did the Plains tribes turn their attention to the spreading bands of wild horses that proliferated along their camp trails. Tribes in the Northwest, however, who were farthest from the primary source of supply, did develop horse-running skills and secured replacements by chasing and noosing pre-selected animals from the wild bands. The High Plateau region in Oregon Territory was also excellent horse country. Ross Cox, an adventurer and noted chronicler of the day, in his *Columbia River* journal, dwells on the vast numbers of wild horses found there during the first quarter of the nineteenth century:

"Thousands are allowed to go wild. . . . We have seen from seven hundred to a thousand wild horses in a band; and some of the party who crossed the continent by the Missouri route told me that in parts of the country belonging to the Snake Indians, bands varying from three to four thousand were frequently seen; and further south are more numerous."

From such enormous herds, by 1969 the wild-horse population in the Northwest had dwindled to perhaps a few thousand head in the three states of Washington, Idaho, and Oregon. Over previous decades untold numbers of wild horses in the area had been rounded up and turned into dog food and sausages by canning factories in Portland. The Bureau of Land Management did not report a single wild herd on public lands in the state of Washington.

Yet the wild horses of this region are credited with saving at least one party of stranded explorers during the first quarter of the nineteenth century. David Thompson, a Canadian surveyor and one of the first men to cross the Northern Rockies and reach the Columbia River (only a year after the departure of the Lewis and Clark expedition from that region), made the following entry in his diary in 1809, indicating that the party was drawing on the wild-horse herds for replacements:

"The Kaotanaes went a hunting the wild horses and brought eight to us. The next day my men and the Indians set off and had a hard day's chase but caught none of them. I have often hunted and taken them. It is a wild and rough-riding business and requires bold, sure-footed horses, for the wild horses are regardless of danger. They descend the steep sides of the hills [the western foothills of the Northern Rockies] with as much readiness as if racing over the finest ground. They appear more headlong than the deer. A dull, mere pack horse was missing and, with a man, I went to look for him and found him among a dozen or so wild horses. When we approached, this dull horse took to himself all the gestures of the wild horses, his nostrils distended, mane erect and tail straight out. We dashed into the herd and flogged him out; an Indian has now eighteen of these wild horses which he has caught and tamed, and we also caught three of them."

Thompson's description of the posturing of wild horses can hardly be improved upon. While photographing the bands, I, too, have been impressed by their defiant poses, their arched necks, and streaming tails. I have also watched them heedlessly plunge down steep hills, their pounding feet loosening stones that cascade into an avalanche which in no way deters their onrush.

In an even earlier entry, Thompson gives evidence that the wild horses he saw so far north were of Spanish origin:

"All Spanish . . . very great bands as every year the mares have a foal. There are several herds of wild horses in places along the mountains, especially on the west side on the pine hills of Mount Nelson. These have all come from tame horses that have been lost or wandered away when sickness prevailed." [Smallpox was decimating the Indian tribes at this time, and many horses, left unguarded during these epidemics, made their escape.]

The above was written in the year 1807, a time when the Blackfoot Indians were beginning to show signs of hostility toward the white trappers, traders, and surveyors infiltrating the Northwest. (Late in the summer of 1807 an Indian chief had been killed by a member of the Lewis and Clark party on that expedition's return journey to the United States, and the incident is thought to have triggered this attitude of hate that the Blackfeet directed toward all whites.) Thompson, sensing that the Blackfeet were on the warpath, was afraid to move from his encampment on the western slope of the Rockies, lest the Indians should spot him. So for two years he and his men were prevented from carrying out their mission, and remained in hiding, surviving by their hunting skill and wits.

Since all hunting had to be done in a circumscribed "safe area," the men in Thompson's party frequently "fasted." At one point they became so famished that they resorted to eating several of their valuable horses, thus destroying hope of eventual escape. Later, however, they were able to capture and successfully break wild horses to replace those that they had been forced to use for food.

Thompson's description of the wild-horse hunts, and the behavior of the wild bands when pursued, is consistent with later accounts of horse running. In his *Narrative of Explorations* . . . , he writes:

"For the greatest part of two summers I hunted them, took several and tamed them. Their feeding places were only about two miles from my residence. When I first made my appearance among them, they were in small herds from five to seven, sometimes of mares and a stallion, others wholly mares. Upon my approaching them, they appeared at a loss what to do; they seemed inclined to run away, yet remained. . . . I shot one of them and they ran off. We now agreed to try to run them down. For this purpose, we took two long-winded horses and started a herd of five. They soon left us, but as these hills are covered with short grass with very little wood, we kept them in sight. It was a wild steeple chase down hills and up others. After a chase of about four hours, they brought us to the place we started them. Here we left them frightened and instead of following them quietly, we dashed at them full speed shouting a hunting halloa and forcing them to their utmost speed; the consequence was two fell dead and a fine iron grey stood still; we alighted and tied his feet together and there left him. Following, we came to another horse and tied his feet and left him, we returned to the first horse. I passed my hand over his nostrils and the skin of his head became contorted. Yet, when tame, the doing of this appeared agreeable. The next day, we went for them on two steady horses with strong lines which we tied around his neck, put a bit in his mouth with a short bridle through which lines were passed, untied his feet, brought him to the house where he was broken to the bit and saddle. They lose all their fat and became lean and it takes about two months to recover them to a good condition. When in this last state they are made use of to hunt and ride down more wild horses."

When Thompson stated that two horses fell dead and a third stood still when the men merely "shouted a hunting halloa" and dashed at them, he was only the first of many horse runners who followed to report the extreme sensitivity and vulnerability of wild horses to pursuit and captivity. Stallions commonly seem unable to survive the ordeal of being captured and often seem to "will to die" within hours or days of being deprived of their freedom and of their sultanic power over their harems. But sometimes whole bands have succumbed when subjected to the experience of being rounded up and corralled.

The methods and tricks of the first cowboys, who seventy-five years after Thompson's successful experiment in capturing and breaking wild horses, developed the art of "mustanging" to its highest form, will be discussed in a later chapter. For the moment suffice it to say that the high attrition among the animals pursued, even by these later-day experts, was no secret and has been attested to in countless tales in which they themselves tell of their adventures.

But in the year 1807, before the wild horses were subjected to such systematic, methodical, and relentless persecution, they were not yet the wary creatures that they were destined to become. When Thompson first approached the wild herd, "they appeared at a loss what to do, they seemed inclined to run away, yet remained."

I can confirm from personal experience that a wild horse will not invariably spook when he detects the presence of a man in his habitat, but sometimes will hold his ground while he sizes up the threat. On such occasions, I have been able to snap many pictures of wild horses looking directly at my camera, and sometimes, while the animals stand transfixed, I have even managed to talk my way closer to the herd. Some wild horses, it would seem, are fascinated by man and, as a consequence, are vulnerable to capture.

Thus by hesitating, the horse-gone-wild once again began to lose its freedom, passing into the hands of its old master who, even at this late date, was still very much dependent on the services of a good horse.

12. *The Question of Size*

Despite the Indian pony's noble Spanish ancestry, he was frequently scrubby from poor or intermittent feeding, wild-eyed and ragged from excessive independence and no grooming, and stunted from being put to work too young.

No reputable horse breeder breaks a horse to the saddle before the animal is at least two years old; and, if possible, he will delay training for yet another year. A young horse has to metabolize a lot of grass, air, and sunshine to develop into the animated muscular system it is destined to become, and by burdening its body with weight and stress during this critical stage of development, its growth is irreparably stunted.

The Indians did not understand this principle, so they took no special precautions with their young animals. Like the squaws, the children, and the dogs, the horses had specific roles to play and duties to perform whenever camp was moved. All had to work if the tribe were to keep up with its ever-shifting food supply and outwit its ever-lurking enemies.

On moving day, the squaws and the common horses apparently bore the heaviest burdens. It was the duty of the women to feed the tribe, break camp, pack the tents and belongings and strap them on the horses, organize the food for the trek, and then proceed on foot if the horse herd had suffered a raid and mounts were scarce.

The war-horses on the other hand were neither packed nor ridden but, like the warriors, traveled unburdened and unfettered—at instant readiness for an enemy ambush. Horses trained to be buffalo hunters were also exempted from pack duty. But all remaining animals (dogs included) were required to serve the business of moving people and baggage. Of course, if the herd was sufficiently large and there were superfluous animals, the spare horses were simply herded along the trail by the young boys.

Children under three were lifted on top of the horse packs and tied in place, and as the pack train plodded along, the infants often napped, their heads bobbing to the sway of the horses. It is hardly surprising that when grown they became such extraordinary horsemen; their first rocking horses had been the real thing.

Children over five or six had specific responsibilities. They were required to guard the war-horses, help carry objects if pack animals were lacking, and keep an eye on the younger children.

Only the men were unencumbered. Many rode in style, having spent the early hours before the journey painting their faces and decorating their mounts.

This division of labor might seem lopsided except for the fact that every tribe was in constant danger of attack from its enemies. It was essential, therefore, that the men conserve their strength for the sudden, exhausting, and savagely violent battles that so frequently erupted.

No one—whether man, woman, child, or beast—escaped his or her obligations to the welfare of the tribe, so it would have been inconceivable that young horses should be spared from service until their bones had time to harden. Consequently, most of the horses were strong but not handsome; had bottom but no shape; were healthy and intelligent but undersized.

The forebears of the Indian ponies, namely the Spanish horse of the Conquest, had been small to begin with, rarely attaining fifteen hands. The average Spaniard is small himself; four centuries ago he was a good deal smaller. But some of the Indian mounts were only twelve and thirteen hands and could truly be classified as "ponies." Obviously, harsh conditions, poor grazing, and overwork at an early age all played a part in limiting the size of the animals.

Many have claimed that the "dwarfed" horses of the Indians were the result of inbreeding. Such a theory, however, becomes untenable when one examines the unstable lot of any group of Indian horses. They were constantly changing hands, being stolen, traded, passed from tribe to tribe, lost, and recovered. Moreover, since only one tribe seems to have understood how to practice gelding, the random breeding by so many male horses would create more genetic combinations than are possible in any breeding program where a few stallions father all of the offspring.

Mutual grooming. A foal nibbles cockleburrs from her mother's mane (above).

A stallion watches over his mares (left).

Neither was the horses' diminished size a product of natural selection, a process by which natural conditions would favor the survival of only those animals genetically destined to be small and thus, in time, eliminating from the strain the gene for large-sized horses. The offspring of the Indians' horses, when raised under favorable conditions, regained the normal some-what larger stature of their earlier ancestors. Major General Harding Carter, who led the cavalry attacks against the great Apache chief, Vitorio, observed that "whenever Indian horses are transferred to the easier conditions enjoyed by their stable-fed relatives, they invariably produce offspring that are restored to a larger size." Ranchers who have captured wild horses and bred them agree that this is so.

If it is true, then, that the wild horses can produce larger-sized offspring than themselves, it is logical to conclude that the animals have not been altered genetically. Nature has simply limited the ultimate growth of each individual horse in the wild herds to correspond to the food supply in their habitats. The cause and effect are reciprocal, the reduced animal being the product of an insufficient food supply during its early years, and conversely later requiring less food to sustain life in its poor habitat.

Today, wherever wild horses are found, they are generally small. Many are of pony stature. Wild stallions rarely exceed a thousand pounds, and some mares weigh as little as seven hundred pounds. In their steady retreat to poorer and poorer habitats, the horses have adapted to scant and unpredictable food supplies. In the past when drought or winterkill ruined their range, wild animals migrated, not returning to their home range until the crop had recovered. Now man and fences prevent the wild horses from reaching greener pastures. Consequently, nature, unable to provide the animals with a dependable food supply, has compensated by reducing their physical size and requirements.

The maturation rate of wild horses also seems to occur at a slower rate than that of their stable-fed counterparts. Two- and three-year-old mustangs frequently appear to be yearlings. Though many well-meaning people view this slower growth as a sign that the animals are not faring well, there is no reason to believe that such is the case.

According to experiments performed on rats and mice by Clive M. McCay of Cornell University, animals kept artificially immature by being placed on a restricted diet during their early development will ultimately live up to twice the normal life-span of their strain. McCay interprets the results of his experiments as meaning that prolonging the period of early development also postpones senility and death.

Nature's concept of what a wild horse should look like does not always conform to man's notions, but, as Dobie pointed out, man, habitually, makes a mistake when he equates size with quality. Nature has produced a very durable animal in the wild horse.

13. The Appaloosa Horse

One tribe of Indians in the Northwest, the Nez Percé, is credited with having selectively bred the horse known today as the Appaloosa.

It is interesting that the Nez Percés (the Coppanish of the Lewis and Clark journals) should have wanted to own horses at all. They were not nomadic buffalo hunters, as were the Plains Indians, but were a "collecting and gathering" tribe that harvested the annual salmon run on the Columbia River. They certainly had no need of horses to help them net the thousands of fish that struggled upstream to spawn each spring. Neither could horses be of any use in the mountain meadows where the edible camas roots, so relished by the Nez Percés, grew without tilling.

Nevertheless, they adopted the horse and adopted it early. It has been said of this tribe that they were the most "adopting and adapting" Indians of North America. So eager were they to possess the goods or new ideas of friend and foe alike that, on encountering an enemy in the field, they sometimes delayed fighting, under a flag of truce, for however long it took them to exchange goods. Not until the bartering was completed would lines be drawn and the two tribes withdraw to begin the conflict.

In their passion for novelty, the Nez Percés are even reputed to have once sent scouts to spy on Crow ceremonies in order to obtain new dances, and shortly after meeting Lewis and Clark they sent three tribesmen as far as the frontier town of St. Louis in order to obtain the white man's religion.

So it is not surprising after all that upon hearing exciting reports regarding horses, the Nez Percés quickly came to the conclusion that they ought to have some. Around 1740 they pooled the resources of several villages and sent an emissary loaded with goods to Ute territory to trade for some of the strange beasts, although they had no notion how to ride the animal and no near neighbor to teach them.

It is interesting to compare the initiative of this tribe with the Sanpoils of the Spokans, their nearest neighbor to the north, who waited and watched the Nez Percés experiment in breeding, riding, and raising horses for one hundred years before adopting the animal themselves. More enterprising neighbors, however, particularly the Cayuses, the Bannocks, and the Shoshonis, benefited greatly from the Nez Percés' success in horse breeding. Soon all had excellent herds. The Cayuses, especially, picked up breeding tricks from the Nez Percés, as well as stock whenever they had a chance. As a result, the Cayuses soon accumulated such numbers of horses that the name "Cayuse" has become synonymous with all Indian horses. The wild horses found in the West today are also referred to as "Cayuses" —a fact that points to their close identity to the pony of the Indian. The horse that the Nez Percés went to such trouble to obtain did not essentially change their way of life, but like most things adopted by this tribe, simply helped to enrich it. Now buffalo-hunting expeditions were mounted and sent to the Plains to obtain dried meat and skin for teepees (another innovation), but the tribe itself did not become nomadic. The Nez Percé people were much too peace-loving and fond of their hunting ground in northeastern Oregon and western Idaho to dream of following a migratory animal about the war-torn Plains. Their horses were primarily used for racing and bred to be beautiful in ceremony and parade.

How the Nez Percé Indians, who lived on an isolated plateau where the three states of Washington, Oregon, and Idaho join, chanced to hit on the idea of selective breeding is a mystery. They seem to have discovered by themselves how to perform gelding without first having watched the operation practiced by someone else, for the technique they used was original and apparently superior to the white man's method. After observing the Nez Percé method, Lewis and Clark adopted it. In the *History of the Expedition* Clark writes:

"The stone [stallions] horses we found so troublesome that we endeavored to exchange them for either mares or geldings, but though we offered two for one, the Indians were unwilling to barter. It was therefore determined to castrate them; and being desirous of ascertaining the best method of performing this operation, two were gelded in the usual manner, while one of the natives tried the experiment of the Indian way, which he assured us was much the better plan. All the horses recovered; but we afterward found that those on which the Indian mode had been tried,

though they bled more profusely, neither swelled nor appeared to suffer as much as the others, and recovered sooner."

Through the practice of gelding inferior stallions, and by trading off low-grade or poorly marked mares to their neighbors, the Nez Percés in a relatively short time possessed a quantity of very distinctively marked animals. In fact, so elaborately spotted were these horses that they hardly needed to be touched up with paint for the extravagant ceremonies in which they played such a significant role.

These Appaloosa horses, named after the Palouse River along which they once grazed, have been facetiously called the two-toned, polka-dotted ponies, and the description can hardly be more accurate. There are six color types, but the two most common patterns are as follows: The front half of the animal is either white or roanish, meaning that it is a solid color, interspersed with white hairs, giving that part of the horse an almost iridescent cast—much like "shot silk"—when the light hits it in a particular way. If the basic color of the roan is black, this half of the animal sometimes appears blue; if the basic color is brown, it reflects shades of red. The rear half of the Nez Percé horse is either white, spattered with small roan polka dots, or roan with a scattering of small white polka dots. A third type of Appaloosa is called the leopard phase, and an animal so marked is covered with round polka dots over its entire white or gray body.

One other characteristic of Appaloosa horses bears mentioning. Their eyes are completely circled with white, giving the animal an expression of eternal surprise.

These fancy animals, which delighted the Indians, have become very popular again today as evidenced by the ever-growing membership of the Appaloosa Horse Club in Moscow, Idaho. This club (actually a registry for Appaloosa horses) was based on the best Nez Percé foundation stock that could be located when, in 1938, efforts were made by a few dedicated individuals to rescue the "Indian-bred horse" from oblivion. However, the breed cannot be said to have actually been restored by this organization's work, for from time to time steps were taken by the club to improve the Appaloosa by crossing it with Quarter Horses, Thoroughbreds, and Arabians. Animals that displayed the right color pattern among these various breeds were accepted for registration. Today there are three distinct classes of Appaloosa horses, none of which contain horses that are pure descendants of those animals first seen by Lewis and Clark when they visited the High Plateau country and met the Nez Percé Indians. But like the leopard, the Appaloosa cannot hide its spots; though it is more of a color phase than a breed, nevertheless, it obviously traces a good deal—if not most—of its ancestry to the Indian stock that was responsible for the telltale polka dots.

The spots that distinguish this unusual animal also serve to mark its trail through a long course of history, for the spotted horse that showed up in Oregon Territory in the eighteenth and nineteenth centuries bears a striking resemblance to horses depicted in fourteenth-century Persian art. There are also parallels between the Appaloosa horse and drawings of horses appearing in Chinese art dating as far back as 500 B.C.

Whatever the horses' ancient history might have been, their sojourn with the Nez Percé tribe was highly salutary. Whereas the Plains tribes in their continual wandering and warfare put their animals to constant and hard use and exposed them to stress from the earliest years, the horses of the High Plateau enjoyed a better life, good feed, a mild climate, and plenty of leisure in natural "horse country." That this treatment agreed with them soon became apparent. The horses of this region did not become stunted. Ross Cox estimated that many were even fifteen hands tall.

The Nez Percés, though essentially not hunters or warriors, found other uses for their horses. They raced them and placed high wagers of blankets on the outcome. Early trappers and mountain men, forced to remain in this isolated region for several years, found such entertainment a welcome relief from the lonely monotony of life in the wilderness. Cox, in *The Columbia River,* describes a typical contest as follows:

"The horses were ridden by their respective owners, and I have sometimes seen upwards of thirty running a five-mile heat. The course was a perfect plain, with a light gravelly bottom, and some of the rearward jockeys were occasionally severely peppered in the face from the small pebbles thrown up by the hoofs of the horses in front."

When these mountain trappers had served out their contracts and returned to civilization, so lavish was their praise and so extravagant was their description of the Indian horse races that Captain Bonneville, when he broke the first wagon trail from Independence, Missouri, to the Columbia River, brought with him American horses, the first to reach the region. One of his prime objects was to test the relative merits of his carefully selected "blooded-stock" against the Plateau Indians' much-vaunted horses. Hence a race was planned.

Involved in the contest was an Indian horse which Bonneville had purchased from the Skynse village, a Shoshoni horse, and one of his own homebred animals. Washington Irving, in *The Adventures of Captain Bonneville,* describes the event as follows:

"The race course was for a distance of one mile and a half, out and back. For the first half mile, the American took the lead, by a few hands; but losing wind, soon fell behind; leaving the Shoshoni and the Skynse to contend together. For a mile and a half, they went head and head; but at the turn, the Skynse took the lead, and won the race with great ease, scarce drawing a breath when all was over."

It is not known that the winner of the race was an Appaloosa. It is known, however, that through selective breeding the Nez Percé Indians were instrumental in upgrading the stock of the entire region. Not only did these Plateau horses demonstrate to Bonneville that they were superior to American horses on the race track, they also impressed him with their powers of endurance. In a complete report to the United States army regarding the Indians in this far region, Bonneville describes the Nez Percés as superior horsemen, "who own horses 14 to 14½ hands high, stout built, and upon which the Indians gallop all day." He also noted that certain individual tribesmen possessed as many as three thousand horses.

Inadvertently, of course, the Nez Percés' concern for their horses affected the health and good looks of their neighbors' stock as well—horse stealing being as much a way of life on the High Plateau as it was on the Plains. But near neighbors were not the only ones to benefit from the extreme care taken by the Nez Percés to improve their herds. Across the Rockies the Crows of Wyoming, allies and friends of this tribe, received large numbers of these splotched horses as gifts. Chief Bobby Yellowtail of the Crows, in an interview, told me some of the details of these exchanges of horses:

"The Nez Percés would come and stay with the Crows for a year or two in order to hunt buffalo. Now it's a peculiar thing that the buffalo didn't seem to go over on the west side of the Rockies cause if they did the Nez Percés would never have come to hunt with the Crows. They'd stay here for two years and get all kinds of pelts to make teepees with and get the dried meat and the pounded meat and then they'd go back. Then in another year or two there would be another great big caravan of Nez Percés coming over here. Well, as a result, we had marriages between the tribes and we had Crow-Nez Percés. And naturally there would be a lot of horses given as gifts. They'd come and bring those horses—where they developed them we don't know—but we had just a profusion of Appaloosa horses here."

Since it was the oversized herds of the Indians that continually supplied fresh blood to the wild bands, this "profusion of Appaloosa horses" on both sides of the Rockies no doubt also infused vigor into the wild horse herds across a wide region. Documentation that Appaloosas were frequently seen with the wild bands is evidenced by several of Charles Russell's paintings in which he invariably depicts an Indian's noose about to fall over the neck of a wild horse with spots on its rump.

Though in recent years few Appaloosas have been sighted in the wild, only five years ago reports were more common. Since their genes remain masked in the herds, Appaloosas may again show up in numbers. However, since an Appaloosa horse seems to be as prized by whites today as his ancestors were coveted by the Indians of yesterday, it is unlikely that a wild horse so marked would long escape the attention of the "mustangers."

Since any Appaloosa recovered from the wild today would not have been "upgraded" by the special breeding program initiated by the Appaloosa Club, it could logically turn out to bear an even closer relationship to the horses of the Conquest than any registered animals. It might even qualify for registration in the Spanish Mustang Registry as well as in the Appaloosa Horse Club. At the present time, Robert Brislawn has in his possession two Appaloosa-marked mares whose purity is still in question, and so they have not yet been admitted to membership in the Spanish Mustang Registry.

14. Settlers Use the "Cayuses"

When Lewis and Clark first appeared among the Nez Percés, the "adopting and adapting" Indians, characteristically, tried to establish good relations and trade with the strange white tribesmen who appeared in their country and whose knives and guns of polished metal, magic compasses, telescopes, and mirrors so intrigued them. The Indians embraced and fed the weary travelers and offered them tribal status in a formal ceremony. Perhaps more important from the point of view of the explorers, the Nez Percés willingly supplied them with fresh horses.

Lewis and Clark on their part behaved well with this tribe of Indians and favorably impressed them. Captain Clark, with the help of Sacajawea, the Indian wife of a member of his party, and four translators, made a speech before them in which he extended greetings from the Great White Chief, President Jefferson, and told them the news that their lands had been annexed by the white nation far away to the east. He also delivered the President's admonition to all Indians in the West to put an immediate end to intertribal warfare and live in peace.

The Nez Percés accepted the news with equanimity. They responded that they were happy to accept the friendship of the Big-hearted White Men, but that it would be necessary for Captain Clark to speak to the Blackfeet and the Shoshonis about the warfare. The Nez Percés added that they would be very happy if the white nation that had annexed their lands would, in fact, restrain these terrible enemies.

Only the women expressed uneasiness over the news of the annexation. As a token of their misgivings, they mussed their hair at the feast given to honor Lewis and Clark. The men, however, bent on establishing trade with the white explorers, did not share their wives' forebodings.

The good relations established by Lewis and Clark were soon undone by the men who immediately followed. Shortly after the John Jacob Astor expedition reached the mouth of the great river and completed the building of the Fort Astoria Trading Post, two small detachments of trappers were dispatched into the wilderness to found sub-posts for the Pacific Fur Company. The sites chosen for these sub-posts were in Nez Percé territory, situated along the tributaries of the Palouse River and the Salmon River known to be rich in beaver. These two locations were selected because they provided river transportation to the main post, Fort Astoria, and because the Nez Percé were reputed to be friendly and desirous of trade. This latter point was a major consideration as the trappers were counting on the Indians to supply them with horses to use for food throughout the winter.

Trouble began immediately. The Nez Percés did not wish to sell their horses for this purpose, and even their passion for the white man's goods was not inducement enough. They flatly refused.

A John Clarke, who headed this Palouse River operation, was a man of impatient temperament and he regarded the Indians' refusal to sell him horses as a personal affront. He expressed himself in ways that easily surmounted any language barrier existing between the Indians and the whites. Then, when a silver goblet that Clarke had managed to carry throughout his arduous travels (an object with which he planned to impress the village chief) was discovered to be missing, Clarke lost all control. In a rage, he ransacked the village until the treasured object was found, and then he hanged the thief as a lesson to the Indians.

This act had a profound effect on the Indians. They were appalled at the uncontrolled behavior of this stranger, and they refused to extend hunting privileges to him within the boundaries of their territory. As a consequence, John Clarke and his party of men were forced to move to the Spokane River and live among the Sanpoils, who were horseless.

Donald McKenzie, who headed the detachment assigned to the Salmon River sub-post, fared no better with the Nez Percés. McKenzie's first mistake was to suggest to the braves that they trap beaver for him, an insulting proposition, since trapping was the work of women. But when he attempted to buy their horses for food, the outraged Indians would not hear of it.

McKenzie, however, was not a man to take "No" for an answer. Whenever he needed meat, he simply shot the horses he wanted from the Indians' herd, leaving a bundle of goods in payment beside the severed head of the beast he had slaughtered. It wasn't long before McKenzie, too, was forced to move out of Nez Percé territory, and he shifted his operation to Walla Walla on the Columbia River.

But the coming of the white man to the region had already complicated the lives of the Indians. By introducing the Indians to the use of weapons, the explorers had created an arms race among the tribes. So when the Shoshonis, who were already well supplied with guns, began pressing the Nez Percé nation from the south, it soon became evident to the Nez Percé chiefs that it was imperative that they, too, trade with the white man for firearms. And so they reconciled themselves to the white man's appalling diet, and according to records led 350 horses a year to Walla Walla to be exchanged for guns.

Though both Clarke and McKenzie had gotten off on the wrong foot with the Nez Percés, most of the mountain men of this early period succeeded quite well in winning the friendship of these Indians. Many of the trappers were contracted by fur companies to remain in the territory for a period of years, and the longer they were separated from civilization and family life, the more they appreciated the warmth and diversity of Indian tribal life. Many took squaws for wives and adopted the Indian mode of dress and customs. The only other diversion offered to these isolated white men was the annual fur rendezvous at which the lonely trappers gathered for a few weeks of revelry before heading back into the woods. So all sought relaxation and pleasure in the company of friendly tribes, attending their dances and especially their horse races.

For thirty years this pleasant Indian-white relationship existed. But it was bound to change as soon as the region became more accessible to other interest groups. Washington Irving, in *The Adventures of Captain Bonneville,* speculated on the future of the area:

"We are aware that this singular state of things is full of mutation, and must soon undergo great changes, if not entirely pass away. The fur trade, itself, which has given life to this portraiture [of Captain Bonneville], is essentially evanescent. Rival parties of trappers soon exhaust the streams, especially when competition renders them heedless and wasteful of beaver. The fur-bearing animals, extinct, a complete change will come over the scene: the gay trapper and his steed, decked out in wild array, and tinkling with bells and trinketry; the savage war chief, plumed and painted, and ever on the prowl; the trader's cavalcade, winding through defiles or over naked plains, with the stealthy war party lurking on its trail; the buffalo chase, the hunting camp, the mad carouse in the midst of danger, the night attack, the stampede, the scamper, the fierce skirmish among rocks and cliffs, all this romance of savage life, which yet exists among the mountains, will then exist but in frontier story, and seem like the fictions of chivalry or fairy tale. Some new system of things . . . will succeed among the roving people of this vast wilderness; but just as opposite perhaps to the habitudes of civilization."

It can readily be discerned from this wonderful summary of the "romance of savage Life" that the early mountain trappers would not have long survived without the help of the Indians' horses. The "buffalo chase . . . the stampede . . . and the fierce skirmish among rocks and cliffs," all took place on the backs of fiery little ponies provided by the tribes of the Far West, and the significance of these often scrawny-looking creatures was not lost on the mountain men. When at last their term of service to the fur companies had been fulfilled and they returned to civilization, they carried home amazing stories of the horses to be found in this faraway realm.

The "new system of things" predicted by Irving took place swiftly and brought to the Northwest an entirely different type of American—people whose attitude toward the Indians' horses was completely negative.

In 1843, shortly after the discovery of a pass over the Blue Mountains that could be crossed on wheels, immigrants began inching their way along this "Oregon Trail," pausing at Fort Boise for a short rest before attempting the steep mountain range directly ahead. These immigrants were of a totally different character than the wild mountain men who had preceded them by four decades.

Most of the early trappers had been men who were nonconformists, bachelors who sought adventure and escape from the restrictions of civilized living. Life among the Indians had suited them very well, and they had eagerly adapted themselves to the wilderness. The immigrants, by contrast, brought their civilization with them and had no intention of living a primitive life and integrating with the Indian tribes. Their families were in their wagons.

As word spread among the Northwest tribes of the arrival of these "different whites," tribesmen from far and near gathered along the trail to get a first look at white women and children. Eager to trade with the newcomers, each Indian brought with him dozens of horses to be exchanged for gingham aprons and other trifles that struck his fancy. Since most of the oxen and horse teams were completely spent after pulling the prairie schooners as far as Idaho, the immigrants were only too happy to obtain the Indians' fresh horses. Many of the travelers could not have made the steep ascent that lay just ahead had it not been for these ponies.

The Oregon Trail actually led through Cayuse country, a fact that rankled the Nez Percés, who naturally wanted the trade, and they contended that a better route across the Blue Mountains lay on their lands to the north along an old war trail. Although they tried to divert the traffic, the travelers refused to believe that the long detour proposed by the Nez Percés would be less time-consuming than the short but difficult climb they were about to face west of the Snake River.

As it turned out, it was fortunate for the Nez Percé nation that the white immigrants wouldn't listen to their good advice. In addition to the gingham aprons, the travelers carried measles, scarlet fever, and smallpox in their caravans, and the Indians, possessing no immunity to these diseases, succumbed by the thousands to epidemics that struck down whole villages. By 1847 the Cayuse nation was no more, its people virtually extinct, and all that remains of this tribe today is its name, which has come to mean an Indian horse.

Though the first immigrants obtained horses from tribes other than the Cayuse, they were unable to distinguish one Indian from another, and they assumed, since their route lay through Cayuse territory, that all the horses they acquired from tribesmen lined up along the trail were "Cayuse" horses. The name stuck.

This inability on the part of the newcomers to discriminate between the various Indian nations might well have served as a forewarning to the tribes of the trouble they would soon have with the settlers. Many of the immigrants to the Pacific Northwest were second-generation farmers from the Middle West, whose parents had pioneered the Ohio River Valley. Raised on horror stories of Shawnee Indian resistance and depredation, they were prepared—perhaps even eager—to re-enact the conflicts that their parents had faced a generation earlier. Their view of the red man was one-sided; they regarded all Indians as belonging to one savage race of primitive and wholly untrustworthy individuals, and they failed to differentiate between friendly tribes and hostiles.

The Plateau Indians had greeted these newcomers with friendship and even provided them with fresh horses; nevertheless, when the immigrants began to settle on to the land, they viewed their neighbors, the Nez Percés included, as immoral savages and they looked down on them. This despite the fact that the Nez Percés on their own initiative had persuaded two Protestant missionary families to journey across the wilderness to bring them the white man's religion.

When stock was lost, the farmers were quick to blame the Indians and would organize themselves into posses to raid the Nez Percé herds, helping themselves to whatever horses appealed to them. Rationalizing that their missing animals were more valuable than the spotted stock they were appropriating, they generally took two for one. Nor did they bother to ascertain which Indian had actually made off with their animals, if indeed any had, but availed themselves of horses from the most convenient herd.

Their thinking on such matters was not unlike the Indian idea of justice—any person belonging to the tribe of a guilty man could serve as scapegoat.

Later, when confronted by the angry Indian whose stock they had seized, the whites simply denied all guilt, claiming that their new animals had been captured from the wild bands that abounded in the region. The Nez Percés knew better. They branded the ears of their horses and could recognize their own stock. Moreover, they knew that the white farmers could not have caught a wild horse from the backs of their draft animals.

Though these Cayuse horses now being rustled by the whites had pulled more than one stranded immigrant across the mountains, they were not highly regarded by the farmers. The horses were neither built nor trained to do the work of the ox teams that they were expected to replace. Besides, the immigrant farmers had no comprehension of the basic difference between the hot-blooded Buffalo Runners they now had in their possession and the cold-blooded plow animals they had known all their lives. They regarded the small Indian horses as merely inferior examples of the draft stock they had left back home, and the Cayuse label soon began to mean a low-grade animal. Even today a derogatory connotation is attached to the name "Cayuse," and a prejudice against the small horse persists among many Westerners.

In 1969, when a bill was introduced into the Nevada State Legislature designed to limit the hunting of wild horses from twelve months out of the year to two, an anti-horse assemblyman protested. He argued, "These wild horses are not the romantic mustangs you all read about roaming the hills. They are inbred, Roman-nosed [Barb!], maverick, *Cayuses,* and they are detrimental to fish and game."

Unwittingly, Assemblyman Norman Glaser, by the very language he used to condemn them, confirmed that the horses he did not want protected were of historic interest. Unfortunately, his fellow assemblymen were equally uninformed, and the connotation of the label "Cayuse" prejudiced their judgment. The bill failed to pass.

Not everyone, however, is so ignorant of the facts surrounding this word, or so lacking in accurate knowledge concerning the horse that bears the name. The Canadian Wild Horse Protection Society, located north of the state of Washington in British Columbia, publishes a quarterly magazine edited by a horse expert, Miss Norma Bearcraft. The magazine is titled, *The Cayuse Conserver.*

15. A Psychological Development

A confrontation between the Indians whose way of life was based on the sharing of a communal hunting ground by all the members of the tribe, and the settlers who carefully surveyed the land, laid out their farms in neat squares, and defended their private property against all comers was inevitable. To the American, only recently freed from unfair British land laws which restricted property titles to eldest sons, owning a plot of land represented a sacred right. Therefore, the need of the Indian to make use of a wide sweeping stretch of undelineated hunting ground not only menaced the pioneers' homesteads, but threatened a very deeply felt American political philosophy as well.

The only exception to this prevailing American belief in the sanctity of private land ownership was expressed somewhat later by the cattlemen of the Great Plains, who needed an open range of proportions far beyond an individual's means to possess in order to support their enormous herds of livestock. Like the Indians, whose hunting way of life dictated that they be mobile and roam freely across vast tracts of land, the cattlemen, too, were irked by the settlers who divided the range into paltry squares. The early ranchers often found their cattle cut off from feed and water by these fenced-in farms, and they bitterly resented the homesteaders.

Both the mobile Indians and the early cowboys depended on two things for their existence: an open range and plenty of horses. On the other hand, the settlers regarded these two factors as inimical to "progress" and their particular aims.

But another generation would pass before the Great Plains would be the scene of the final confrontation between the "nesters" (as the farmers were called by the cattlemen) and those whose livelihood depended on their ability and freedom to follow the movements of animals.

In the meantime, in the Northwest the first Americans to arrive were not ranchers but farmers, and they pre-empted the Indians' hunting lands, taking what they needed piece by piece and converting it to farmland. From their viewpoint, the region was unoccupied simply because it had never been divided and claimed. They rationalized that, since the Indian showed no inclination to utilize the fertile farmland that had for so long been at his disposal, he should now be forced to relinquish it to those who would put it to good use. To the hardworking farmers the Indian appeared idle because he did not scratch the soil and watch over a crop.

The restless wandering of the tribes as they followed the seasonal bounties of nature—whether buffalo on the Plains, camas-root harvest on the mountain meadows, or a salmon run in the Columbia River—made no sense whatever to the white settlers who felt the need to put down roots and to impose some kind of stability on the land. Although the intermittent relief granted to the land by the movements of the nomadic tribes was beneficial and promoted its continuing health, the settlers, whose methods were more artificial, could not grasp the fact that the Indian was living in harmony with his environment. They believed that the Indian was just too foolish to recognize the error of his migratory ways, and they blamed his horse for the fact that he refused to settle down.

Horses, according to the white settlers, gave the Indian the mobility he needed to maintain control over wide tracts of undeveloped land, speed to pursue wild prey and so avoid doing any real "work," and a commodity to trade for ammunition to defend his way of life. As long as the Indian possessed vast herds of horses, the whites reasoned, he would continue to resist the advances of civilization, and the wandering tribes would flourish at the expense of the hardworking farmers. The prejudice felt toward the Indian was thus gradually transferred to the Indian's horses.

Even after these ulterior motives had long been forgotten, the negative attitude formed toward the Indians' horses during this period persisted and later colored governmental policy regarding horse herds on reservations.

The military concurred with the settlers that as long as the Indians continued to maintain a nomadic or seminomadic existence there would be no peace in the West. According to John A. Hawgood, author of *America's Western Frontiers,* General William T. Sherman made this report: "All Indians who cling to their old hunting grounds are hostile and will remain so until killed off. . . . We must take chances and clean out Indians as we encounter them."

The ultimate fate of the Indians and the ultimate fate of their horses were so intertwined that it is necessary to review one in order to understand the other. Though each tribe's story was unique, the basic theme of humiliation and deprivation imposed on all the Indian nations was agonizingly similar. The crushing of the Indians, their removal from the "lands where their fathers were buried," and the extinction of their way of life is a brutal story. Whether an account be given of the gunning-down of the surrendered Sioux nation at Wounded Knee, or of Chivington's massacre of a peaceable Cheyenne encampment in Colorado, or of the pursuit of the Nez Percés across fifteen hundred miles of Rocky Mountains by the United States cavalry, they all testify to the greed and inhumanity of the white man.

During the process of the penning up of the Indians, there were moments when bands of horses took advantage of the confusion and broke for freedom. As a result, the wild horse population may have reached a peak, estimated by some as high as seven million. Unfortunately, the Indians were unable to follow the example of their stock and do the same.

The Indian's gradual resignation to his fate and to the destruction of his way of life, as well as the white man's disposal of the living remnants of the Indian's disintegrating culture—his horses—is well illustrated by the sad story of the Nez Percé nation.

The business of moving Indians had long been practiced in the East, but little had been learned from the bitter experiences that had resulted. In 1830 under Andrew Jackson's administration, the Indian Removal Act had become law, blueprinting the process by which the Eastern tribes were driven westward as the frontier shifted, until at last they were dumped on the unwanted Plains. This removal process often meant that tribes were relocated two, three, and even four times on their way to their ultimate destination on the "Great American Desert," the peculiar designation given to the region beyond the Mississippi River.

Now the settlers in the Northwest, though not yet sure in which direction they might later wish to expand, were ready to follow the precedent of earlier pioneers in the East and begin the business of relocating the Indians.

In 1855, the governor of the Oregon Territory, Isaac Stevens, called a council of the Nez Percé nation to meet in the valley of the Walla Walla River for the purpose of discussing "permanent lands" for them. One of his lieutenants, Lawrence Kip, kept a diary of the event, which is quoted by Francis Haines in *The Nez Percé:*

"Governor Stevens, at the opening, gave them the most elaborate address he has yet made, explaining to the chiefs most definitely what lands he wishes them to give up, and what their Great Father [the United States President] would give them in return, together with the benefits they would derive from the exchange. General Palmer, afterwards, made a speech an hour long in which he endeavored to illustrate to his audience the many advantages resulting from their being brought into contact with civilization."

The same Lieutenant Kip reveals that while the white arbitrators were trying to eradicate the Indians' way of life, they were not averse to partaking of its pleasures!

"The races tonight were the most exciting we have seen as the Indians bet some sixteen or eighteen blankets on the result and all the passions of their savage natures were called into play. There was visible none of the Mohawk stoicism of manner which Fenimore Cooper describes."

In the abstract, the untested reservation idea might have seemed a good solution to Governor Stevens who, no doubt, foresaw that the conflict between the Indians and the settlers was certain to escalate. Bringing the Indians "into contact with civilization" certainly sounded progressive, and it was hoped that once the Indian gave up his horse herds and learned to work for a living, the white community would begin to find him an acceptable neighbor.

The offer made to the Nez Percés at this time was not unattractive. Providing the Indians agreed to stay within their borders, they would be allowed to retain all of their customary hunting grounds, would be granted hunting and fishing privileges on public lands off their reserve, and would receive $200,000 for schools and a hospital.

Since it seemed they had little to lose, the Nez Percés agreed to the conditions of this treaty and signed it. But four years later, Congress still had not ratified the agreement drawn up between Governor Stevens and the Nez Percés, and many tribesmen became suspicious. They prophesied that the white man was stalling for time to grow strong enough to seize the Indians' lands without paying. Events proved that this prediction was correct.

In 1860, one installment of the promised $200,000 arrived. It was the first and last payment that the Indians were to receive, for in that year the United States was caught up in a civil war, and the Indians of the remote Western region were forgotten. The Nez Percés had to be content with promises.

16. A Horse-Removal Program

During this period of Civil War in the United States, the white settlers of the faraway Oregon Territory received no more attention from the Government in Washington than did the Indians and, as a result, they took the law into their own hands more and more. Annoyed by the fact that the Indians had been granted excellent land which they themselves coveted, they began encroaching on the reservation, staking out farms and erecting fences on the choicest acreage. The Indians made no protest. There was no one to whom they could protest.

But when gold was discovered in a small stream flowing through the Nez Percé treaty lands, the encroachment turned into an invasion. So many prospectors poured into the reservation that a serious food problem would have been created had it not been for the humanitarian impulses of the Indians, who fed the hungry gold-seekers.

The gold fever soon died down when the stream-yield turned out to be too low to be profitable, and the miners began to abandon their claims. The Indians, hoping to recover their lands from the white farmers squatting on the reservation, registered a strong protest over the treaty violation. The white response to the Indians' complaints can be summed up by an editorial in the Boise newspaper which proposed that the Indians' "problem" be solved by sending the "savages" a shipment of blankets infected with smallpox.

But the whites themselves began to grow uneasy over the illegality of their actions and, on second thought, decided that, since the treaty agreement had indeed been violated, it might be in their best interest to meet with the Indians at another council for the purpose of drawing up a new treaty. The treaty which they proposed at this time reduced the Indians' reservation by seventy-five percent.

The Nez Percés were not so ready to ratify this treaty, and there was much dissension among them over the future course of their nation. Their initial concession to inhabit only the lands ceded to them by the treaty of 1855 had not radically altered the tribe's mode of existence. Under the terms of this agreement they still had considerable room to roam, to harvest the annual salmon run on the Columbia River in the spring, and in the winter to move their horses to the temperate meadows in the Wallowa region of northeastern Oregon.

In some ways this structured isolation permitted them to revert to an earlier and, no doubt, happier period. Disillusioned by the behavior of the white settlers, they expelled the missionaries who had been invited to work among them, protesting that white people did not practice what they taught, and they began again to express their religious fervor in traditional dances and ceremonies. A few members of the tribe remained Christians, however. Chief Joseph, for one, continued to be guided by a New Testament given him by one of the ejected missionaries. The Nez Percés, always democratic in outlook, tolerated this diversity of religious viewpoint within their tribe and made room for it. But the tribal dissension over the ratification of the new treaty which would reduce the reservation lands divided the tribe into three separate religious factions.

A part of the tribe that retained orthodox Christianity favored the signing of the new treaty. These Indians were convinced that the reservation system would teach them farming and would ultimately lead to assimilation. Another faction, also Christian but much more relaxed in outlook, did not agree. This group, led by Chief Joseph, felt that the Indians' hunting way of life was better for Indians, and that they ought not to be reformed. Chief Joseph pointed out that the reduced reservations would not support the Nez Percés' large herds of Appaloosa horses, and he expressed a preference to live in the Wallowa region with the ponies. A third group, anti-Christian, had developed a healthy distrust of the white man and opposed signing any kind of treaty with him. This group was actually quite militant in outlook.

After much wrangling over a period of many days, the three factions finally were able to come to an amicable solution. Their decision reflects the very highly sophisticated democratic philosophy of the Indians, for they agreed to resolve their differences by dissolving the Nez Percé nation, breaking it up into three separate tribes, each to go its own way and do what it wished. In a formal ceremony, they declared their mutual and friendly independence one from another. Only the missionary faction, however, signed the new treaty.

This was not at all to the whites' liking. They wanted all the Indians and their horses removed to the Idaho reservation, and so the United States Government in Washington was advised by the settlers not to honor the tribe's act of self-dissolution. Hence, all the Nez Percé Indians were bound by a treaty signed only by a few. The nonsigners, who refused to move to the reduced reservation area, were thereupon regarded as in violation of a Government treaty, and the United States Militia began to hound them. At this point, Chief Joseph, embittered by the injustice of this action, renounced Christianity and destroyed his New Testament with the words: "I will have nothing more to do with the white man and his ways."

The Government in Washington, too far away to comprehend the true nature of the situation, did nothing to remedy the nontreaty Indians' grievances, but supported instead the view of the American settlers in the region who were anxious to have the Indians penned up, and they finally succeeded in getting an order from General O. O. Howard, saying that the nontreaty Indians should be put on the reservation within thirty days.

The only hope of the nontreaty Nez Percés to escape reservation life was to flee to Canada. So the tribe headed north, breaking trails across fifteen hundred miles of unknown mountain territory while being pursued by the U.S. Cavalry.

As the fugitives hacked their way through the heavily forested mountains on what is now called the Lolo Trail, small detachments of warriors remained in the rear to fight the advancing cavalry. Though skirmish after skirmish ended in the defeat of the American forces, the Nez Percés could not hope for victory. Detachments of fresh soldiers were constantly reinforcing the pursuers. Furthermore, despite their many victories, the Indians were never able to consolidate their position, since they were constantly forced to move backward to catch up with the fleeing tribe.

Defeat for the Nez Percés was inevitable. Paradoxically, it came about through a minor miscalculation. The Indians had long observed that white fugitives who crossed the invisible boundary between the United States and Canada escaped further persecution. Believing that they had already crossed the border and reached Canadian soil, the Indians ended their flight at Bear Paw—a few miles too soon.

The misery endured by the Nez Percé people, and the incredible valor of the horses that carried this tribe through the mountain wilderness at an average speed of sixteen miles a day, is beautifully told by Francis Haines in his book, *The Nez Percé*. Many horses died of starvation, some broke their legs on the log-strewn route, others plunged into ravines when a steep slope suddenly turned into a rock slide under the weight of the animals. Yet the survivors continued. At the final surrender eleven hundred Nez Percé horses were still alive and were turned over to General Howard as the spoils of war.

Thus the Appaloosa horse was scattered to the four corners of the North American continent and, were it not for the intricacies of genetics, would have been completely lost to posterity. But evidence of Appaloosa ancestry—a blanket of spots—turned up on horses of many different breeds and permitted the Appaloosa Horse Club to establish a new line of animals so marked.

As for the treaty signers, their nomadic life was over. A hunting way of life required that the tribe be guaranteed the freedom to pursue game wherever it migrated; and though the original treaty had ceded to the Nez Percés sufficient acreage to support adequate numbers of wildlife, the reduced land offered by the revised treaty did not. This struggle between the two cultures ultimately affected the well-being of the wildlife upon which the Indians depended. With the change in their methods of obtaining food, the Indians soon found their horses to be superfluous. In time they stopped gathering herds, and more animals slipped away to the wild.

The story of the gradual whittling down of reservation lands and the cultural obliteration that resulted was not unique to the Nez Percé tribe. The same policy toward Indians was carried out elsewhere. Wherever the whites located, their settlements quickly expanded, and they soon demanded that the Indians relinquish their "unused" land to make more room for the settlers. During the last half of the nineteenth century, the United States Government solemnly negotiated and ratified 363 treaties with 200 Indian tribes, and it is a matter of record that most of these treaties were later violated by Government action or by acts of Congress.

Not all Americans were unsympathetic with the Indians' cause. The Quakers strongly protested the removal of the tribes from their customary hunting grounds, and expressed shock at the amount of graft in the Bureau of Indian Affairs. Most of the funds marked for Indian education and welfare, it was alleged, were going into the pockets of the Government agents employed to manage the reservations. In the 1870's in response to the Quaker protest, President Grant replaced all the Government agents with clergy, assigning various tribes to the major Protestant denominations and the Roman Catholics.

The Presbyterian ministers who arrived to take charge of that portion of the Nez Percé nation that had come on to the reduced reservation lands were zealous reformers, bent on recasting the Indians' character. It was felt by the Reverend John Monteith, head agent, that his charges would never submit to the civilizing process until they gave up their herds of spotted horses. As he saw it, the Nez Percés' passion for horse racing led to gambling, and their love of buffalo-hunting excursions to the Plains led to the breaking of the Sabbath. Moreover, raising and selling horses gave them an independent income and relieved them of the wholesome necessity of performing work. According to Monteith, horses ate up pasture that could be put to better use, and he made it his number-one priority to get rid of the Indians' horses.

But weaning the Indian from his horses was no easy matter. To him, the horse represented wealth, status, and a meaningful past. The battles between the reservation agents and the various tribes which began over horses at this early date continued for many years.

Agriculture, the Indians were told, would soon bring them to the threshold of an exciting new way of life and give them the same advantages enjoyed by the whites—that large herds of horses were an impediment both to agriculture and to their own future. Moreover, those individuals who agreed to give up their horses were allowed to settle their families on the best sections of the reservations. The goal of the horse-removal programs instituted by Government agents at this time was to convert the Indian from a hunter into an agricultural worker.

Sixty years later when the expected transformation had not come about, the Bureau of Indian Affairs tried another tack. They attempted to make livestock raisers out of the ex-hunters. In 1920, a New York *Times* article signaled this new approach to the "Indian problem" and also indicated that the Indians were still clinging to their ponies:

"The successful future of the Indians depends largely upon their ability to grow livestock. Much of their land is chiefly valuable for grazing. It should be fully productive according to its adaptation. The Indians' native instincts are favorable. He loves animal life and is the natural friend to the flock, but needs protection and sympathetic instruction. . . . He must learn that merit is not in numbers alone . . . that a few good draft horses are worth more than a hundred ponies and that scrub stock consumes as much food as well-bred animals and is much less marketable."

But the fact that the Indian "loved animal life" and was "the natural friend to the flock," did not mean he wanted to go into the meat-producing business. Many tribes preferred to lease their lands to white cattle and sheep men rather than become livestock growers themselves. In 1929, the Crow tribe accepted the Schneider Sheep Company as tenants on their reservation (which incidentally had been reduced by a series of treaties from an original thirty-one and a half million acres to nine million acres). The first move made by the sheep company after putting their flocks on the Crow pastures was to demand that the Indians remove their horses so that the sheep might get the full benefit of the grass. When the Crows ignored this request, the Schneider Sheep Company hired airplanes and pick-up trucks and in one day shot every horse on the range. As one eyewitness, George Lande, told me, "It didn't matter whether they was yours, mine, his, or gentle or wild! They just shot them, you see!"

His wife interrupted: "Some was gentle. We had a nice herd over there . . . our work horses, and we went over to hunt them one day, and they was all laying there dead. They'd shot everything. The Indians, you see, didn't know how to fight back. And they'd get some crooked agent in, and the whites would just buy them off, and the agent just sold what the Indians had to the white men. The Crow Indian agent, who was boss over all the Indians, he upheld Schneider in this."

Though the agents no doubt thought they were doing the Indians a favor in replacing their horses with paying sheep, the Indians did not regard their ponies as worthless despite the fact that the stock was unmarketable. So most of the tribes in the West continued to raise thousands of ponies and pastured them on limited reservation lands. In time the unrelieved grazing caused the grass to disappear, and the land itself began to show signs of erosion. In the 1930's, the Government, alarmed over the deterioration of the reservation lands, convinced several tribes that their horse herds should be reduced, and Government-sponsored roundups were conducted in which tens of thousands of animals were gathered and destroyed.

But the "useless" horse apparently still held sway over the affections of the Indians. Petitions were sent to the White House protesting these stock-reduction programs. In Southern Utah, the Navajos voted to take the war-path if the culling did not cease. Though much time had passed since the Indian horses had aided their masters in making a final stand against the farming culture that engulfed them, the defeated Indians did not quickly forget their cherished horses. Until the end of the Second World War, Indian reservations were overrun with horses.

The pragmatic white man who "cherished nothing" was baffled by the stubborn reluctance on the part of the Indian to accept a sensible economic evaluation of the problem. One writer epitomizes this view:

"Why should the relief agencies pour out money to indigent wards when they could be self-sufficient if they did not possess the 'cultural hang-over,' the love of a worthless horse?"

But the Indian philosophy transcended economic gain and is well articulated by spokesman Paul Bernal of the Pueblo tribe: "It is said that years ago, many years ago, when the Indian was alone in this country, he cherished every little thing. Every living thing that grew from the green earth he cherished. But the white man cherished nothing. He destroyed everything. The Indian was conquered. He was overrun. He was dominated. His lands, his best lands were taken from him. His religious shrines of nature were taken from him. Why? Not because the white man cherished them. No, the white man wanted to destroy them. He wanted to destroy the Indian, to exterminate him. He wanted the Indians to die out completely. The Indian was left naked. He has nothing left but what he can hold in his hands. The earth where he stands. And what he has in his heart. No man can take these things from the Indian. Only God can take these things from the Indian, and the white man is not God."

And so for one hundred years the Indian continued to hold the horse in his heart to the perplexity of the social reformers. Today, however, the picture seems finally to have changed. Many of the reservation Indians have at last replaced their horse herds with cattle and sheep and become competitive stock growers. Furthermore, a large percentage of reservation land is now under lease to white farmers who have altered its pastoral character.

Yet, though domestic herds have been greatly reduced, wild horses can still be found on Indian lands. In rough and broken country, unsuitable for raising livestock, small bands of wild horses continue to eke out a living. Many of these animals have been wild for many generations and should not be confused with those domestic horses still being raised by the tribes. Nevertheless, they have been regarded as tribal property by the Indians, and as such were not molested by "mustangers." Only when these wild herds trespassed on leased land did they become fair game for the white man and run the risk of being shot.

Such a situation existed on the lands of the Gila River Indians in Arizona. Two herds of wild horses, each numbering a dozen or so animals, inhabited a section of the San Tan Mountains that extends on to the Sacaron Reservation. These horses were rarely seen until an alarming drop in the Arizona water table prompted them to make early-morning treks into the valley to drink. The distance from their normal habitat to the irrigation ditches where they watered was considerable, and the horses got footsore making the daily trip. So it was not surprising, that they spent an extra hour grazing on the lessee's field of alfalfa before starting their long climb back up into the mountains. I visited the reservation and witnessed the whole drama one morning between four-thirty and five o'clock.

Afterward Indian councilman Dana Nelson and Indian brand inspector Ralston Allen told me that the lessees had shot several trespassing wild horses and that the tribal council had received many complaints from the tenants, demanding that the horses be destroyed. But no action had been decided upon. The Indians were uncertain whether it was their responsibility to protect the tenant from stray livestock, or the tenant's duty to fence his own farm.

A more practical and cheaper solution than fencing, would be to bulldoze out a trough to catch water for the horses in their mountain habitat, thus relieving the animals of the necessity of making the long trip to the valley. Such a plan to conserve mountain water, I was told, was feasible and had been discussed for a quite different purpose. The horses, however, could benefit from the project if it were carried out.

I suggested that the Indians act quickly in order not to lose their wild horses, which could be a wonderful tourist attraction for the Gila River Tribe. Since the reservation is only an hour's drive from the vacation capitol of Phoenix, the tribe could promote half-day excursions into the San Tan Mountains to see these wild horses. Families, in particular, look for just such activities to fill their time and amuse their children while on vacation. But councilman Dana Nelson was skeptical. "No one is interested in our reservation or our problems," he told me. "All the tourists bypass the reservation. They don't stop. Everyone says about us, 'Yes, I passed through your reservation,' but no one stops."

People might stop, though, if offered an early-morning tour into the wild San Tan Mountains where they might catch a glimpse of a wild stallion with a long mane herding his band of varicolored mares across a ridge.

Judging from the popularity of wildlife excursions from Florida to Africa, it would seem a project guaranteed to succeed. Perhaps, if not in Arizona, some other Indian tribe will see a way to turn that cultural hangover of theirs—"the worthless horse"—into an economic asset.

17. *The Wild Horses Thrive on the Plains*

At the opening of the nineteenth century, the buffalo and the wild horses thrived on the Great Plains. In 1807, explorer Alexander Henry reported that such enormous numbers of animals were found in the region that they represented a hazard to travel. Buffaloes were so numerous, according to reports, that one could ride for as many as seven days across a landscape darkened with their shapes without losing sight of them. Authorities estimated that sixty million of these animals existed on the Plains. Yet within a period of seventy-five years, the buffalo was all but extinct.

Travelers also reported sighting horse bands so large that their movement across the horizon lasted without interruption for an entire day. A wagon train would sometimes surprise a field of horses into flight, creating havoc among the party's domestic horses and causing them to rear and plunge and scream to join the fleeing bands. Only by extreme effort could the men restrain the excited animals from taking off for the wild while still hitched to wagons or carrying packs and saddles.

If descriptions of landscapes flecked with wild mustangs can be believed, the creatures were of uncommon beauty. Their colors varied, ranging in the browns from the palest buckskin to the most purple chestnut, and including also such deviations as blue grullos, red roans, and true blacks.

In addition, the region supported elk, wolves, coyotes, antelope, and a great variety of small game. Yet significantly, prior to the arrival of numbers of white men, there was no indication that the Great Plains had been overgrazed by all the wildlife that fed upon it.

Until the middle of the nineteenth century the vast area lying immediately west of the Missouri River had been totally ignored. Early reports of

(Top) A young stallion circles and eyes another stallion's harem.
(Bottom) And is rewarded by a clip to the chin.

Wild mare with her yearling offspring and colt of the year.
Note stripes on legs.

A rare maneuver—five stallions form a temporary alliance and combine their harems in a retreat. Vulnerable mares and colts run ahead, followed by four "lesser" stallions. Top stallion brings up the rear.

the Plains had convinced most Americans that the land was uninhabitable. Zebulon Pike, in *The Expedition of Zebulon Pike* (*1806–1807*), for example, referred to it as the Great American Desert, a misnomer that created in the public mind the impression that the Plains area was nothing but an impediment to be crossed to reach the more desirable regions beyond.

It is true that despite its gentle appearance the region that was destined to become nine large states in the Union was perhaps the most difficult to settle because it contained scant lumber with which to build cabins, forts, and fences, a new problem for those attuned to a "tree culture."

Nevertheless, the rich soil of this bed of grass lured a few hardy frontiersmen to come out and take a chance on mastering it. But the crops that looked so promising in spring, hung thirsting on brittle stalks by summer, as each day began and ended without a cloud to mar its blue perfection. The twenty inches of annual rain that fell west of the Missouri River was exactly half the amount of moisture that watered the Mississippi Valley. The very earliest immigrant farmers who ventured out on the flat Plains found themselves very quickly deceived and frustrated, and eventually drifted back to the more reliable and productive climate of the Mississippi Valley.

Putting livestock out to graze on the natural pastures afforded by the Plains was, no doubt, an idea that occurred to many pioneer farmers; but without lumber no fences could be constructed to contain the animals, and the concept of an open range upon which great herds of cattle could roam freely, commingling with a neighbor's stock, was still beyond the imagination of the property-minded settlers. How would the animals be controlled, separated, identified, and herded? Until the later emergence of the Texas cowboy—that truly American figure who lived out of doors and moved with the stock, herding the animals from one range to another, rounding them up, cutting them out, branding them for identification, and driving them along trails to market—the immense pasture land was left to buffaloes, the antelope, and the wild horses.

The few early immigrant settlers in the region, who defied the forces of defeat and clung to the fragile grasses, learned in time how to cope with the strange land and invented various methods of "dry farming." Among other devices, they discovered that by packing the soil after every precious rainfall, they could conserve the moisture and thus save their crops.

This technique was learned accidentally by observing acreage that had been trampled by a herd of sheep after a rain. Where the earth had been packed down, moisture was preserved in the soil and plant life was able to thrive. Though all hoofed animals, including wild horses, perform this task in the wild, as soon as man discovered the technique and imitated it artificially, he forgot where he learned it. Hoofed animals, so important to plant health in dry territory, are frequently removed from arid regions in a misguided effort to protect the struggling plant life.

With so many drawbacks to farmers, the Plains was uncoveted and referred to as "Indian Territory" and it soon became a kind of dumping ground for dislocated tribes removed by the Federal Government from the agricultural regions in the East and relocated "permanently" in buffalo country. By the mid-nineteenth century, twenty-three tribes had been moved to the Great Plains.

The Horse Indians, long established on the Plains, did not welcome these newcomers into the region, and the friction that arose among the various tribes became a matter of grave concern to the Government in Washington. Troops were sent to patrol the region and try to maintain peace.

In such an environment, however, the white soldiers were no military match for the Indians. Firearms proved useless here. The Kentucky rifle, with its forty-four-inch muzzle and nine-pound weight, could not be accurately aimed from the back of a horse. Worse, it required reloading after each and every firing, and woe to the unsuccessful marksman who had to stand in an open field and shove powder, wadding, ball and more wadding, caps, and a ramrod into his rifle while quilled arrows whizzed about his ears. The Kentucky rifle, an excellent weapon for use in the woods, or among hills or rocks where there was cover, was only an encumbrance on the flat grasslands. The arrow and the Indian pony were the most effective weapons on the Plains and remained the means by which the Indians protected their last stronghold until the invention of the Colt repeater.

For the most part, however, the "dragoons" who patrolled this desolate region were not looking for conflict and, in fact, represented themselves as arbitrators who had come to resolve the skirmishes that constantly flared up among the various Indian tribes. It was tacitly understood that this large, unwanted section of the continent would remain Indian land forever, and that the United States' only interest here was to safeguard the passage of her citizens along the Santa Fe Trail in the south and the route to Oregon Territory in the north.

Thus many platoons served a tour of duty on the prairies without seeing much action, and the soldiers amused themselves during the long months in the wilderness by hunting animals and chasing wild horses. Many wrote stories of their adventures which were published by popular magazines of the day.

In the 1830's the *American Turf Registry* printed a series of letters which indicated a difference of opinion among the horse-minded soldiers regarding the worth of the wild horse flesh they had seen on the prairies.

To settle the dispute, a breeding project was planned. A Major Mason, whose personal mount was a Thoroughbred, objected to the praise constantly being heaped upon the Western mustang. He believed the animal was overrated, and he made up his mind to settle the issue. From the Plains Indians, he purchased a mare which he bred to a pedigreed horse. His object, he stated, was to test "the outcome, but with no expectation."

At the same time, a Lieutenant S. W. Moore returned to the United States with two prairie studs purchased from the Osage Indians. It is not clear whether these animals had been captured from the wild or belonged to an Indian herd. The studs were described as being hard of hoof, fourteen and one-half hands high, and both white. The size was already beginning to seem small to American horsemen, who themselves were growing taller with every generation.

An editorial in the *Turf* raised objections to the experiment planned by Major Mason. The editor pointed out that rearing a colt on forage and not subjecting it to the rigorous life of the prairie would create conditions that could alter the outcome. A stable-fed colt, he contended, would grow up "soft," and he went on to say, "I believe Major Mason would do better to employ Indians to catch a stallion for the test rather than endeavor to raise a colt."

In the next issue of the magazine Major Mason retorted that after seeing four thousand Indian horses, he wouldn't give fifty dollars for any four. "The best ones are stolen, the wild ones they will sell for a trinket," he asserted.

An irate reader responded to this slur on the wild horses with the following impassioned letter dated November 5, 1835:

"I see that a major of the dragoons has given you an article in which he depreciates the wild horse. The excursions of the dragoons have never extended beyond the hunting ground of the Osage . . . about one hundred miles above the Cross Timbers. . . . They cannot be supposed to have seen much of the prairie or the horses on it. I have been the route from St. Louis to Santa Fe, thence around the head to the Red River, to the heads of the Colorado of Texas . . . thence across the Red River by way of Washita to Fort Nash. I have seen tens of thousands of wild horses . . . have killed and eaten them . . . and may be supposed to know something about them. All the wild horses brought into the United States are caught on the way, and I have been with the Osages while catching them. A herd of horses makes their appearances, the Osages start out on horseback, each man supplied with a noose at the end of a pole. They take their stations on every side of the wild horses and commence running them until they overtake and noose some among them. Of course in this chase the good horses invariably escape, while the mean ones are taken and brought into the United States as choice wild horses. . . . If fine delicate heads, wide nostrils, slim and tapering and clean limbs . . . small and hard hoofs and an Arabian symmetry of form will make a fine horse, there are fine horses in abundance on the prairie. I have seen one leader of a herd, while the whole body was running at full speed, circle around and around the herd like a hawk, driving up the laggards in the rear and then returning to the front, seemingly with all the ease imaginable."

The account given by this wild-horse enthusiast is probably accurate. Stallions seem to have amazingly little difficulty catching up with their fleeing harems, although they make frequent stops to "stare-down" their pursuers. A buckskin stallion I observed in the Red Desert drove twenty-five mares and four stallions ahead of him to safety, and though he frequently slowed down almost to a halt in order to keep a wary eye on me, yet he was able to pull alongside his stampeding subjects with the greatest ease and even circle the herd once in order to force them into a more compact unit. The photographs on pages 126-127 illustrate this feat.

The *American Turf Registry* does not reveal the results of Major Mason's breeding experiment. Yet many continued to admire the wild horses, as is clearly revealed in Matt Field's description of one encountered along the Santa Fe Trail in the year 1839:

> 'Twas a beautiful animal . . . a sorrel, with a jet black mane and tail. [sic] We could see the muscles quiver in his glossy limbs as he moved; and when, half playfully and half in fright, he tossed his flowing mane in the air, and flourished his long silky tail, our admiration knew no bounds, and we longed . . . hopelessly, vexatiously longed to possess him.
>
> Of all the brute creation the horse is the most admired by men. Combining beauty with usefulness, all countries and all ages yield it their admiration. But, though the finest specimen of its kind, a domestic horse will ever lack that magic and indescribable charm that beams like

In a burst of speed, a stallion circles his mares while in flight.

a halo around the simple name of freedom. The wild horse roving the prairie wilderness knows no master . . . has never felt the whip . . . never clasped in its teeth the bit to curb its native freedom, but gambols, unmolested over its grassy home where Nature has given it a bountiful supply of provender. Lordly man has never sat upon its back; the spur and the bridle are unknown to it, and when the Spaniard comes on his fleet trained steed, with noose in hand, to ensnare him, he bounds away, over the velvet carpet of the prairie, swift as the arrow of the Indian's bow, or even the lightning darting from the cloud. We might have shot him from where we stood, but had we been starving, we would scarcely have done it. He was *free,* and we loved him for the very possession of that liberty we longed to take from him . . . but we could not kill him.

But though the wild horse of the Plains was experiencing his golden age when the above was written, the end of his unmolested freedom was soon to come. The beautiful and free horse with the black mane that so delighted Matt Field and his traveling companions was one of the last generation of his kind to escape from the persecution of man. Within fifty years the rush to the Plains by the "boomers" began to transform the beautiful grassland, hitherto known as "Indian Territory," into a countryside of economic priorities.

The beauty, significance, and cultural heritage of the region which was so quickly lost, along with sixty million buffaloes and several million wild horses, can hardly be assessed in terms of esthetic, moral, and long-range values. Though many sections of the Plains were wholly unsuited for cultivation, and the economic gains achieved by turning the sod were often short-lived and costly in terms of soil erosion and permanent damage to the land, no thought was given to preserving any segment of the Plains intact in a state of natural equilibrium. No National Park was set aside to preserve the unique features of the Plains, its rich plant and animal life. Neither Indian priority, nor conservation principle carried enough weight to prevent the land from being senselessly drained of all its wealth as completely and as rapidly as possible. Today dust bowls and serious erosion scar much of the region where the "economy of scales" of the nineteenth century wrote its indelible signature on the earth.

Had a section of the Plains been set aside for observation and study, before the interlocking food chains of the region, its ecology, were totally obliterated, such a section might serve us now and teach us how to heal the wounds of the vast region and how to make use of it in the future in ways that are more consistent with its own peculiar nature.

Obviously, we have made a great many mistakes. Certainly a region that could support sixty million buffaloes and several million wild horses should not have become overgrazed—as it did—by a fraction that number of livestock. Did we remove a link from the life-chain of the region? Did fences destroy the range? Did plowing create conditions that led to erosion? We can see isolated effects of some of these things, but nowhere do we have a "control" area in which to observe the *natural condition* of the Plains.

Perhaps it yet would be possible for the Department of the Interior to establish a kind of laboratory on some remaining virgin tract of Plains where the plant and animal life that originally thrived in the region might be reintroduced and studied.

18. The Wild Stallion: Overlord and Defender

Though the Great Plains may have held little to interest the earliest settlers who bypassed it for richer territories beyond, literary figures such as Washington Irving were fascinated by the region and eager to savor the aboriginal life that existed there. So in the year 1832, Irving readily accepted an invitation to accompany Henry Ellsworth, a newly appointed commissioner of Indian Affairs, on a good-will tour among the Plains Indians.

Naturally, the party traveled by horseback and without the benefit of roads. Guided across the sea of grass by a platoon of somewhat inexperienced rangers, Irving was introduced to the primitive wildness of Indian Territory and so was able to give posterity his view of this region. In *A Tour of the Prairies,* he describes the Plains dotted with countless buffaloes and with wild horses capering on the horizon, and characterizes the Indian tribes, "before they disappear forever as independent nations."

But perhaps his most revealing description is of the rangers who escorted the expedition. For the most part, he writes, they consisted of wild farm youngsters from the Mississippi frontier, undisciplined, and without military training. Nevertheless, these raw, young soldiers believed that they made quite an impression on the Indians with their military appearance. Irving observed, however, that the Indians humored the young men, maintaining a serious attitude in their presence, while mimicking them behind their backs.

It is easy to see how Ellsworth and his diplomatic mission might have struck the Indians as being somewhat ridiculous. Wherever this entourage on horseback encountered an Indian, be he a hunter chasing buffalo, or a warrior in full paint and regalia, they halted, and Ellsworth proceeded to deliver an impassioned speech, admonishing the Indian to renounce his warlike habits.

At one point the party met a group of Osage hunters intent on obtaining Pawnee scalps. The warriors patiently and politely listened to Ellsworth's speech on universal brotherhood, then departed, as he fondly believed, with peace in their hearts. But a French-Indian member of the platoon who understood the Osage language later informed Irving privately that the Indians had concluded among themselves that they had better redouble their zeal as it sounded ominously as though the Great White Father meant to put an end to their horse stealing.

On this trip Irving is the first person to mention sighting the "pacing white stallion," a wild horse that was to become legendary and would be reported by travelers in areas as remote from one another as Texas and Montana. This fabled creature was said to be able to outpace the fleetest ordinary horse. (A pacing horse moves his front and back leg simultaneously, first on one side and then on the other, instead of alternating front right and back left, then front left and back right.) High prizes were offered to any man who could capture him alive, but no one could ever approach near enough to rope him.

The Indians, particularly the Osage, believed the stallion to be a ghost. The white men, although they did not accept that view, had their own private superstitions regarding this creature who covered such a vast range. It never seemed to occur to anyone that there might be a number of white pacers among the millions of horses which then inhabited the Plains. Every white stallion, whether sighted east or west of the Rockies, was immediately assumed to be THE white stallion. The legend grew, stories were published, and prize money multiplied, but the fabled stallion always eluded capture. He apparently lived to a very ripe old age, for his activities continued to be reported for more than sixty years.

The New York *Times* in 1882 published a full-column description of this famous animal doing battle with a pack of wolves. General Abe Buford told the story of an event which had taken place on the Western prairies forty years earlier, when he was still a lieutenant with the dragoons in the company of Captain Nathan Boone. He wrote:

"During the night we could hear the distant neighing and snorting of horses and the barking and howling of wolves. Our horses were breaking loose from their lariats frequently during the night. No one in camp could design the cause of the trouble save Captain Boone, who said there must be a battle of the wolves and horses raging, and ordered the guards to be

After being ousted from their parental bands,
lone adolescent males often form temporary friendships.

doubled to prevent a stampede of our own horses. At daylight the command was mounted and Boone said we would have an opportunity to catch a horse or two. So Anderson and Chilton and myself selected three squads of the best mounted dragoons in the command. We moved down the creek in the direction of the sound of the neighing and barking and all were on tiptoe to witness the battle. Going about a mile under cover of the bank of the little creek, the noise growing more distinct every moment until we got opposite the field of battle, which was upon the level prairie about 300 yards from the bluff bank; here we halted and the three officers went upon the bank to reconnoitre. We saw the battle raging. The herd of horses was about 150 strong, and the most prominent one among them was the 'Great White Horse of the Plains' which many of you have doubtless often read of. He seemed to be the commander and had formed the mares in a circle with their heels to the enemy, or outward.* The diameter of this circle was about 100 yards with all the foals and younger colts in the center; all the stallions with the 'white horse' in command on the outside and surrounding the circle of mares, who were fighting the wolves. The wolves retreated rapidly from us over the beautiful prairie, and we gave chase with all the speed we could. The 'white horse' apparently gave the signal to retreat and in this retreat commanded the rear guard. Before the retreat commenced, I noticed a squad of stallions approach the circle of mares. They pawed the earth, neighed, snorted fiercely and started off, leading the retreat. The mares opened the circle and the colts went out, following a squad of mares and the other horses in the rear, and the 'white horse' still in the rear. I was mounted on a thorough-bred horse sired by Sidi Hamet. I gave Cid the spur and moved directly at the White King with pistol in hand thinking I might crease him if I could ever get by his side. (Creasing' is sending a ball through the upper muscle of the neck which stuns the horse and he falls helpless for a few moments and can be secured by a lariat while in this condition.†) . . . As we approached the herd, the white horse would go slow and let us come up to within 20 yards of him but could go away from us at his ease. . . . On the return from the chase to our camp where we found Boone and Johnson roasting buffalo hump and jerking beef, we passed the battle-ground where were many evidences of the battle, quite a number of dead wolves and horses, some carcasses of horses on the outer edge of the battle-field that had fallen in some of the charges and evidence that the wolves had devoured their carcasses. When we returned to camp

* Horses do not fight with their back heels, but face their enemies. General Buford's description is inaccurate on this point.

† Nearly always killed the horse.

Boone laughed heartily and said: 'Why, Medoc, I thought you were going to capture the great "white horse" mounted on your thorough-bred from the Blue grass region.' . . . Such my friends is a hastily prepared description of the battle of the horses and the wolves in which we plainly see the reasoning powers of this great 'white horse of the plains' fully developed. We also plainly see his military idea brought fully into play. In his assaults upon his enemy, he first organized his assaulting parties, and in his retreat from his more formidable opponent, the dragoons, he covers the retreat of his army. This is certainly the strongest of evidence that he possesses reasoning powers, and is therefore a fit associate and companion for man."

General Buford's military description of the white stallion's heroic masterful defense of his band when under attack might appear a bit overdrawn. However, the reports of other competent firsthand observers tend to confirm Buford's strange story, and I myself have seen a "mustang ring" etched into the earth in northeastern Wyoming—a depressed scar on the land that bears testimony to the fact that once a circle of horses dug their hard hoofs into the ground on this spot and defended their colts from attack by wolves.*

I have also witnessed how several stallion-dominated harems will combine on occasion to form a united band under the single leadership of a particular stallion. Under normal circumstances such co-operation among the male animals is contrary to their very nature. In general, each harem of mares is dominated by a single stallion, who will not tolerate the approach of another male. Stud colts are permitted to remain in their mother's band only until they reach approximately two years of age, after which they are driven off by their sire. Prior to expelling his offspring, however, the lordly father may occasionally engage his son in mock combat, thus preparing the young horse for the more serious battles he must later fight in order to win his own harem.

At the age of two years, however, the young males are hardly sufficiently strong or militant in spirit to acquire a group of females. As a result, since horses are extremely sociable by nature, two or three young males may band together for company. These small groups of adolescents are unusually quick and aggressive, and it is very difficult to approach them. They often remain near the area in which they were born, and usually run close behind their former band. In time of danger, they may even reunite

---

*Such depressions in the soil last for decades. Ruts created by prairie schooners are still visible from the air.

An eyeball-to-eyeball confrontation between two stallions escalates into a battle while the unconcerned mares look on.

temporarily with their parental herd.

In any contest in which several stallions take part, or in any retreat involving more than one male in the herd, only one of the stallions appears to be in charge, and he invariably runs in the flank position. The lesser stallions will herd their individual harems into a single group, then wheeling into a position behind them, will run abreast and slightly forward of the male in command.

On the Red Desert in the summer of 1969, I witnessed such an operation. Five stallions rallied their five harems into a herd containing twenty females, including colts and yearlings. Just as General Buford described, the maneuver had the appearance of a very well-drilled military tactic. The lesser stallions galloped at the rear of the herd of mares directly in front of the head stallion who covered the "retreat." The commanding stallion, alone, stopped from time to time and turned to face the enemy—who in this case, happened to be me.

Ordinarily, each of the four stallions would have held this "rear" position behind his own harem, and would have asserted himself by posturing and displaying menacing behavior to the enemy. But the four stallions, on this occasion, chose to relinquish their authority to a single male.

Unlike the horses in General Buford's account, however, the forward position was at no time taken by lesser stallion, but invariably was held by a mare. In each harem there is one mare who consistently assumes this place, and it is she who determines the "escape trails" that the band will follow. Normally, the other mares run single file, but I have not been able to observe whether any distinct order is maintained in their lineup. The mare or filly on the end, of course, runs the unenviable risk of being bitten by the stallion should the mares ahead fail to keep the pace he requires.

Though individual animals differ, and individual stallions, therefore, do not always behave predictably, generally speaking, the male horse is by nature extremely domineering and keeps a very strict watch over his females, herding and harassing them almost incessantly. Each stallion has had to engage in a fierce battle to win every female added to his harem, and mares are not permitted to wander off. Stallions generally keep very busy herding them into a compact unit so they can keep a watchful eye on them. Obviously, they do not permit their charges to cross into another stallion's range. Although territory in itself is not of prime importance to horses, and two bunches of horses that are contiguous may even share a spring, taking care not to go to water at the same time, woe to the trespasser that approaches too close to a stallion's mares!

An unaccepted challenge. A Barb-type stallion succeeds in discomfiting an inter-loper, then returns to drive his mares to a safer portion of his territory.

Though the vegetarian horse is gentle by nature, when he does decide to fight, the conflict is a shockingly vicious and bloody affair. Consequently, two stallions may try to avoid this confrontation through a strange ritual of posturing. In such instances the two males will confront each other, their manes bristling and their tails highly arched, and will press their foreheads together and stare at each other, eyeball to eyeball, until one of them backs down. After such a display, the discomfited animal may gallop off, leaving the other the victor. However, if it proves to be a fight to the finish, the two horses will rear up on their hind legs and begin to pound at each other with their hoofs. Manes are bitten and torn off, legs broken, and ribs crushed as the stomping, biting, kicking combatants lunge at each other. During the greater part of the battle both horses fight in an erect position, standing on their hind legs, and should one fall, he is immediately stomped upon by the other. Throughout the fight, the stallions shriek, snort, and scream at each other as their hoofs crack together. Meanwhile, their mares stand huddled together awaiting the outcome, seemingly oblivious to the fact that they are the cause of all the commotion.

In contrast to the males, a mare seems to reveal no possessive spirit whatsoever toward her mate. The glue that binds a harem seems to be the females' mutual affection. This is reinforced through mutual grooming. I have observed no particular show of loyalty to the stallion on the part of harem members. It is he, however, who prevents wayward mares from deserting.

I observed one old mare try to slip away to freedom while the harem was in flight, only to be retrieved later by the stallion after he had chased the other females to safety. This incident took place in the Pryor Mountains, and as usual the horses were running away from me. Inadvertently I had blocked the horses' trail and literally cornered them in a rocky canyon, giving the stallion no choice but to drive his mares up a steep embankment. This canyon wall was so overgrown with mountain mahogany and small juniper trees that instead of climbing single file as is usual with wild horses, each animal broke its own trail through the tangles of underbrush. Just as the stallion passed behind a large clump of mountain mahogany, one old mare turned and started to run downhill, stumbling and slipping on the loose stones in her haste to escape.

The stallion at first gave no indication that he missed a member of his harem, and he continued to struggle to the top, where he drove his remaining females out of sight. But in a moment he reappeared on the rimrocks, posed briefly, and then sighting the runaway, began his swift descent, weaving back and forth among the trees as gracefully as a skier.

In a short time he overtook the renegade mare and confronted her with the ominous message of his weaving, outstretched neck. The old mare's head sagged as she turned and started to trudge back up the hill, while the stallion impatiently nudged, bit, and all but boosted her along.

The technique by which the stallion maintains control over his mares is straightforward and unsubtle. He bites them. But he also employs a kind of shorthand method of communicating his displeasure, which is understood by the females and enables them to get into line and avoid being nipped. This threatening behavior consists of a grotesque elongation of his neck, and a rhythmic weaving back and forth of his head, giving him the appearance of a snake swaying under the hypnotic influence of music. Whenever the stallion makes this gesture, the mares are quick to get the message.

Only when a mare is about to give birth does her mate allow her to roam. At that time she is permitted to leave the band and seek a secluded spot to drop her foal. But the young colt * must quickly be on its legs and running, for the stallion will soon reappear to herd the mare and her newborn back to the harem.

Despite the possessive nature of the wild stallion toward his collection of females, he does not invariably display interest in every mare he encounters, and will on occasion drive one out of his territory if she does not appeal to him. San Domingo, the Medicine Hat horse on the Brislawn's Cayuse Ranch, is typical of this kind of discriminating stallion. Some male horses even seem to have a predilection for mares of a particular color, accepting no off shades in their harem. I have seen an all-bay harem, though the stud was black; and I have also seen an all-black harem, and a solid sorrel-colored harem.

It is difficult to see how such a collection of mares could have occurred by chance when mares in contiguous bands are of assorted colors. The stallion, it would seem, has exercised some preference in the matter. But a stallion's preferences in females does not always conform with man's ideas of beauty. Though the all-bay harem, I observed, contained many swaybacked and decrepit animals, the young stud guarded his bevy of brunettes jealously. Robert Brislawn commented on this unaccountable lack of taste exhibited by certain stallions, remarking that it is probably lucky for all of us that we don't see alike.

Indirectly the overbearing nature of the stallion actually serves his subjugated mares and benefits the herd. His jealousy causes him to be constantly on the alert for a contender and, as a result, wolves, mountain lions, bears—and especially man—do not escape his detection. Further-

---

*Technically, a colt is always male, but in this book I use "foal" and "colt" interchangeably, in accordance with Western custom.

Hours old, a foal sees its first dawn as its mother enjoys solitude and a respite from the possessive tyranny of her mate.

more, by driving trespassing horses away from his mares, he prevents his loosely defined territory from becoming overgrazed. In addition, his contentiousness and willingness to face an enemy and fight give his mares lead time in which to escape; and his suspiciousness, which causes him to test water holes and trails for signs of danger or competition, protects his mares from falling into traps.

In time of danger, the stallion shows no forbearance toward any lagging colts. If a mare falls behind to stay close to her tired offspring, the stallion has been known to grab the little creature in his teeth, give it a shake to break its neck, and then continue to drive the mother forward. The mares, however, display behavior that indicates mourning when a colt is killed. "Aunts" too will show a great deal of interest in a newborn foal and have been known to try to take a baby away from its mother. The sterile hybrid mules are particularly apt to do this and are called "colt crazy" by those familiar with their ways.

Though most mares passively accept the tyrannical harassment of the stallion, certain females play more active roles. The lead mare not only determines the trails to be taken in time of danger, she sometimes acts as a second sentinel and will alert the horses to any unusual activity the stallion may overlook. She is much more casual about this duty, however, than is the stallion, who is always anticipating a rival. But when she does detect something that arouses her suspicion, her behavior is strangely similar to that of the male. Like the stallion, she will often approach a few steps closer for a better look while displaying some menacing gestures before giving the danger signal to the other horses.

A stallion who attempts to lead his band instead of taking the hindmost position, according to J. Frank Dobie, is not a reliable horse and will not hold his band together for long. I have seen only one stallion "head" his retreating mares, and as he began to outdistance them, I wondered if his mares might decide not to follow him.

Since the wild horse surpasses all of his enemies in speed, his natural defense is to run away, and horses will try to avoid battle if possible. The wild horse, for all of his arrogant behavior, does not threaten man. Though there have been a few authenticated reports of stallions attacking human beings, such incidents are extremely rare and when investigated, it is usually disclosed that the belligerent horse was previously harassed by mustangers or possibly even lost his mares in a roundup. Occasionally, however, a stud will not tolerate the presence of a human onlooker while engaged in a battle with a rival, and will attack a man who approaches too close. In the spring of 1969, an official of the Bureau of Land Management was treed by a wild "combatant" in the Pryor Mountains while trying to take a picture of a stallion fight.

But every stallion will display threatening gestures toward human intruders and give his mares time to get away. Then, if retreat is open to him, he, too, will gallop after his harem before the mares have had a chance to outdistance him. Nevertheless, his menacing behavior can be very convincing. I have personally had the experience of being "charged" by a stallion that I surprised at extremely close range. When it became clear to me that the horse was enraged by my intrusion, I stood motionless, taking care to make no menacing gestures myself that might further aggravate him. For what seemed like minutes, we confronted each other a few feet apart. The stallion stomped his feet, tossed his mane, and from time to time blew his nostrils clean to get a better "sniff" of me; then, after what seemed like hours, he turned and galloped after his retreating females. I missed a good close-up picture, but I really did not have the courage to point a camera at that snorting animal.

19. Cow Ponies

Many people have wondered what became of the enormous population of wild horses—numbering in the millions—that only a century ago thundered across the Plains. Unlike the buffaloes, the horses were not slaughtered and brought to near extinction for their hides, yet before the nineteenth century closed, their numbers had decreased, perhaps by fifty percent.

To understand this abrupt decline, it is necessary to consider yet another role that the wild mustang played in the unfolding story of the West—a role in which he not only contributed to the development of a whole new industry, but made possible the opening of the last American frontier, the Great Plains. Had it not been for the hundreds of thousands of mustangs that were retrieved from the wild and converted into a new kind of horse called a "cow pony," the middle section of the continent would have been even more difficult to subdue. For it was not until the emergence of the mounted cowboy that this intractable grassland was finally overcome. Moreover, it wasn't until the early Texans discovered how to transform the ex-Buffalo Runners that ran wild in the Nueces Valley into clever herding and cutting ponies that cattle could be handled in the lumber-less wide-open spaces (not to be fenced until the invention of barbed wire in 1873).

In the United States the use of the open range upon which cattle circulated freely across many miles was a concept born in Texas, though in Mexico, Spanish ranchers had handled cattle in this way for some time. As it happened, it was a system that was eminently beneficial to the entire Plains region, where land was plentiful and water scarce, and where plant life needed frequent relief from grazing animals. The native prairie grasses that had evolved here thrived in the spring when rain fell and matured early, spilling their seeds before the droughts of summer destroyed them. Even six months of uninterrupted grazing could interfere with this rapid reproductive cycle, though the seed-carrying wind might repair damage that did not involve too extensive an area.

The herds of buffaloes that so frustrated the Indians by their incessant shifting had, in actual fact, by thus changing their grazing grounds, been acting in complete harmony with the grasses upon which they fed. In one area they cropped, in another they trampled and thus sowed.

Perhaps the early cowboys had observed the buffaloes and taken a lesson from nature, for they too trailed their cattle to fresh grass long before a particular section showed signs of becoming overgrazed. Like the Indians who moved camp frequently to follow the herds of buffaloes, the first cowboys were mobile-minded and lived outdoors with their animals. Thus they were better attuned to the Plains environment than were the early farmers. For unlike the farmers, they did not bring to the dry region fixed ideas based on life in America's more humid belt, but improvised, invented, and adapted themselves to what they slowly discovered the region would yield.

The other characteristic of the Plains, the great distances that lay between its shallow rivers, also made it particularly unsuitable for division into small, privately owned units. Where the riverbanks were claimed by a few settlers, vast stretches of intervening dry land had no access to water and consequently remained uninhabitable. Free access to water resources made an open-range policy imperative.

Unfortunately, the humid-area legislators in faraway Washington had no concept of the peculiarities of this region, nor did they take a lesson from the Indians who had utilized all of the vast Plains rather than breaking it up into small pieces. The Land Acts which were introduced in Congress from 1841 to 1894, though logical for the well-watered East, divided the dry Plains into homesteads too small and too distant from water to be functional.

Most of the claim-stakers who were lured to the Plains by the offer of free land had no understanding of these serious drawbacks. Their farming techniques had been learned in other climates, and they suffered terrible setbacks when the sporadic rainfall completely ceased in early summer, and in the resulting drought, the wind carried off the soil they had worked so hard to loosen.

The passage of the Homestead Act in 1862, which offered free land to the poor and unemployed, though in intent a progressive measure, designed to give relief to cities that were becoming crowded with European immigrants, in reality brought much hardship to the very people it was meant to serve. The Plains could not be conquered by the usual methods of agriculture. Perhaps even more regrettable in the larger picture, the Homestead Act destroyed the highly relevant concept of an open-range land policy that would have been so natural for the region.

But before the homesteaders brought their fences, the cowboys for a while enjoyed unlimited freedom across hundreds of miles of open range, and the cattle they herded, which were the property of numerous owners, commingled at watering holes and on the grassy prairies.

The feasibility of handling cattle in this way depended on two important developments: first, the adoption of a system of branding whereby the steers could be positively identified at roundup time; and secondly, the observation that trained Mexican horses could be used to help perform the difficult work of herding, roping, and trailing the cattle with the long horns found running wild in the Nueces Valley of Texas.

These "cimarrones," as the longhorns were called, were the offspring of animals abandoned by Spanish missionaries who had retreated from the Apache Indians after failing to convert them. For a time, the government in Mexico, fearful of French encroachment from the east, promoted ranching along the San Antonio River, and the abandoned missions were secularized and turned into private ranches. But after 1762, when France ceded Louisiana to Spain, ranching in this area lost its political relevance. According to Mari Sandoz in *The Cattlemen:* ". . . after 1770 ranching along the San Antonio River withered as under the hot winds from the Staked Plains, although the wild cattle kept spreading."

Unlike the wild mustangs, also found in profuse numbers, especially in the valley between the Nueces and the Rio Grande, the wild bulls were not scattered by the Horse Indians, but remained in a confined area bordered by the Red River on the north and the Brazos on the west. The very isolation of this habitat served to protect the cattle from exploitation.

The first Anglo-Americans to settle in the area prior to the Mexican Revolution in 1821, could not resist trying to drive free beef across the hundreds of intervening miles to distant New Orleans. These early enterprises were for the most part colossal failures. Large numbers of animals were lost in wild stampedes en route or drowned when forced to ford the wide Mississippi River. What few head finally arrived at market were thin and stringy, making the venture anything but profitable for the Texas entrepreneurs.

Shipping the herds from Shreveport by flatboats to New Orleans by way of the Gulf of Mexico was less hazardous, but a steer brought only $10 a head when sold at Shreveport, whereas the same animal was worth $45 in New Orleans. Profit lay in successfully driving the animals to market.

Notwithstanding their losses, these early drovers were not discouraged by their failures. They concluded, instead, that what was needed were more tractable steers and the right kind of horses trained to herd them. Both these types of animals had already been observed by the Texans on the Mexican ranches below the Rio Grande border. The result was that the Spanish ranchers, long victimized by Comanche horse thieves, now began to lose their stock to the G.T.T.s (meaning Gone to Texas), as the Americans were called.

These Mexican horses carried much the same blood and displayed many of the same characteristics as the Andalusian stock brought to Mexico by the Conquistadors in the sixteenth century. Although infusion of new blood from later imports had modified the Mexican breed, the horse still reflected the hardy qualities and the intelligence of their early ancestors. In addition, these horses had for long generations been schooled to herd livestock; the ability to work cattle seemed to have become bred into them. Now, together with the readily available wild mustangs of the region, they became the foundation stock of the Texas cow pony. As a result, San Antonio soon became one of the largest horse markets in the world.

Buying horses was expensive, stealing them was dangerous, while capturing them from the wild was fun. Once the cowboys had mastered the Mexican art of training a horse, they raided the border ranches less frequently. Instead, they began to capture the superabundant wild Texas mustangs (estimated by Dobie to have reached the million mark in this state alone) and to break them for the herding task. It was soon discovered that the purer strains found in the wild-horse population often made the better cow ponies. So once again the wild horse of the Spaniard was cast in a new role.

The early cowboy not only adopted the horse of the Spaniard and imitated his method of handling cattle, but also affected the costume of the vaquero (Mexican ranch hand) and brightened his vocabulary with Spanish words. The Mexican *lazo* became a lasso, the *la reata* was Anglicized to become a lariat, and even the Spanish word *remuda* became the name given to the unit of cow ponies that worked a cattle drive.

A remuda was the large herd of cow ponies embracing all the horses belonging to the cowboys of an outfit. Since the nomadic cowboys literally lived in the saddle, moving from place to place with the cattle, they needed a frequent change of mount to prevent any one animal from becoming played out. Consequently, when a man joined a cattle drive, he brought with him a "string" of perhaps a dozen horses. All these "extra" ponies were herded along the trail in a group by a horse wrangler. A roundup of two thousand to four thousand head of cattle might require a *remuda* of anywhere from three hundred to five hundred horses.

At dawn the wrangler would rope out a horse for each man in the outfit to saddle and ride. But certain of the animals became wary of the wrangler's noose, were rarely ridden, and consequently grew wild again. When these semibroken horses or "broncs," as they were called, occasionally did find themselves snared and put to work, they required considerable "unlimbering" by their riders. Cowboys either learned to master such animals or gave up herding cattle, for it was a rare morning when the horse wrangler did not try to deliver a rebellious bronc to some poor cowboy, who then faced the task of subduing it while the others looked on.

This regular morning performance provided amusement for the men, relieving the monotony of the long trail rides. Of course, any man who lost his seat when his horse pitched, likewise lost face with his companions, for men were judged by how they rode a horse. "Sun-fishing" and "bogging its head" were two of many ways by which a bronc unseated its rider. Yet somehow, the cowboys did learn to ride these wild creatures, mastering the full repertoire of tricks the horses were capable of.

At the shipping towns where men from far-flung outfits gathered at the end of their cattle drives, they proudly demonstrated their horsemanship. Riding exhibitions were held on the open prairies along the railroad sidings where spectators simply formed a circle and leaped out of the way when the action got rough. An unbroken horse, penned in a makeshift corral, would, when released, come out bucking wildly, his rider standing high in the stirrups while the crowd cheered.

Most of the animals ridden in these events were unbroken mustangs captured from the wild. Horse hunts were organized specifically to gather animals for this purpose. Horses from the *remuda,* however "spoiled" they might be, were not rough enough to please the crowd when "bronc riders" were making fifty cents, or whatever sum could be collected, for "sampling" bad horses. Out of this tradition has grown the big business of rodeo, which today offers more than three million dollars in prize money in nearly six hundred shows held annually across the country.

Though a cowboy's saddle string often contained enough "bad actors" to keep their owner in practice for rodeo events, usually these animals, after an initial display of temperament, would settle down and enjoy herding cattle. In fact, such "snakey" horses often proved to be the quietest and most efficient when at work. Were this not the case, they would not be used on a subsequent trail ride, for the cowboys attempted to fatten the steers on the drive to market and had little patience with a flighty horse that might cause the cattle to stampede. Beef, after all, was sold by the pound, and in a single stampede thousands of pounds of beef could be lost, converted into body energy. Herds were encouraged to move slowly and to take frequent rests. Hence, a bit-chewing, prancing horse, though an interesting diversion in the early morning, was expected to have enough "cow-sense" not to stir up the cattle during the remainder of the day. A good cow pony carried his head low and "padded along" around steers. Western movies that depict horses pounding across the range, forcing cattle to move at a trot, are ridiculed by cowboys.

The little Spanish horses seemed to understand instinctively what was expected of them, and soon adapted themselves to the moods of their riders. Blooded horses imported to Texas from Kentucky to work on the range, on the other hand, frequently proved too wild when around the stock and not quite temperamental enough to provide entertainment around the camp. Sometimes a cross between a Thoroughbred and a local mustang produced an excellent cow pony. However, many cattlemen objected to the cross, claiming that the gain in weight produced by this mixing was offset by the loss of a mustang's special qualities.

The early Western cow horse, though usually of mixed ancestry, was predominately Spanish. He resembled the Indians' Spanish ponies in that he, too, was not always beautiful and often was ewe-necked and deer-legged, although he differed from the Indian ponies in that he was more frequently a solid color than a pinto. He combined the dauntless spirit of the Indians' cherished Buffalo Runners, with an inborn aptitude for herding; some said he instinctively knew more about steers than many of the men who rode him.

The cow ponies did not all perform the same kind of work. Many were trained to be specialists as "cutting horses" or "ropers." A cutting horse was considered to be the most intelligent of the range horses, and when a cowboy told a man he was as "smart as a cutting horse," he meant it as a compliment. The cutting horse was trained to trail a steer and drive him out of a herd, to turn on a dime, and to follow a specific animal regardless of how much it darted, shifted, and changed direction.

Some cowboys bragged that their favorite cutting horse could work without any guidance from them, claiming, for example, that when cutting yearlings out of a herd, all they had to do was show the horse the first animal, and from then on he picked out the yearlings by himself and trailed them all day without any further advice from his rider. Others boasted that their cutting horse could trail a jackrabbit out of a herd of cattle if they indicated that he should do so.

In *Cow People,* J. Frank Dobie tells the story of George Bosler's horse, Bosler's Blue, that could even work alone with no one in the saddle and, on his own initiative, push steers out of a herd with his shoulder. Buffalo Bill once lost a bet to George Bosler when he doubted that the steel-blue cutting horse could actually work in this way. The incident is not so hard to believe, however, when one recalls the difficulties experienced by Sergeant Pryor when he tried to drive some Indian ponies, trained to hunt buffaloes, through the Pryor Mountains to rendezvous with Lewis and Clark at the Bighorn River. The riderless horses, it will be remembered, upon sighting buffaloes, galloped after them and surrounded the herd alone. After that experience, Sergeant Pryor sent a man ahead on horseback to clear the trail of buffaloes.

A roping horse had entirely different duties from those of a cutting horse. First used by Mexican vaqueros, the roping horse understood how to pull up the slack when he felt the tug of a two-thousand-pound steer on the end of the rope snubbed to his saddle horn. By sidestepping and backing, he would hold the line taut and prevent the steer from lowering his head for a charge. While the cowboy worked to secure the enraged animal, the horse carefully "played" the steer like a fish, but would give way to release the noose when he felt the signal from his rider, a single jerk on the rope.

The work of the cow pony was exacting and physically hard, and the work of its rider was monotonous and sometimes even dangerous. For little pay, perhaps thirty dollars a month, the range rider worked a hundred-hour week, traveling across dangerous Indian country, subsisting on poor food, and often finding his best company to be his horse. Frequently, his fellow workers were outlaws who made the cattle trail their hideout for a season or two. Misunderstandings were often settled with guns, and many a cowboy was buried in an unmarked grave hastily dug along an old cattle trail.

During this early period, many cowboys were also killed by Indians, who resented the fact that white men were "whooping away" the buffalo herds in Indian territory. But trailing cattle through Apache country was hardly more dangerous than herding them across an agricultural strip in eastern Kansas populated with white settlers. This land had been ceded to the United States by the Indians in the Kansas-Nebraska Act of 1854; and the American farmers who lived there, fearful that their own live-stock might contract cattle fever from the tick-infested Texas longhorns, met the herds with guns and pitchforks, and barricaded the route that led across Kansas to the Eastern markets.

Even after the completion of the Kansas Pacific Railroad had brought profit to the local boom towns that sprang up along the shipping route, Kansas farmers did not want cattle trailed into their state, and they made life difficult for the cowboys. The cattlemen, in turn, tried to drive out the "nesters," as they called these homesteaders, and the conflict between the property holders and the nomadic cowboys escalated until drought and big business eventually foreclosed on both groups.

Though the period of the open range was short-lived, the figure of the American cowboy, which had its birth in those days, has enjoyed amazing durability. John Hawgood, in his book *America's Western Frontiers,* points out that though the mountain trappers of the Pacific Northwest experienced some brief public adulation, and though the Indian fighters of Kentucky also were heroes-of-the-hour for a short time, no American character has so seized and held the imagination of the world as has the cowboy.

No doubt his youthful, prankish, and unrestrained personality has had something to do with this sustained popularity, but Hawgood believes that his horse might be the key factor responsible for making the Western cowboy appear a little bigger than life. Like the image of the Plains Indian mounted on a pony, the cowboy and his horse have become inextricably and unconsciously merged into one centaurlike figure in the public eye. And though the horse upon which he actually sat was hardly larger or more impressive in appearance than the pony of the Plains Indian (being in most cases one and the same animal), the very fact that he was mounted added to his image that touch of glamour and romance that earlier heroes lacked.

This close association of the cowboy with his horse, however, was not the mere fantasy of an admiring public, but was a very real fact. Like the Horse Indians, the cowboy enjoyed an almost mystical relationship with his mounts. Riding alone all day gave him an opportunity to know his string of animals well, and he came to look upon each saddle horse in much the same way that he regarded people. He expected a lot from both, and if either let him down, he gave way to anger, granting his horse no easier forgiveness than he granted to a man. Such a concession would have been patronizing and an insult to his animal. However, though he might remain angry with his horse for several days, his complaints about the animal's tricky behavior often sound like boasting. Dobie made the observation that when a cowboy bragged, it was often difficult to determine if he was talking about himself or about his horse.

Through this close relationship between rider and horse, the cowboy developed an almost uncanny knowledge of cow ponies, making it possible for him to recognize an animal's worth almost instantly. He might point to the sorriest-looking nag in a sales ring and, without further examination, know that he had just bought for himself a "performing" horse. He was no snob about appearances and rode an undersized scrub horse caught on the Apache reservation or taken from some Texas bottomland as happily as horses whose appearance more closely resembled their Arabian ancestors. In fact, the early cowboys often prized their runted horses above the more handsome ones, claiming an ugly horse was always smarter. One early Texan expressed his preference for a small horse by saying, "I'm looking for a pony. I'm not fixing to ride one of those big Dutch trottin' horses."

In later years when size became more equated with masculinity, Western men "bred up" their saddle stock and rejected the mustangs that often did not exceed thirteen hands. It must be admitted, of course, that the average Texan of recent years is a larger man and consequently needs a larger horse to carry him.

Despite the fact that the early cowboys' favorite horses were frequently captured from the wild, the wild-horse herds that raised the dust in Texas held little romance for the hardworking cowpunchers. Wild horses stampeded their cattle and upset the labor of many days. Furthermore, the *remuda* horses became excited at the sight of the wild ones, and often would compound the cowboys' troubles by joining a roving band.

But in spite of this annoyance, the cowboys' natural affection for horses prevented them from participating in any scheme to rid the range of the mustangs. Most of them preferred to live with the problem rather than shoot a horse. Their stockmen employers, however, did not share such sentiments and tried to enlist their aid in extermination programs, even offering a bounty of two dollars for every pair of wild horse ears. According to cowboy-author Will James, the cowboys were disgusted by the proposition.

But capturing wild mustangs to obtain another saddle horse was quite a different matter. Enormous numbers were gathered, and the young ones broken and pressed into service. From the brushy bottoms of Texas to the

Bighorn Basin in Montana, wherever the first cowboys trailed cattle, there also the wild horses existed. And with time on their hands, the horse-crazy cowboys could not resist putting themselves to the test of catching still another horse to be added to their saddle string. It will never be known how many thousands of wild horses were brought back to a domestic condition during this period. But the wild-horse population that had been steadily escalating since the first day the horse was reintroduced to his native habitat in western North America now took a downward turn.

20. Scapegoats

Though the early cowboys refused to shoot the wild horses as ordered by their stockmen employers, wild-horse extermination programs were nevertheless effectively carried out by the early cattle barons.

Almost as soon as a profitable system for marketing cattle was devised, financiers took over the livestock industry, forcing many cowboys out of ranching and making employees of them. These businessmen had little personal contact or experience with the region they were exploiting, and they gave no thought to the concept of preserving a natural balance among the various plant and animal forms on the Plains. Most livestock owners managed their gigantic spreads "in absentia," hiring efficiency experts to oversee operations and tell the cowboys how to do their work.

And so the fragile and poorly understood Great Plains passed out of the hands of its inhabitants and became the "property" of business interests whose only concern was the rate at which they could force the region to yield a profit. As a result, what wildlife was not crowded off the range by overstocking was persecuted by the ranch supervisors. The heyday of the wild horse was over.

And wild horses were not alone in feeling the harsh effects of the massive exploitation that rapidly denuded the grass, exterminated the game, and ultimately left so much of the West bankrupt. Wildlife, plant life, and the earth itself have never recovered from the ecological shock that occurred on the Great Plains during the last third of the nineteenth century.

The transfer of the grazing lands into the hands of Wall Street brokers was brought about by the construction of a railroad across the continent. In the year 1867, a Chicagoan, Joseph G. McCoy, had an idea that changed the character of the West irrevocably. McCoy, the original "Real McCoy," conjectured that with the opening of the Kansas Pacific Railroad then under construction, cattle could be shipped directly to market in Chicago; and with the opening of a market for the previously worthless beef of Texas, the longhorns would become a negotiable commodity.

Early in July of that year he began constructing shipping yards on the lonely Kansas prairie, selecting a spot almost in the exact middle of the continent through which he knew the railroad was destined to pass. To this location he hoped to attract drovers.

As work proceeded on his corrals, he sent out an agent to search for "every straggling drover possible to tell them of Abilene and what was being done there toward making a market and outlet for Texas cattle." The cowboys, with good reason, were incredulous at first. McCoy, in his *Historical Sketches of the Cattle Trade* . . ., writes of their reaction:

"This was joyous news to the drover, for the fear of trouble and violence hung like an incubus over his waking thoughts alike with his sleeping moments. It was almost too good to be believed; could it be possible that someone was about to afford a Texan drover any reception other than outrage and robbery? They were very suspicious that some trap was set, to be sprung on them; they were not ready to credit the proposition that the day of fair dealing had dawned for Texas drovers. Yet they turned their herds toward the point designated and slowly and cautiously moved on northward."

By the end of the year thirty-five thousand steers had been driven into the Abilene corrals constructed by Joseph McCoy. There they were loaded on cattle cars and sent by rail to Chicago. McCoy had proved that he was indeed the real thing.

Now that an outlet had been provided for the longhorns, stock raising became a profitable investment, and speculators were quick to get into it. The Texans who had developed the skills necessary to handle the livestock, to trail the animals to grass, and to drive them to market, soon found themselves competing with gigantic cattle corporations, owned and controlled by Eastern and British interests. Unable to match such fabulous capitalization themselves, most of the small-time ranchers sold out to these corporations and went to work for them as cowhands.

The new livestock industry expanded rapidly, for it promised a twenty percent return on money and offered an apparently unlimited growth potential. As long as cattle continued to breed, the brokers pointed out, profits, too, would multiply.* There seemed no reason why the bonanza should ever end.

Soon Texas had cattle occupying every available acre of her vast range, and the stockmen began to look around for new pastures on which to expand. Most of the northern Plains, the region that was to become Wyoming, Montana, and the Dakotas, had recently been ceded to the United States by the Indians. Still unsurveyed in 1869, it was a part of the public domain, and the precedent of utilizing such untitled government land for grazing purposes had long been established by the small rancher. It was generally recognized that whoever occupied a given section of land possessed a "prior right" to it. As a result, the large outfits now began to search out every unused piece of grazing land they could find throughout the North and stocked it with cattle to establish their "priority claim."

Under such a "no-overhead" arrangement, where land and feed cost nothing, only one factor limited profits—the size of the herd. Increased propagation was now emphasized, and brood stock was at a premium. For a time, more animals seemed to be shipped to the northern Plains for breeding purposes than were sent away to packers. Cattle brought west from Ohio and Illinois, east from Oregon, and even imported from faraway England, were crossed with longhorns trailed up from Texas.

Before long these cattle enterprises in Wyoming and Nebraska had swelled into kingdoms. One, the Nebraska Bay State, extended across seven counties and was larger than certain Eastern states. Another, the Swan Land and Cattle Company in Wyoming, stretched along the banks of the Laramie River for one hundred thirty miles and continued south for an additional three hundred miles.

Such conspicuous success had the effect of attracting still more money and creating even greater expansion. Most of the small operators were forced out of business, and the Western cattle industry was left almost entirely in the hands of outside corporate manipulators.

To deal with any local or political repercussions that might arise to oppose their monopolistic interests, the cattle corporations formed stockmen associations. These powerful associations enforced their own rules and even hired vigilantes to guard the "priority rights" of members to choice stretches of the public lands. Independent ranchers, sheepmen, and

* Immediate sale of steers was not necessary to show profit on the books. The trick was to get the livestock to reproduce at the fastest possible rate, and the paper stock, automatically reflecting the growth of the herd, would do the same.

farmers soon found themselves excluded from water sources "claimed" by the big stockmen.

The few small operators who struggled to compete did so by following the example of the corporations and filling the range with more stock than it could carry. Soon the bellowing of hungry steers could be heard in the West, indicating that all was not well on the Plains.

The exploitation of the Great Plains, though late in starting, once begun, proceeded at an astonishing rate. E. S. Osgood describes the phenomenon in *Day of the Cattleman:*

"With a rapidity that could almost be measured in months rather than years, every available bit of range in north and central Wyoming was soon occupied, the country in eastern Montana north of the Yellowstone to the boundary of the Indians' reservation was filled up, and herds began to look for favorable locations beyond the international boundary along the Saskatchewan River."

That the vast northern Plains was rich and well suited for the grazing of cattle was undeniable. For long ages it had supported and given rise to a great diversity of animal life. In prehistoric times it had served four kinds of elephant, the imperial and woolly mammoths, the mastodon, many species of bison, camels, rhinoceroses, a giant pig, all the evolutionary forms of the horse, and a giant and a small ground sloth. In more recent times, it had accommodated such familiar animals as buffaloes, horses, elk, antelope, and deer. Not only had the Plains demonstrated its capacity to support wildlife in great diversity, it had also carried animals in numbers far exceeding the herds of domestic livestock which were now arbitrarily placed upon it. Yet, under the management of the cattlemen, the land rapidly began to show signs of losing its health and vitality.

Whereas the wild animals such as the bison had mystified the Indians by responding to some unknown signal from nature and, at intervals, had vacated certain regions upon which they had for a time feasted, crossing miles of seed-laden grass (which they incidentally trampled, sowed, and planted with their hoofs during the migration process), now cattlemen used the newly invented barbed wire to fence their herds within large, but nevertheless restricted areas.

The fencing of the public domain was illegal, and complaints from settlers who were looking for land to homestead brought action from Congress. In 1885, a law was passed that prohibited the cattle outfits from setting up barbed-wire kingdoms on land that was not their own. Settlers were advised to cut the illegal fences and to homestead on the land of their choice. But the powerful stockmen's associations made such action too dangerous.

In the long run, however, the fencing proved to be as detrimental to the interests of the cattle barons as it was to the settlers it was intended to barricade. E. S. Osgood writes: "In the first place, by limiting the free movement of the herds, it prevented even grazing; and, in the second place, it increased winter losses. Cattle drifted for miles before a blizzard, and if they could keep moving tails to the wind, they would probably survive. Once they came to a halt before an impassable barrier, they were lost, unless the storm abated."

Ironically, the principle of the open range, so wholesome for the plant life of the semiarid Plains, and so practical for the animals that inhabited its treeless stretches, was defeated by the cattlemen themselves. Overstocked "enclosures" were rapidly denuded of grass and, without ground cover, the earth began to wash away, cracks opened, and the precious topsoil was carried off into ever-widening gullies. Though it was recognized that the damage being done was irreversible, the popular viewpoint held by Americans was that the country was big enough and rich enough to accommodate everybody and every interest indefinitely.

The Indians alone protested that the bright sunsets in the West were forebodings of disaster, indicating that the Great Spirit was in a vengeful mood because of the white man's destruction of the buffalo range. They watched in amazement as the whites chased the buffaloes off the land to make room for more hungry cattle, and they inquired why an animal that didn't require any care should be replaced by one that caused so much work and trouble. Interestingly, bright sunsets may sometimes be caused by dust in the atmosphere.

But the white man, then as now, prided himself on his superior ability to exploit the land at a faster rate than his predecessor. The absentee cattle lords consulted their books and proudly announced that the cattle business had yielded a one-hundred-percent annual increase since "big business" had taken it over, and they argued that if left to expand unimpeded, states such as Wyoming would soon become the richest in America. Besides, the corporate heads argued, agriculture had never lowered the productivity of the land anywhere, and cattle raising, after all, was agriculture.

The cattle interests, of course, would not share a blade of the dwindling grass with the wild horses. Consequently, the horses that were bold enough to poach on the public grazing land acquired their most formidable enemy. The stockmen blamed the wild horses for the clearly visible deterioration of the land, and they organized posses to hunt and shoot them.

Though the horses had lived in the West for three centuries without destroying their habitat, no one now questioned that the horses were responsible for the poor conditions of the range. A story in the Chicago *Tribune,* datelined Cheyenne, December 12, 1884, and titled "War on the Wild Horses," was reprinted in the New York *Times* two weeks later. It reports on the efforts made by stockmen to exterminate the wild horses:

"Wild horses have become so numerous on the Plains that some of the stockmen in the vicinity have organized a hunting party whose objective will be to thin them out. The hunters are provided with long-range rifles, fleet ponies, and supplies and forage enough to last all winter.

"These horses have existed on the Plains for many years, but of late have been increasing very fast [contradicted later in the story]. They are quick to scent the approach of foes, fleet as the antelope that may often be seen browsing in security at their side, and as unmanageable as the wind. . . . The wild stallions are guardians of the bands. Always on sentinel duty, they give the alarm when the enemy approaches.

"Five or six years ago they could be found on the divide between Sidney and Sterling, in bunches of 50 to 75, but now a bunch of 25 is considered large. [The reporter had said they were on the increase!]

"Wild horses when captured or trained are superior to other horses of the same size. Many of them are used by the cowboys, and others are broken to the harness and driven as carriage horses, being entirely reliable. Several men living in Sidney make a living by catching wild horses.

"The present movement of the stock raisers threatens to put a stop to this business. Mounted on grain-fed horses the hunters will pursue the wild bands when they are somewhat weakened by the rigors of winter. Riding as close as possible, the men will shoot the stallions from time to time. It is hoped that by spring nearly all the stallions will have been killed and the the capture of the mares by the wholesale will then be made possible."

Less than six months after the publication of the above news story, the price of beef fell drastically. The range was so overstocked that cattle had become a glut on the market, and Chicago packers slashed the price of steers from thirty-five dollars to eight dollars a head. Although the public had evinced little interest in the deterioration of the public range from overstocking, now that pocketbooks were affected, grave concern was ex-

Two stallions wage a battle when they meet at a stream.

Dun-colored mare and foal.

The natural gait and neck arch of this beautiful wild horse would make him a good candidate for the highly esteemed Spanish Riding School.

A high-stepping foal might also qualify for admission to that school.

Some horse hands are luckier than others, depending on the home range they have claimed. Water is available year-round here.

A wild horse circles me on the Nevada testing grounds.

Mares with foals at sunset.

High on a mountain meadow a stallion and his ten mares size me up.

A beautiful grullo-colored mustang with dorsal stripe and "broom tail" that sweeps the ground.

pressed that the cattle industry should have so overextended itself and brought ruin to its investors.

But nature had worse things in store for her despoilers. The following winter, a blizzard which began in late January, was followed by storms and below-zero weather almost without relief for two months. Temperatures in Wyoming dropped to 50 below zero and hundreds of thousands of cattle drifted with the wind and piled up at fences where their frozen carcasses were found the following spring.

Since no provision was made to feed cattle during the winter months, there was no stored forage available to meet the emergency. Losses were devastating, and cattle suffered miserably. They bawled for food as they slowly died from hunger and the unrelieved cold. Out of desperation some animals tried to eat the tar paper from ranch shacks, and the occupants were forced to stand guard and drive the suffering beasts away with clubs in order to keep their homes intact. When at last the Chinook wind whistled up from the southwest and melted the snow, only a few bony creatures were still alive. Eighty-five percent of the stock had died. The West was bankrupt.

Winter attrition normally killed from five to ten percent of the cattle, a loss that had not been considered significant enough to warrant providing expensive feed for the stock. During ordinary winters, the cattle used their noses to dig through the snow and uncover feed, and though February and March usually were grim endurance contests between the animals and starvation, most of them "hung on" and managed to survive.

Unlike the cattle, whose noses were apt to grow sore and bloody from pushing away ice and snow, the wild horses used their hoofs to paw the snow off the ground and uncover the grass. Under the stressful conditions of the winter of 1886–87, some of the raw-nosed cattle, too badly injured to forage for themselves, began to follow the horse herds around and feed in areas the mustangs had opened up. Though it is doubtful that the horses could have helped them much in view of the duration of the bad weather, nevertheless it is ironic that only the previous winter the stockmen had waged their all-out war against these wild horses.

The concept that animals benefit from a multiformity of life within their habitat was apparently an insight that was beyond the comprehension of the nineteenth-century cattle barons. Yet they might have noticed the vigorous condition of the Plains wildlife upon their arrival, when mustangs abounded and buffaloes and antelope coexisted in enormous herds.

Many early visitors to the West had observed and even pondered the strange fact that wild horses and buffaloes were so frequently seen grazing together in pastoral harmony. Antelope, too, stayed close to the wild horses, taking advantage of the careful sentry work of the stallions who alerted them to approaching enemies. Though to the careful observer it is usually obvious that an affinity between two species of animals results in benefit to both, at times it is difficult to detect the services being performed. Sometimes it takes a catastrophe such as the blizzard of 1886–87 to suggest a new symbiotic link.

Today it is generally acknowledged by cattle raisers that the wild horses aid livestock by opening up trails in winter and breaking thick surface ice on water holes. Furthermore, by eating dry winter grass, the horses speed up the spring growth. The concept that even the plant life of a habitat might derive benefit from a multiform of animals dwelling on it was an even more alien thought to the cattle magnates, and they blithely removed the wild animals, claiming they were "competing" with the domestic stock. Yet to the extent that a variety of grazing animals eat different types of plants, their combined effect on a habitat will keep plant life in balance. When any one species of animal is removed, its normal forage soon begins to outcompete other plants, thus altering the environment to the detriment of the remaining animals. Furthermore, the stockmen put two steers in the place of each wild animal they removed from the range. The result was not the reduction of foraging animals but the elimination of diversity.

Yet diversity may have been what the Plains required. For again, the stockmen could not have failed to notice the lush condition of the prairie grasses on their arrival when a variety of species feasted on them in numbers even exceeding the livestock that now destroyed the range. Certainly on other continents, such as Africa, habitats sustain an incredible assortment of animal forms. Perhaps the affinities and the antipathies of one species toward another create the proper tensions that cause the animals to shift their territory and thus relieve any one part of the land from continuous use by a single form. In any case, common sense should have told the cattlemen that any animal, whether wild or domestic, when imprisoned in a limited pasture, sooner or later will consume all its forage.

It is perhaps understandable that these early stockmen should have overlooked some of the more mysterious roles that animals play in helping to cycle plant life, and failed to realize that by substituting one species for many, they would inevitably create subtle changes in the total environment. Even now such effects are not all known or understood. One contribution to the habitat that is made solely by the horse, however, is certainly worth mentioning. Many people have noticed that the greenest pastures are those upon which horses once fed. The reason for this is that horses are "seed-ers." Whereas cud-chewing cattle thoroughly masticate and destroy any seeds they may incidentally ingest, the horse does not. His inefficient diges-tive system passes grass seeds, and these are stored in manure piles; sometimes these seeds remain dormant for several years, or until the right conditions of moisture cause them to germinate and take root.

Thus by "storing" seeds against a catastrophe such as a prairie fire, a grasshopper plague, or a disease that might wipe out a plant species prior to its seasonal maturation, nature safeguards the continuity of that plant life. And so the horse, by "banking seeds," insures the perpetuation of its own forage.

But such ecological observations were beyond the imagination of the nineteenth-century stockmen who were confident of their methods, and who firmly believed that man was created to dominate nature, not to understand it. The American approach to the opening of the West, put simply, was "Get rich now and pay later." The price that will ultimately be exacted has not yet been assessed. It takes one thousand years for the earth to produce a single inch of topsoil, and the soil on the Plains averages less than nine inches. In the short time that the white man has imposed his will on the West, he has permanently and irretrievably destroyed an area twice the size of the fertile croplands of California and seriously damaged, per-haps beyond reclaim, five more Californias. Aldous Huxley sums up this irresponsible attitude toward nature with the following comment: "Fore-thought is incompatible with now-greed."

Unfortunately, Americans have always been able to rationalize damage to natural resources by pointing to the immediate profits that they have been able to realize.

Perhaps the cattle crash of 1886–87 did shock some people and alert them to the almost criminal abuses inflicted on both land and animals by commercial interests. E. S. Osgood, in *Day of the Cattleman,* quotes one bankrupt stockman, Granville Stuart, as saying, "A business that had been fascinating to me before, suddenly became distasteful. I never again wanted to own an animal I could not feed and shelter."

Nevertheless by the mid-nineties cattle had once more built up on the Northern range, and the voices of the stockmen began to demand what little land remained to the Indians. On the Great Plains (that Great Ameri-can Desert guaranteed to the red man forever) all that remained of Indian

Desert dawn may spell sunset for endangered kit foxes who watch a newborn foal being guarded by a wild mare and "aunt." A camouflaged badger shares their desert habitat.

Territory was what is now the state of Oklahoma. And the cattlemen, fearing another winter catastrophe on the northern Plains, demanded this land for winter pasture.

The exploitative attitude of the early stockmen set a precedent in the West of callous disregard for land, ecology, and wildlife. Today Americans continue to accept destructive and even inhumane practices of commercial interests, viewing them as legitimate so long as it can be shown that some-one is realizing a profit from them whatever be the long-range cost in terms of wilderness values and the ecological health of the land. While such a materialistic view prevails, it is unlikely that wild horses or any other noncommercial animal will have much chance of surviving.

21. The Slaughter of the Buffaloes

The wild horse of the Plains was not the only animal to feel the effects of the white man's exploitative greed. While the mustangs were being persecuted by the stockmen, hide hunters preyed upon the buffalo herds and white settlers confiscated the domestic ponies of the Indians.

Whereas for centuries the Indian ponies had served as reserve stock from which the wild-horse herds gained new blood, now the best ponies of the Plains tribes were appropriated by the settlers and either converted to their own use, or driven to Eastern markets for sale. The Indians were left with only poor specimens, many of which were not sufficiently hardy to earn their way in the wild.

In the case of the buffalo, by 1880 the enormous herds had been decimated. Of the sixty million beasts estimated to have roamed the Plains at the opening of the century, only ten million remained, and during the following decade all but a few hundred of these were wiped out. Yet, even while the extermination was accelerating, Americans denied that the buffalo was threatened. The American people, then as now, were firmly convinced that they lived in a land of endless plenty, and they refused to heed warnings against exhaustion of natural resources. Not until the buffalo tally had dropped to under a hundred animals did the general public believe there might be cause for alarm.

The wild-horse herds that grazed peacefully alongside the buffaloes, interacting with their shaggy companions in some way, fared somewhat better. Being a more flexible animal, the horse could adapt to a wider range of habitats, and wisely the bands began to retreat from the Plains to inaccessible mountain heights, rocky canyons, and desert wastelands. There, in poor but uncoveted abodes, they grew wilder and remained relatively safe from extinction. Thus the Great Plains, though once their principal habitat, was largely abandoned by the mustangs. (Incidentally the elk also left the Plains and went to the high mountains at this time.)

Today the Plains supports fewer wild horses than do the desert regions of Nevada and Utah, or the mountainous terrains of western Colorado, southern Montana, and northern Wyoming.

Though the disposal of the buffaloes and the Indian ponies was actually carried out by private citizens and by commercial operators, the United States Government gave its tacit approval to the process. For now that the Great American Desert had begun to show signs that it might yield to settlement after all, the Government re-examined its concession of this "useless" piece of real estate to the Indians. Here, as in the Pacific Northwest, the Indians' nomadic way of life stood in the way of mass settlement; on the Plains, however, there were *two* animals that sustained and served the hunting tribes, the buffalo and the Indian pony, and both these animals now became the targets of the encroaching whites.

In this treeless environment, the buffalo provided the Indian with all he needed for survival: meat for food, skins for shelter, and chips for fuel. It also provided him with nonessential items important to the human spirit such as horn spoons, rawhide saddles, and bone combs. To all the members of a Plains tribe, but especially to the hunter, the buffalo represented life, religion, and identity; and with the destruction of the herds, the Indian was reduced physically, psychologically, and even spiritually. In two decades brave warriors and courageous hunters were transformed into mere wards of the white man.

If a period can be known by the men it calls its heroes, then Buffalo Bill who boasted that he once killed 4,280 buffaloes in a seventeen-month period expresses the spirit of the third quarter of the nineteenth century when the Great Plains was being exploited by the cattle kings and opened to settlement. In a personal account of a buffalo-killing match waged between himself and a friend, Cody, in *Buffalo Bill's Life Story* reveals not the slightest sign of any misgivings over this extravagant and senseless waste of animal life. He writes:

"At last the time came to begin the match. Comstock and I dashed into a herd, followed by the referee. The buffaloes separated; Comstock took the left bunch and I the right. My great forte in killing buffaloes from horseback was to get them circling by riding my horse at the head of the herd, shooting the leaders, thus crowding their followers to the left, till they would finally circle round and round.

"This particular morning the buffaloes were very accommodating, and I soon had them running in a beautiful circle. I dropped them thick and fast, until I had killed thirty-eight; which finished my 'run.'

"Comstock began shooting at the rear of the buffaloes he was chasing, and they kept on in a straight line. He succeeded in killing twenty-three, but they were scattered over a distance of three miles. The animals I had shot lay close together.

"Our St. Louis friends set out champagne when the result of the first run was announced. It proved a good drink on a Kansas prairie, and a buffalo hunter proved a good man to dispose of it.

"While we were resting we espied another herd approaching. It was a small drove, but we prepared to make it serve our purpose. The buffaloes were cows and calves, quicker in their movements than the bulls. We charged in among them and I got eighteen to Comstock's fourteen."

Before the contestants tired of their afternoon amusement, Cody had killed sixty-nine buffalo and Comstock forty-six. Even while this contest was being waged, the Canadian Government, alarmed over the sharp decrease in buffalo numbers, enacted legislation that would prohibit such wholesale slaughter of the great beast so important to the survival of the Indians. But, due to a famine that had already struck the Northern hunting tribes, the law had to be repealed immediately. It had been passed too late.

In 1872, the United States Congress also passed legislation to restrict the mass killing of the buffalo, but President Grant busy with higher priorities did not bother to sign the measure. Granville Stuart, looking forward to the fortune he was soon to make in the cattle business, fought the bill, arguing that the extermination of the buffalo was the most expedient method of subjugating the Plains Indians. Most Government officials agreed. The Indians, they insisted, would never learn to become productive farmers until the buffalo was gone. The story had a familiar ring, as once again the removal of an animal was the means by which the white man tried to reinforce his stolen position in Indian territory.

The construction of the transcontinental railroad, which had made cattle big business, also signaled the end of the Buffalo Era. In the years immediately following the Civil War, when the deep wounds of that conflict were still being felt, the concept of a railroad that would span the continent and open up the virgin tracts of the West to settlement appealed to Northerners and Southerners alike. The undefiled West stood as a symbol of hope to the war-weary Americans, and the very effort of building a railroad across this

A remnant of history in Yellowstone National Park.

Mustangs gallop on rare stretch of undespoiled prairie.

promised land gave a sense of unity and purpose, especially to the thousands of men who worked on it.

But despite the enthusiasm of the construction gangs who graded the land and laid the ties, the emptiness of the Great Plains and the monotony of the landscape after a time began to pall. To relieve their boredom, the men hunted, and as the track steadily advanced across the country, a lifeless swath several miles wide attended it. Ten thousand workers, all armed with breechloaders, shot everything that stirred along the route, and soon the stinking carcasses of uncounted buffaloes began to pile up beside the newly made roadbed.

Even the herds that were not directly in the path of the Union Pacific or the Kansas Pacific were searched out and ravaged by hunters employed by the railroads to provide fresh meat for the construction workers every day. Unlike the Indians who jerked strips of meat, drying and preserving what they did not immediately consume, the work gangs feasted only on fresh hump and tongue, leaving the remainder of the carcass to the flocks of scavenger birds that quickly learned to follow these wasteful predators. Bill Cody, known to the public as Buffalo Bill, got his start as a hired hunter for the Kansas Pacific Railroad.

The wanton slaying of the buffaloes did not cease with the completion of the roadbeds. The railroad companies were interested in attracting passengers, and they catered to the whims of their first customers who demanded that the train slow down whenever a herd of buffaloes was encountered so the passengers could have the pleasure of shooting the animals from the car windows. William Webb, author of *Buffalo Land,* has given this firsthand description of one of these "hunts" that occurred during a trip taken in 1872:

"During these races [with the buffaloes] the car windows are opened, and numerous breech-loaders fling hundreds of bullets among the densely crowded and flying masses. Many of the poor animals fall, and more go on to die in the ravines. The train speeds on, and the scene is repeated every few miles until Buffalo Land is passed. . . . All over the plains, lying in disgusting masses of putrefaction along valley and hill, are strewn immense carcasses of wantonly slain buffalo. They line the Kansas Pacific Railroad for two hundred miles."

The railroads quickly recognized that buffalo hunting was a resource to be exploited; they seized on the hunting theme and promoted excursion trips planned especially for hunters. Grand Duke Alexis of Russia helped to make the sport popular by chartering a special train for the sole purpose of shooting buffaloes from the ease and comfort of a parlor car.

But though the railroads were eager to please, they stopped short of allowing their passengers to drag the undressed carcasses of their "kill" on board. The animals had to be left where they fell along the tracks, and it wasn't long before all runs had to be made with the train windows tightly closed.

Such blatant contempt for their most important source of food alarmed the Indians. At the Medicine Lodge Treaty Conference they attempted to raise the question, "Why do you kill and not eat?" But the conference had been called for the purpose of getting the Indians removed from treaty lands to the south in order to build a third railroad, the Atchison, Topeka and Santa Fe, and the question of how to save the buffalo was given no consideration.

In yet another way the railroads played a major role in the extermination of the buffalo herds. During the 1860's and 70's their principal freight aside from cattle, consisted of untanned buffalo hides. The Plains held little else to export since the near extinction of the beaver had put an end to the early fur trade of the Northwest. So buffalo hunters were hired to go West to harvest the shaggy skins, and buffalo robes were briskly promoted in the United States. These robes became fashionable and remained so for fifteen years, or until the animal that produced them was gone forever from the Great Plains.

It was this professional hunter more than the so-called sportsmen who most alarmed the Indians, because of the method by which he brought down his prey. The professional hunter early discovered that herds could be stymied merely by killing the lead buffalo and, for a few minutes, until a new leader had been accepted by the various male contenders for the top position, the buffaloes were unable to run. As the frustrated animals impatiently awaited the signal that would allow them to stampede to safety, they would mill about, bellow, and paw the ground, and the hunters could easily pick off the tenderest calves and cows.

The Indians complained that this type of mass slaughter created so much anxiety among the animals that it permanently changed their nature and habits. Frenzied by the smell of blood, the agitated buffaloes would sometimes even add to the carnage by madly attacking one another, and goring and trampling the injured and dying. Any herd that had been through such ordeal never entirely recovered from it. The experience seemed to derange the animals and they became extremely wild. The Indians claimed they were unable to approach and hunt such a herd on horseback using their customary weapon, the bow and arrow.

The wanton destruction of the buffaloes, the mainstay of the Indians, by white profiteers was not without serious repercussions. During the sixties and the seventies, the most dedicated Indians of the various Plains tribes attempted to lead resistance movements in an effort to drive the whites out. Riding their war horses, many of which were Medicine Hats, the Cheyenne and the Sioux attacked white buffalo hunters in Indian territory. But these attacks only led to cruel reprisals and aroused more fear and hatred among Americans, who were unable to comprehend the issue at stake. The Indian, on the other hand, understood clearly that he was fighting to save his culture from total obliteration.

The American farmers also played a part in undermining the Indians' culture. From their agriculture-based perspective, they viewed the red man as indolent. Pawnee Bill, a white man who later led the "Boomer Raid" on Indian Territory in the Cherokee Strip, aroused public opinion by demanding that the Indians should be required to explain why they should "enjoy their herds of horses and hunting and not farm." He was even more indignant toward those "reservation" Indians who leased their lands to the cattle interests, accusing them of "fancying themselves to be in the real estate business, now that the game was disappearing." Even the news media in the United States seemed blind to the real meaning behind the Western conflicts and depicted the Indian as a backward savage, thirsting for warfare.

To the Government of the United States other national objectives took precedence over the issue of justice for a primitive people who were accused of standing in the way of progress. The profiteers who were arousing the Indians to war by robbing them of their game were actually carrying out an ugly task that the Government was secretly happy to see performed. Besides, the United States Government, then as now, held the view that it is morally justifiable to consume resources belonging to another nation as long as that nation has shown no inclination or ability commercially to exploit its own wealth. The Governor of Colorado expressed the philosophy of the period in a speech to his constituents: "God gave us the earth and the fullness thereof. I do not believe in donating to these indolent savages the best portion of my territory, and I do not believe in placing the Indians on an equality with the white man as landholder."

During these two decades while the white man proudly demonstrated to the Indian his superior ingenuity at turning a natural resource into a quick profit, the Indians who had utilized the same resource for many long centuries without exhausting it, shook their heads in sorrow.

22. *The Poaching of the Ponies*

Not content with the slow process of starving the Plains tribes into submission by exterminating their principal food supply, the white man also seized the Indians' horses. The government as well as the settlers, sensing that the Indians' very life and culture were tied up with their animals, began to realize that the Indian would fall with the loss of his prized possession and not before. The Indians' horse thereupon became a target.

To a certain extent government policy toward the small horses of the Indians, and opinions of Westerners regarding these animals, still reflect the attitudes formed at this early date. Just as the Nez Percé tribe had been brought under control by the disposal of their ponies, now the horses of the Plains tribes, the Sioux and the Cheyennes, were confiscated illegally.

A story dated August 8, 1876, appeared in the New York *Times* giving the details of a telegram sent by General Sheridan to the War Department in which he requested permission to sell Indian ponies either captured or surrendered "at such prices as can be obtained for them, the funds so accumulated to be held for the purchase of cattle for the Indians at the proper time." General Sheridan went on to say that the ponies would not sell for much, "but the main objective is to get them away from the Indians." The story concluded with the statement that the Commissioner of Indian Affairs would no doubt concur with General Sheridan's view of the matter.

Two years earlier the best horses of the southern Comanche and Kiowa tribes had been given no quarter after a skirmish with General McKenzie, and thousands of the animals had been slaughtered at Tule Canyon near the Texas Panhandle, where their whitened bones can still be seen. The American public, however, had begun to object to this waste of the spoils of battle, hence auctions to dispose of the captured ponies thereafter became the order of the day.

It was not only the rebellious Indians, however, who lost their most prized possessions to the white intruders. Even the peaceable "reservation Indians" also had their stock stolen or confiscated. This is brought out in another news story in the New York *Times* which recounts the theft of seven hundred Indian horses from the Red Cloud Reservation by white men who drove their booty past Camp Sheridan and Camp Robinson without being apprehended by the military authorities. The writer goes on to explain that the Federal authorities were bowing to the *posse comitatus* law passed the previous year and therefore would not interfere with the internal affairs of the Territories. The article continues:

"The Indian agent [on the reservation] having no armed force at his command is powerless to stop the depredations and for the present they seem likely to continue. The Indians notwithstanding their keen sense of injury, arising from this want of adequate protection, manifest no symptoms of insubordination but remain entirely peaceable and are beginning to devote themselves to farming. . . . The Spotted Tail Indians [a branch of the Sioux] within the past two years have lost several thousand horses in the same way."

The settlers, it might appear, were only too eager to appropriate the "worthless ponies of the Indians" that Sheridan reported would not sell for much, and even people to the east seemed pleased to acquire "aboriginal horse-flesh." Thousands of Indian ponies were driven hundreds of miles across the Plains to cities and towns in Illinois and Minnesota and Iowa, where they were sold at auction.

A story from the St. Paul *Pioneer Press,* dated December 23, 1876, and later reprinted in the New York *Times,* describes "the sensation of the hour," namely, the sale of five hundred Indian ponies taken from the hostile Sioux and driven nine hundred miles across the snowy plains of the Dakotas and into the stockyards in St. Paul, Minnesota, where a large crowd assembled to bid on them. The article gives remarkable details of the event:

"The streets leading to the stockyards were densely crowded with sleighs, omnibuses, and pedestrians, all hurrying to the general center of the attraction. The rush was unprecedented and everybody was astonished at the extraordinary interest which was manifested by citizens and strangers alike in this sale of aboriginal horse flesh. . . . The weather was raw and cold; no fires were burning anywhere; no warm reception rooms were at hand; everything was frigid and cheerless and yet some 4,000 to 5,000 men at the least calculation crowded around the auctioneer, or wandered over Martin Delaney's spacious grounds inspecting the ponies that were picketed around in every direction.

"The ponies were small and lean, showing the hardships they had endured in their long march of eight or nine hundred miles across the snowy plains of Dakota and across the whole state of Minnesota, but nevertheless the little fellows generally showed a snap and pluck and life that seemed to win the sympathy and good opinion of every beholder. A very little nag, scarcely over four feet tall, would be trotted out, his only bridle being a thin rope with a loop and enclosing the lower jaw. Then one of the government employees, clothed in a buffalo overcoat, would bestride the animal which looked smaller and lighter than his rider and yet at the word 'go' that little pony would get up and dash around the ring with a velocity that elicited rounds of laughter and applause, and which necessarily served to raise him high in the estimation of the beholders."

These five hundred ponies that had survived the long trek to St. Paul were only a small portion of the number that had actually been taken from the Sioux. The story goes on to tell of the losses incurred en route. Some of the horses were lamed by the long, hard journey and had to be destroyed. But many were acquired by settlers who followed the herd in the hope of picking up a straggler or two. The article tells of their methods:

"At times there were hundreds of men and boys with teams and on horseback. It not infrequently happened that two men would claim the prize and the dispute would end in a free fight during which some other fellow would walk off with the 'ho'ses.' Occasionally the settlers, it is said, availed themselves of an opportunity to get a haul on the sly, or now and then purchased ponies from the drovers, who had no right whatever to sell them."

Thus the best of the Indians' ponies were gradually confiscated by the white man, and many were driven east where they lost their identity through crossbreeding with American stock. The Indians still maintained large herds of ponies, it is true, but many of these were sorry specimens. Yet even these inferior scrub animals were prized by the red man above all his other possessions. Horse stealing from neighboring reservations was still the surest means for an Indian to obtain honor and earn the right to wear another feather in his headdress. And with the buffaloes nearly extinct on the Plains, horse stealing was, in fact, the only means by which a brave could distinguish himself and demonstrate his prowess.

In a pathetic effort to retain one manly activity behind which to hide their badly injured pride, the Plains tribes continued to carry out horse-stealing raids, rustling animals from one another's reservations. As late as 1886, a party of Piegans traveled south from Canada, entered the Crow treaty lands in southern Montana, and made off with sixty animals from Pryor Creek. This creek is in the general vicinity where Sergeant Pryor camped eighty years earlier, and where he lost the horses he was driving to a rendezvous with Lewis and Clark. It is not far from the present-day habitat of the Pryor Mountain wild horses.

The Crows pursued the thieving Piegans, but recovered only forty of the sixty stolen ponies, and the following day the Piegans swooped down again upon the Crows, making off with an additional fifteen horses.*

At this point a United States Cavalry detachment was sent in pursuit of the Piegans and reported sighting them with ninety animals, mostly Crow ponies, but also a few stolen from local white ranchers. The Piegans, however, were too elusive for the soldiers who were mounted on cavalry stock. The result was that the Piegans outdistanced their pursuers and succeeded in driving ninety horses three hundred miles to safety across the Canadian border.

However, the Crows were not willing to submit to this humiliation, and a year later a party of Crow braves under the leadership of Thunder-and-Lightning, returned triumphantly from a horse raid against the Piegans with a booty of sixty horses in their possession. The score between the Crows and the Piegans should then have been considered even but, according to a New York *Times'* report of the affair, the whites were unwilling to let the matter drop. The article reads:

"The Crows were celebrating their return when Agent H. E. Williamson [Crow agency head] ordered his police to arrest the entire party for horse stealing. This incensed the Indians to such an extent that they commenced firing into the agency, riddling the building with bullets, but fortunately no one was hurt. The agent immediately sent a scout to Fort Custer for troops."

The offending Crows were about to be taught the sobering lesson that horse stealing was illegal and would not be tolerated by their white

---

* Crow Chief Bobby Yellowtail, in an interview during the summer of 1969, reflected on the traditional rivalry between the Piegans and the Crows regarding horses. Raids continued to take place throughout his very early childhood in the 1890's, and he expressed the opinion that such horse stealing had a certain value in that the raids were exciting and relieved the monotony of life on a reservation.

guardians, at least not when the Indians were the guilty parties. Moreover, it was also to be demonstrated that the law which prohibited it, though often flouted by the whites, would be strictly enforced whenever Indians were involved. The news report continues:

"Arrests are to be made by the civil authorities. The Indians say they will resist any attempt of the police to arrest them as they know they will be tried and convicted for horse stealing and severely dealt with. . . .

"An ugly feeling is shown among them as a short time ago a large party of them were arrested and their outfits were confiscated by the Wyoming authorities for hunting outside of their reserve. The excitement on the reservation is intense and all whites are warned not to trespass for fear of further outrages."

One hardly needs further verification that the attempt on the part of the reservation officials to separate Indians from horses was calculated, and its objective was to undermine the Indians' attachment to a hunting culture. For despite the severity of the penalty for horse stealing—offenders could be hanged—the West was rife with *white* horse thieves whose "long ropes" had helped to set them up in the cattle business.

During the excitement of horse raids, the stolen animals frequently were abandoned or escaped in flight. Moreover, those that were successfully driven to a faraway reservation did not always adapt themselves to their new and unfamiliar surroundings, and many broke free and traveled great distances in search of the region where they had been born. However, this instinct of horses to return to their home range is not invariably coupled with an ability to find the way. As a consequence many became wild.

To a certain extent the Indians depended on this love-of-the-home-range instinct in most horses to hold their semiwild herds on reservation lands, and they never bothered to picket their ponies. But not all horses reveal this trait, and many unpicketed Indian ponies took advantage of the first opportunity afforded them to join a wild herd.

The effect on the mustangs of the continuing infusion of fresh blood was beneficial. Not only did it prevent inbreeding but it kept the population stable. Later, when reinforcements from domestic stock were no longer forthcoming, the wild-horse population dropped sharply.

As the nineteenth century waned, the wildness and dramatic color that had so long characterized the Great Plains gradually faded, and a certain "tameness" was imposed on the Plains states. The painted warriors were settled on reservations and growing apathetic with boredom, the massive herds of shaggy buffaloes were gone forever from the grasslands, and the

Spanish-blooded Buffalo Runners were herding bawling cattle on a range that had become fenced. The war between two cultures was over, and the buffaloes, the Indian ponies, and the Indians had been defeated.

Only the wild horses still remained unvanquished, and their fugitive existence was like a reproach to the settlers who regarded these animals as relics of the Indians. As a reminder of the role played by the white man in the tragic events that crushed the nomadic culture of the Great Plains, the wild horses had an unsettling effect on the Westerners, and they gave "the no-good Cayuses" no quarter.

23. *Who Owns the Wild Horses?*

Though the wild horses were historically and symbolically linked with the Indians' ponies, white people too contributed stock to the wild herds. Sometimes this happened inadvertently when a range horse escaped and joined a wild band, but often domestic stallions were intentionally released by a horse rancher who hoped that the males would acquire wild mares which could later be gathered and domesticated. So horses moved in two directions; while a certain number of domestic animals escaped to the wild, conversely, many wild horses were brought into a domestic state, broken, and sold for profit.

Since in the white man's view all facets of nature are resources to be claimed by him, the wild horses were no exception. Like gold nuggets, the buffaloes, the beaver, and the grassy plains, wild horses were eyed as a potential source of revenue, and Westerners looked to exploit the herds in any way that might bring them a profit.

Some ranchers tried experiments to "breed up" the little horse found in the wilderness in order to make them more marketable. In Oregon, horse ranchers turned Clydesdales loose with the wild herds hoping to obtain offspring that had the size of the work horse and the "know how" of the mustangs. But the result was somewhat grotesque. Though the crossbreed had a willing heart (a gift from Dobbin), his thick, hairy legs could not execute the fancy footwork that his mustang spirit wanted to display.

In Montana horse ranchers advertised: "A cross between the Indian Cayuse and a well-bred stallion makes the best horse for a cattle outfit," and they turned Percheron, Kent, and Norman stallions loose with the local mares found in the wild or with brood stock taken from the Indians.

Whether or not the horse breeders actually believed that the blood of draft animals would improve the fiery little herding ponies is a moot question; they were in business to make other people believe it would, and with so many Cayuses available for little or nothing, the cowboys would have to be convinced of the advantage of purchasing the specially bred stock. The common range horses, therefore, were belittled; whereas the mixed bloods, by contrast, were extolled.

Nevertheless, though the average price of a crossbreed was high, usually between fifty and one hundred dollars, the cost certainly did not accurately reflect the rather dim view that most cowboys took of the animal. They complained that the horse's feet were too big and, as a consequence, it was unable to make a fast turn when "cutting" cattle. They dubbed the mixture a "Percheron Pudding Foot."

The working cowboys were not easily fooled by appearances, and though the "broomtails," or "fuzztails," or "slicks" as the wild horses were variously called were worthless in the sense that they were free for the catching, cowboys continued to regard them as the best animals for working cattle. Will James, in an article in the *Saturday Evening Post,* expressed his feelings in picturesque language:

"If I had my pick between a $1,000 Arabian steed and a common fuzztail, I'd much rather select the one with the snort and the buck, cause I know the trail between suns is never too long for him, no matter how scarce the feed and water may be."

Only in the Southwest did the horse ranchers try a cross that was more compatible with the local stock. Fast horses trained for racing were imported from Kentucky and Virginia and put on the range with the Spanish herding ponies, and from this mixture of hot blood with hot blood, good "Sunday cutting horses" began to show up. These animals, variously called Kentucky Whips, Steel Dusts, and other now all-but-forgotten names, gradually evolved into the very fine Quarter Horse so popular with Westerners today. But at the turn of the century the Quarter Horse was still undefined, and it was the Spanish horse that continued to break the records.

In 1897, when the United States Bureau of Animal Industry arranged a twenty-four-hundred-mile endurance ride from Sheridan, Wyoming, to Galena, Illinois, two brothers, Bill and Bert Gabriel, each caught and broke a broomtail from the wild and entered the competition. During the long and arduous journey, no horse was allowed a mouthful of grain, nor were they shod, though the route crossed rough and broken country. Only when the horses came upon grasslands did they benefit from nourishing fodder;

otherwise, they grazed on poor food, since one of the regulations of the contest was that no provisions be carried for the animals.

Yet ninety-one days after the grueling contest began in Wyoming, the two broomtails trotted down the Main Street of Galena as fit as on the day they had set out. These prize winners were true Spanish-blooded Indian Cayuses, as evidenced by their low weights of 750 and 900 pounds respectively, in contrast with some of the larger mixed breeds that tipped the scales at 1,000 pounds and up.

The purpose behind this endurance trial set up by the Bureau of Animal Industry had been to demonstrate to the world the value of the Western-bred horse and to create a market for the animals, particularly in South Africa for use in the Boer War. Although it was the ordinary Cayuse that actually proved its worth and superiority in the contest, paradoxically, the ultimate result of its victory was the promotion and sale of much other "bred-up stock." Understandably, the foreigners who came to the Northern range to negotiate for horses were not familiar with the types of horses being bred there, and were easily dissuaded from buying the small and sickle-hocked animal whose reputation had lured them to America in the first place. On the other hand, horse raisers had no difficulty selling cross-bred animals that looked better under a saddle but were not their equal.

The increased demand for horses in South Africa also had the effect of pushing up prices in St. Louis and other markets as well, and a great many persons who had not previously been in the horse-raising business tried various devices to get in on the bonanza. For instance, the owner of a branded horse might turn his animal loose among a group of unbranded wild mustangs as a stratagem for claiming ownership of the entire band. This devious practice of obtaining possession of wild horses created bitter controversy among the horse ranchers.

Actually, it was not clear to anyone who actually possessed a legal right to the wild mustangs. Any rancher who discovered a herd of unbranded horses grazing on the section of the public land that he was using for his range took it for granted that he was entitled to the animals. Somehow, it was hard for a stockman to keep in mind that the range itself was by no means his legal property.

The stockmen's associations, on the other hand, held the view that they owned the wild horses. Inasmuch as it had become their practice to realize revenue for their treasury by appropriating and selling maverick steers, they rationalized that the slicks (unbranded horses over six months of age) also fell into this category.

After the cattle crash of 1887, these once-powerful but now defunct corporations or associations had been reorganized as civil agencies, or commissions, under the jurisdiction of territorial or state governments. For the most part, however, the same people who had dominated the old stockmen's associations were now appointed to the new government commissions. Governors often owed much of their political success to these influential constituents.

The official titles of these government stockmen's associations differed from one state to the next. In some they were known as State Stockgrowers' Associations; in others, as State Branding Boards; and in still others, as State Livestock Commissions. But by whatever name they were known, their functions were very much the same: to inspect brands, to regulate roundups, to police the range, and to promote the interests of cattle raisers in Eastern markets and with the Federal Government in Washington.

As organized pressure groups, these state commissions were of great value to the cattle rancher. However, as regulators of his affairs, the commissioners were often resented by the stockman they served. The Western rancher, whose life was difficult enough to begin with, did not relish anything that smacked of government interference. Though the work of the commissions was practical, and no doubt some such regulatory agency was necessary, the government officials had difficulty overcoming the stigma inherited from the days when they were "strong arms" for the giant cattle monopolies.

Another difficulty encountered by the old stockmen's associations in becoming agencies of the states was a lack of operating capital. General taxpayers, and the farmers in particular, were not at all enthusiastic about supporting a public commission whose sole activity was to promote the welfare of the cattlemen. As a result, another plan had to be devised to raise money in order that they might be able to function.

It was finally agreed that each stockman should be assessed a few cents on every head of cattle that he sold, and in addition to this, the commission should also receive the proceeds from the sale of "mavericks," as all unbranded stock were called.

The plan had considerable advantages. Primarily, it helped to fill the coffers of the commissions, but it also helped to bring about a measure of peace among quarreling stockmen. Ranchers often overlooked some of their calves and colts during the spring branding, and mavericks were found in every herd. Since cattle and horses belonging to various owners mingled indiscriminately on the range, ownership of these unbranded "critters" often became a matter of bitter dispute. The new plan put an end to this source of trouble, as the state commission now claimed the mavericks, and a commission brand inspector was present at all sales in order to enforce the law. Appropriation of any unbranded animal by private individuals was strictly prohibited, being defined as a misdemeanor punishable by a fine and, in some states, by several months' imprisonment. Though rigorously enforced, this penalty was mild compared with the one usually meted out to horse thieves who could be hung for their crime.

A maverick was defined as any steer, heifer, bull, stag, cow, calf, horse, mare, gelding, or colt not wearing a brand. It is easy to see how this definition affected wild horses, for with the formulation of such regulations in every state in the West, the wild horse, which fit perfectly into the definition of a maverick, could no longer be regarded as an unowned animal. Despite his many centuries of freedom in the wilderness, he was now legally defined variously as an "estray," "unbranded stock," or as a "maverick," and as such, he was the property of his most formidable enemy—the stockmen.

It is generally conceded that the commissioners who devised this money-raising scheme never conceived that the law would eventually be a weapon they could use against the wild horses. They simply regarded it as a convenient method of taxing their clients. Nor were the state lawmakers who enacted the measure aware of the adverse effect it would have on the status of wild horses.

Nevertheless, though the "estray laws" may not have been designed to rid the range of mustangs, the fact remained that they could be applied for that purpose. A state stock commission, after all, was. an organization dedicated solely to the interest of the cattle raisers; hence, when the stockmen wanted to declare war on the wild horses, they had their official allies in the commission and its members.

In the beginning the stockmen's associations seemed almost surprised to find themselves suddenly the legal owners of the wild horses, and they evinced little interest in gathering and selling the herds for their own profit. Instead, they tacitly sanctioned horse running. As cattlemen, they understood altogether too well the difficulties of running the broomtails, and they left the job to the mustangers. Anyone who corralled mustangs was permitted to retain the profits from their sale in return for service to the stockmen's associations in "getting the horses off the range." Thus the mustanger was enfranchised by the government agency with jurisdiction over the wild horses to "get rid of them totally." It seems extraordinary that man could have become so estranged from the one animal that had shared so many of his adventures and adversities in peace and war over so many thousands of years.

When this book was first published, in 1969, the maverick or estray laws remained the major obstacle preventing concerned horse lovers from finding a means by which wild horses might be managed like wildlife. Individual citizens who would seek to protect them from abuse, or who hoped that a law would be enacted to prevent them from being completely exterminated, were advised that wild horses on the Western plains could not be considered "unowned" by legal definition. Instead, they were the property of the appointed livestock commissions in every state, and as such, wild horses at that time could not be protected by law.

24. The Mustangers

Not all stockmen viewed the wild horse as an enemy. Many, particularly the small operators who managed their own ranches, loved the wild horses and enjoyed catching a glimpse of a favorite band standing on the brow of a hill, or silhouetted against the sky. They came to recognize certain animals and gave them nicknames such as, "The Red Volcano," "Old Red Ears," or "Black Dynamite." Some even protected the horse bands that grazed on their range, claiming that the unbranded animals in the region were their own stock.

This kind of loose sponsorship of a band of wild horses was a ploy used by sympathetic ranchers in various parts of the West to prevent horse runners from preying on the wild herds. For a number of years the Tillett family in the Pryor Mountains "claimed" the wild horses in an attempt to discourage mustangers from hunting the animals.

And another stockman who lived in the Western Rockies fiercely denied that the horses seen ranging in the Cedar Breaks, which extend from his land onto the public domain, were wild. He insisted that the animals were some of his own stock that were difficult to round up. Though old-timers told of seeing horse bands running wild in that particular region before the rancher was born, the stratagem was, nevertheless, effective. Outsiders did not bother "his" horses.

But many Westerners looked at wild horses and saw only the possibility of turning them into profit. Some entrepreneurs even used the feral bands as a kind of resource and deliberately released stallions among them to build up the size of the wild herds for a future harvest.*

* Since herds that had been "bred-up" in this manner were the ones selectively removed from the wilderness by man, the smaller, less desirable Spanish-blooded horses grew wilder and more difficult to capture with the passing of time.

During the opening years of the twentieth century, markets and buyers for wild horses alternately appeared and vanished. After the Boer War the price of horses plummeted. However, a new outlet soon opened in the South, where mules and small horses were needed to pull the cultivators used to irrigate the cotton fields. During World War I, English, French, and Italian agents came to America to purchase cavalry stock, placing orders for thousands of animals.

When a buyer appeared, horses were rounded up, and the stockmen's associations, lawful owners of the unbranded horses, closed their eyes to the illegal horse running that took place all around them. Since they wanted the horses removed from the range anyway, they regarded the mustangers' private efforts to capture the animals as a service to the stock industry, and permitted them to keep the proceeds from the sale of any they gathered. To give the practice an air of legality, state brand inspectors who were always present at the consignment, sale, and disposal of all livestock, collusively burned a fresh brand on each wild horse in the sales ring, thus identifying it as the property of the mustanger. A Wyoming brand inspector explained the process to me:

"I'd inspect the horses and order that they be fed and watered. Those were my orders, to feed and water the horses. There was no law that required it be done. A lot of horses were shipped out of here to California packing plants, and it was a long trip. So I ordered them fed and watered.

"Now whoever corralled them got them. The state owned them, it's true. But the state didn't want to be bothered going out and getting them, so it was up to me to do what I pleased. I'd give them to the man who corralled them. Now I had to report that there was a proper brand on every animal that was sold, so we'd just burn one on lightly—not even burn the hide—just the hair. It seems crazy to brand an animal that is going to be butchered the next day, but that was the law. No one could sell the unbranded ones 'cause they belonged to the state of Wyoming."

Since the wild horses had become exceedingly difficult to catch, it is easy to see why the stockmen's associations did not attempt to gather and remove the horses themselves, but left the job to the mustangers. Under pressure of so much persecution by stock interests and incessant harassment from amateur and professional mustangers, the wild horses became most elusive. It took extraordinary horsemen to corral them, men who knew how to outpsych, outrun, and outthink them.

It was no longer practical even to attempt to run down the horses and noose them one at a time on horseback. The slow ones that could be taken in such a manner had been captured years earlier, and the survivors were too fast and too crafty. The only realistic method of gathering the horses was to trick them into entering a corral.

In Utah sheep and cattle men, anxious to crowd more livestock onto the desert range, called on the services of veteran cowboy Will James to round up the wily horses. James, in the *Saturday Evening Post* article mentioned earlier, describes the "fuzztails" of this period:

"Plenty of times I've heard fellows talk of running down the wild ones with grained horses in the spring of the year when the fuzz tail is supposed to be weak. I've seen it tried, on occasions done, but I've rarely seen the fuzz tails when they were weak and unless a fellow had a lot of good saddle horses to run the legs off and an income that relieves him of worrying about a living, I'd call it a mighty poor way to go at it. The wild one is ready to go a long way, spring, summer, fall, or winter; he can usually show you where the trail ends, and you'll be by your lonesome when he does."

The method used by Will James and others like him to capture horses was to drive a band into a dead-end canyon, force the animals to circle until they were played out, and then rope them one at a time. If canyons were nonexistent in a particular region, the men built a concealed corral and tricked or drove the horses into it.

These corrals had to be constructed cleverly so as not to arouse the horses' suspicion. The posts and the poles were sometimes covered with green foliage to disguise them. More important, care had to be taken that the cottonwood logs that formed the frame of the corral, and the branches which were intertwined to camouflage the trap, were arranged so that all sharp ends projected outside of the enclosure. Otherwise, in their panic at being confined, the horses would impale themselves.

Beyond these basic requirements, corrals varied in construction according to the method of capture being employed. When men on horseback intended to drive horses into a corral, wide wings were built which formed an immense V funneling into the pen. At the point of entrance, a gate was placed which could be sprung shut, or a canvas flap was attached which could be dropped by jerking a rope.

Riders posted themselves on both sides of the wings, and as the wild horses thundered past, the men on horseback steered the herd into the funnel by whooping and hazing them from both sides. If the animals were discovered a long way from the corral, relays of relief riders were stationed

No exit. Thirsty horses, who have pushed their way between these sharpened poles to water, face unyielding bayonets when they attempt to leave the trap.

at intervals along the way to take up the chase as the wild horses passed, thus saving the saddle horses from exhaustion.

Other methods of corralling or capturing wild horses were devised by individuals who were not keen on the dangerous sport of mustanging. One of the simplest ways to capture a single animal was by means of a small box trap, a kind of foot snare. This contraption was planted on a horse trail known to be followed by a band of horses and was attached to a line tied to a stone or a log. The buried trap was then covered with loose dirt and leaves, and when a horse put his foot in it, a spring released a snare which encircled the animal's leg. Thus encumbered and forced to drag the loose stone or log, the handicapped horse was soon left behind by his band and easily roped by the trappers.

One drawback to the use of the box trap was that one could never predict what kind of animal would be caught by it. Usually an old lead mare hit the trap first and was snared. But deer, cattle, and sheep were also frequently found on the range dragging a loose stone or a log. Still the method was relatively humane so long as the trapper did not delay searching for the encumbered animal. Sometimes, the log or stone would become snagged on a tree or a bush and prevent the animal from reaching water, and the victim might die before being found.

When judiciously used, however, a box trap was perhaps the best method of capturing a single horse for private use. If the snared horse seemed too old to be broken, or too spirited to accept captivity, it could always be set free again.

The Pelligrini family of Yerington, Nevada, set out a homemade box trap in the Wassuk Range in the spring of 1963 and watched it closely. On Easter Sunday they found a four-month old colt caught in their snare. They named the little blue roan mustang "Chico," and succeeded in raising him. Today Chico, who has many points in common with Spanish-blooded horses, weighs no more than eight hundred pounds at his adult growth. His disposition is very much like that of a pet dog. He is so curious and so affectionate that I had difficulty getting far enough away from him to take his picture. Each time I looked into the viewfinder, I saw only the blurred image of a horse's muzzle, and discovered that he had followed me closely. Finally, when his owner, Bill Pelligrini, distracted the horse with sweet talk, I succeeded in getting one shot of him. In his eagerness for affection, Chico then backed me into a fence where I was forced to reward him with undivided attention. Obviously, this horse's disposition had not been soured by captivity.

Another method of capturing horses which did not require pursuing them on horseback was to build a trap around their water hole. Some water-hole traps were constructed with an opening slightly too narrow for a horse to get through, but both sides of this opening were loosely hung and yielded enough to permit the animal to push it apart with his body and squeeze into the corral. Once inside, however, the sides would fall back into position and when the horse attempted to leave, the pointed logs around the edge of the too-narrow opening angled toward him like bayonets. If the animal tried to force his way out, he would become impaled on the logs. This type of trap was used when the primary purpose was to rid the range of horses and not to take them uninjured.

Less lethal corrals, with wide openings, were also built around springs,

(ABOVE) *The wilderness yields ranch recruits. A wild horse is led from the*
Pryor Mountains by cowboy-rancher Lloyd Tillett.
(BELOW) *Brown Hoss, a Pryor Mountain mustang,*
became the Tillett's best cow pony.

and men were stationed in trees and other hiding places, waiting to drop a gate on any horses that might enter to drink. To make certain that sooner or later horses would enter such a water trap, all surrounding springs were blocked up, wherefore thirst would eventually impel some animals to run the risk. It is asserted, however, that some of the more cagey animals refused to walk into the suspicious contraptions and consequently died for want of water.

Will James tells how he watched a black stallion tentatively test the ground around a water corral for several days, and then in a frenzy for water, impulsively rush into the trap. No sooner had he begun to drink than he heard the corral gate drop with a thud. Instantly, without a backward look, the animal knew what had happened and in one incredible leap, cleared the nine-foot corral wall and was gone!

When men like Will James, who appreciated the wild spirit of the mustang, witnessed such resolute defiance in a horse, they did not begrudge the animal his freedom. In later years James confessed that his only regret was for the ones that didn't get away. In his *Saturday Evening Post* article, he said:

"The satisfaction that I'd get at catching some wise bunch didn't last long when I'd remember that they'd be shipped, put to work, and maybe starved into being good by some hombre who was afraid of them and didn't savvy them at all. For they really belonged, not to man, but to the country of junipers and sages, of deep arroyos, mesas, and freedom."

Unfortunately, not all horse runners felt the same compassion for the wild horses. In the Wyoming Red Desert near Rock Springs, mares captured by mustangers were gentled and released to run again with the wild herds, but not until their nostrils had been sewed almost completely shut with rawhide rope or pinched together with barbed wire.

In this pitiful condition the animal would live all year on the hot desert with her nostril flare so restricted that she was unable to draw a full breath of air. Thus handicapped, she would act as a brake on the band, slowing the pace of the entire herd and making them an easy prey for the men who hunted them the following spring.

According to one horse runner who participated in these operations, a mare of high quality was always chosen as the victim so she could perform double duty by bearing a good colt for the mustangers during the year she was free on the desert.

Another method employed by horse runners in that region to slow down the fleet-footed mustangs was to bend a horseshoe around the ankle of a mare and release her with a wild band. The bent horseshoe would not hurt her when she walked, but it would hit and bruise her legs whenever she began to run. The mustanger who told me about this questionable practice explained why he felt such tactics were necessary:

"A lot of horses," said he, "took getaway trails that no man could ride, and there was no way a rider could turn a bunch unless they did something like this, so the same mares were used again and again for this purpose."

He added, however, that he hadn't heard of anything like this being done in recent years. "Not since the use of airplanes made rounding up horses so easy," he explained.

As it was a Federal offense to run wild, unbranded horses with aircraft on the public lands, I asked if horses were still being chased on the Red Desert by air and was told that they were.

"Well, yes, it's illegal," said the mustanger, "but how else are you going to catch the horses? They now live in such remote places that you just would never get what's still out there on horseback."

To the obvious and final question of why bother to get "what's still out there" if the horses were in such remote places, he answered, "Well, why leave them there? What good are they?"

It is doubtful that there were enough wild horses left in any one place in the West in 1969 to be an economic threat to local cattle and sheep interests. Yet the wild horse remained a controversial subject among livestock holders. Some ranchers were wild-horse enthusiasts. Yet many stockmen arbitrarily resented anyone who advocated protective legislation. They said that they could not understand why people concerned themselves over the use or the abuse of an animal that didn't belong to anyone. They seemed to fear that the animals would overrun the range, and it was difficult to convince these people that, like the buffalo, the wild horse could disappear. Unfortunately, there were those who expressed undue optimism regarding their chances of survival. One writer of note, Walker D. Wyman, in *The Wild Horse of the West,* asserted confidently, "There are places in the West where a horse can go that a man with a Winchester cannot or will not unless there is more remuneration than the income from a horse hide. When the horse does not compete with the stock interests, the Grazing Service will probably not be vitally concerned about its elimination. The wild horse will always be found in the West."

Although the wild horses that persisted represented no real threat to the stock interests, and although so little remuneration was realized from their sale that it would seem impractical for mustangers to flush them from their remote hideaways with expensive airplanes, they, nevertheless, were pursued. Often the cost of the fuel burned in the planes exceeded the money earned from the sale of the horses.

Why then did the wild horses continue to be harassed? In reply to this question I invariably received not an answer, but another question: "Well, why leave them there? What good are they?"

The concept that an animal has a definite value in the framework of creation other than how it serves man was puzzling to many people. It was probably most baffling to those who raise livestock for a living. The subtle but very deep pleasure that an animal's existence gives to human beings who inhabit a planet that is becoming ever more mechanized with each turn on its axis was not yet strongly felt by people still lucky enough to be surrounded by plenty of empty land. Yet those very people were the ones who would feel the qualitative loss most severely when the animals were gone. And unless steps were to be taken soon to preserve those creatures that had proved they could survive in the poor habitats willed to them by man, one day soon all of us would live with the same vain regret.

25. On the Track of Wild-Horse History

Western residents bordering wild-horse habitats do not always know or believe the long and colorful history of America's wild horses. Many people presume that the animals in their particular locality are simply the remnants of neglected range stock. This is often not the true story. But men who have run, captured, and sold members of a local herd to canneries sometimes find it difficult to accept the fact that animals worth only three dollars a head at market may have historical value.

Yet in the 1960s I found a number of the first settlers—then in their eighties or nineties—who could recollect having seen wild-horse bands when they arrived. In tracking the history of individual wild-horse bands, I obtained my most valuable information from octogenarians whose memories of the past were sharp. Such old-timers were not always easy to locate, though it was relatively easy to find people who, during and after World War I, were horse runners. Before the invention of the automobile took the profit out of it, nearly every young man tried his skill at raising, gathering, running, or stealing horses. Whenever a hide buyer, a cavalry scout, a Southern farmer, or a chicken-feed dealer came to a Western community to inquire about horses, local people organized a roundup and nearly everybody who could ride a horse sought to get in on the action.

The people who speak of these roundups recall them with nostalgia. They were exciting events that required weeks of planning, camping in the mountains or on the desert, the construction of a proper corral, the tracking of the animals, and finally the big chase. A man who took part in a wild-horse roundup never forgot the experience.

But though the passing of time seems not to have dulled the memory of the event itself, the inglorious objects of the roundup, the horses, are recalled pragmatically by these twentieth-century mustangers. Said one, "Well, sometimes there was a pretty good market for them, but most of the time they weren't worth anything at all. We had too many horses."

To many Westerners during the early part of the century, the wild horse held little fascination outside of what money it could bring, and the market for horses fluctuated considerably. Sometimes the price of horses dropped as low as three dollars a head. On the other hand, during World War I an unbroken horse brought as much as two hundred dollars. The horses were alternately valued and ignored, according to their market price.

Children born in the West at the opening of the twentieth century took the wild horses for granted. They grew up believing that all the unbranded animals on the range were neglected stock, descendants of horses brought west by their parents' generation. Most people tend to take for granted the world as it appeared to them when they were youngsters. Parents usually forget to explain to their children how certain things came to be the way they are.

Perhaps many Western parents preferred to forget that they had gotten their start in the ranching business using common broomtails taken from the wild and Cayuses appropriated from the Indians. Horses seen on Indian reservations after the turn of the century were exceedingly scrawny, mere shadows of their former selves, and were ridiculed by the white community. The Indians' better horses had been taken from them in one way or another, not always honorably, and few people were willing to confess that their own range stock had been based on the Indian pony. The wild broomtails, being Cayuses, carried the same stigma.

Besides, over the course of time, nearly every rancher managed to acquire at least one good stallion, perhaps a Hambletonian or even a Morgan stud, and after his pedigreed horse had been released with his range stock, no more mention was made of broomtails or Cayuses. That rancher now owned "blooded" horses.

One second-generation Westerner who as a youth "ran" horses in the Pryor Mountains was incredulous when told that wild horses had existed in northern Wyoming and southern Montana before his dad had settled in the region. As a young man during the teens of the century, he had never made any distinction between wild horses and the neglected range animals that could readily be found on the mountain meadows, especially since, in his view, all horses, by virtue of their being horses, automatically belong to man in either case.

"You'd go out and gather horses, and they'd run from you and everything. But at that time we didn't know what a wild horse was. We gathered them all in," he volunteered.

During World War I the Army Remount systematically planted stallions among the wild-horse herds in many places (though not in the Pryor Mountains) in the hope of obtaining a tougher cavalry horse. Shortly after the war, when the army became almost entirely mechanized, this plan was abandoned and a great many animals were never gathered.

A widespread supposition that all wild horses were either stray stock or left over from the Remount program was reinforced by the fact that brood stock behaved much like wild mustangs; a single stallion herded and bred his bunch of mares and fought off all contending stallions. If left ungathered for a few years, these range horses also grew wild and were difficult to round up, and many of them, particularly young animals, did not bear brands.

To further complicate the picture, branded range mares were frequently abducted by wild stallions. So branded animals were sometimes seen running in the wild herds. The horses did not remain where their owners had put them, and it was no simple matter determining who owned which horses and, in fact, which horses were owned.

More confusion was created by the fact that on occasion, during some big stock roundup, wild horses were inadvertently corralled, branded, and released again. Once captured, these horses became doubly shy.

The wild herds had plenty of opportunity to cross with domestic stock, and did. But the real question I was interested to have answered was not whether a particular band was pure-blooded, but whether it had existed in the region prior to white settlement.

The Pryor Mountain range, which has long been the home for a variety of owned and unowned, branded and unbranded horses stretches from the Wyoming border across southern Montana and extends onto the Crow Indian Reservation. Periodically, cattle and sheep have grazed its lower plateaus and in the valleys that lie between this range and the surrounding mountain chains. Here there was little need for fences; livestock could be contained by the natural barriers—canyons and steep cliffs—that surround the mountain pastures.

Though ranch horses could easily scale cliffs and rimrocks that were too rugged to be maneuvered by less agile stock, they nevertheless could also be relied upon to remain in the vicinity of their birth range, so an open-range policy had persisted in the area for a number of years after much of the West had been fenced. As a result, horses roamed freely across the mountains and could join or become a wild band with ease.

During the first quarter of the twentieth century a profusion of horses existed in the region, and only when the appearance of an occasional buyer made the effort worthwhile did the local ranchers bother to claim and gather these wild and semiwild creatures. Animals that were not sold were branded and turned loose again. But brands were not necessary in order to claim ownership of a band of horses. If the animals had their habitat on a portion of range used by a particular rancher, they were conceded to be his property, and he was even paid a percentage of the profit earned by any mustanger who bothered to capture them. This was regarded as simple range courtesy.

"Even when I gathered unbranded horses in thirty-one," I was told by one horse runner, "we paid for what we took off a person's range. Paid two dollars a head. Didn't matter if they'd never been caught before. They were all owned horses as far as we were concerned. In nineteen sixteen when I was a kid, I know for a fact, we turned loose a Hambletonian stallion out there and just let it run, just the same as anything else. They were people's owned horses out there."

During years when horse prices dropped, people paid scant attention to the herds that gathered and posed like stags high on the mountain ledges. The horses were there and theirs for the taking whenever it was convenient and profitable to do so. As for the question of where the horses had come from, the answer was irrelevant to the economics of the situation.

One man who pondered the question came up with the following conjecture: "Well, I don't know where they came from first. My father was a trail herder from Texas, came up in eighteen eighty-six. At that time maybe they turned a lot of good brood mares loose 'cause they were settling this country. I don't know if there is anyone alive who can still remember."

Fortunately, in nearly every wild-horse locale, I was able to locate some people who could remember. In the shadow of the Pryor Mountains, I talked with Bessie Tillett, who at eighty still knew her way around with horses. Dressed in blue jeans and perched on the top rail of a corral, she watched her granddaughter break a three-year-old strawberry roan, the offspring of a horse captured out of the wild. Speaking of the past, she said:

"These wild horses were already here when I came, and I came in eighteen ninety-four. We were one of the very first families to come, and the horses were here then and as wild as can be. My father worked to lay the Burlington Railroad when a spur came through just up here in Montana. When we came, they were trying to make the Crows stay on their reservations. The Indians were moving around with big bunches of horses. I wouldn't be surprised if the wild horses up there now are some of theirs. They looked then just like they do now. They were always broomtails. Their manes were long and had witch knots in them, and their tails all but drug the ground. Not much difference in 'em now.

"When we come out to this country, there were wild horses running all over. People here would go up this side of Cody at what they call McCullock Peak and run horses—wild horses. And they would run them down here, you see. I suppose somebody had the idea they were going to get rich with horses."

In answer to my questions: "What kind of horses did the Indians own?" and "Where had they gotten them?", she replied, "In the early days there was so much horse stealing. The Piegans was stealing in the north and bringing horses down here to the Crows. And the Crows was going up and stealing Piegan horses. There would have to be a lot of mixing. That's all I know."

Bessie Tillett's recollections of wild horses during the early days of her childhood dovetailed with stories I had found in nineteenth-century newspapers regarding Wyoming wild horses. She confirmed that the horses were already flourishing when the first settlers arrived.

Yet Bessie Tillett's version and the opinions of the veteran horse runners could actually be reconciled. If, as Bessie claimed, the pioneers had found wild horses in the region and had used them as a resource from which to obtain stock, this would not preclude the possibility that these early settlers also released some of their own horses in the area to mix with the wild herds. The horse bands would still have a historical lineage, although their bloodline would be mixed.

It was improbable that full-blooded Spanish ponies could be found in the region, but I was nevertheless struck by the fact that some of the Pryor Mountain horses had the look of Brislawn's registered Spanish Mustangs. So, in 1969, when I discovered a pile of bleached horse bones scattered on the top of one of the mountains, I sat down on the ground and pieced them together. I was curious to see if the spinal column would lack a final vertebra and indicate a link with the Spanish horse of yesterday.

Not being familiar with every bone in a horse's anatomy, and not having a chart in my possession, it took me a good deal of time to fit the puzzle together, but when I finally completed the task, I was more than rewarded for my work. For, when I counted the segments, I found to my astonishment that the last two lumbar vertebrae were fused, proof that the Pryor Mountain horses did indeed carry the blood of the Conquistador's horse.

Triumphantly, I packed up the evidence and carried it to the town of Lovell, Wyoming, where I presented the bones to the mayor, Clyde Reynolds, who incidentally was a wild-horse enthusiast. Several citizens of Lovell who inspected the find speculated on the persistence of Spanish horse traits over such a long span of time, and one person offered a plausible explanation:

"The longer a horse had been a wild animal, the harder he would be to catch. The big ones, the domestic horses we turned out on the range, sooner or later were run down and taken out of the wild again. The little ones, the ones we didn't bother with, just kept getting wilder and more impossible to catch all the time. We never got those. I guess they are still up there."

From one state to the next, wherever I found a band of horses, the same local lack of knowledge about them prevailed. People were contented with the assumption that the herds were stray stock dating from the period of the First World War. Since that was the period when interest in horse running declined, due to the introduction of the automobile, it was automatically assumed that was when and how the wild horse bands now roaming the West had their origin. But whenever I was able to locate an old-timer who had lived in the region during the 1890's, I invariably heard a different tale.

In attempting to trace the background of a band of horses in the wooded Bookcliff Mountains in western Colorado, I was informed by people who could remember as far back as World War I that these had belonged to a man by the name of Dave Knight, who was somewhat of a legend in that region. Knight had "roughed it" in the mountains, camping out of doors with his horse herds, subsisting on a diet of jerky. I was told that he "could rope a horse around the forefeet and, with no more help than a snubbing post, lay the animal on the ground." Knight's horses were first-rate and at one time were renowned among cow outfits throughout the West. They could readily be recognized by the distinctive garter brand they wore around one leg. But when the bottom fell out of the horse business Knight had been forced to let his herd go wild.

The story was interesting and was confirmed by everyone I interviewed in the region. However, I was curious to know where Knight had obtained his horses in the first place. Whenever I attempted to find out, I ran up against a familiar response: "Oh, he had good 'blooded' horses up there. He must have bought them. I believe he once put out a Steel Dust stallion. His horses were good."

I didn't doubt the authenticity of what I had heard, and the information that Knight had "put out" a Steel Dust stallion on his range was particularly convincing, since everybody who raised horses in those days made it a point to introduce at least one good stallion into his herd. The Steel Dust horse was an excellent cow pony bred-up in Texas out of mustangs and a race horse, and would be the right choice of a man who knew about horses. But I did not believe that Knight's foundation mares had also been "blooded." I guessed they had been broomtails. Accordingly, I called on an old citizen of DeBeque, John Armstrong by name, to learn if he could enlighten me on Dave Knight's horses.

Armstrong, then eighty, had been born and raised at the base of the Bookcliffs, was a horsebreaker in his youth, and remembered the day when Dave Knight had arrived from Oklahoma and gone into the horse business.

Armstrong told me: "When Dave Knight came here, he purchased thirty head of horses from a man named Ira Boice over at Piceance Creek and set himself up in the horse business. Now Ira Boice got his horses from the wild. They were broomtails that he caught and broke to sell. He gathered some of his wild horses right up here in the Bookcliffs, 'cause wild horses were running all over in those days. I imagine that Knight's horses had come right off of this mountain, and he just brought them back here again, where he wouldn't have any trouble holding them on their home range."

With this information I wrote a short article on the Bookcliff wild horses which was published in the Grand Junction *Daily Sentinel*. As a result, I received some information on the Bookcliff wild horses that even predated Armstrong's knowledge and definitely linked the present-day herd with Indian pony strays.

One letter, which came from Roy Hungerford, eighty-one years old, stated that two brothers Mark and Luther Hulburt, then ninety and ninety-three years old respectively, had told him that their father had found two horses in the Bookcliffs, left there by Colorow, the Ute chief, when he retreated from the whites in 1887.

Hungerford wrote: "Now Colorow was a Ute chief and when they drove the Utes off of Bookcliff, they [the Indians] left a mare and a yearling on a high ridge, and that winter was not too rough, so the horses managed to live on some grass and brush and one of the first settlers at Grand Valley, Hulburt was his name, managed to catch them.

"And he [Hulburt] added on a few and increased the herd. And at one time the herd had grown to between 400 and 500 horses. I will help you all I can as I am a lover of history and horses, and still ride almost every day . . . (signed) Roy, the old 6-foot, 150-pound Range Rider, Hungerford."

Visits and inquiries at local Bureau of Land Management offices seldom brought information that was relevant. I was generally told: "The wild horses in our district are not the romantic mustangs that you read about, but are descendants of work stock turned loose in the nineteen thirties when farmers made the transition from horses to tractors."*

This construction of history was indiscriminately stated by Government officials, often in regions where farming had never been practiced. Since I had rarely seen wild-horse bands whose conformation indicated that their ancestors were predominantly draft animals, the explanation did not offer me much of a starting point. It was hard to believe that the little, eight-hundred-pound desert and mountain horses, with the small hoofs and narrow chests, were the runted offspring of big, blocky, three-quarter-ton work horses.

To many people, however, it is easier to believe that nature has wrought such a transformation (in one generation) than to be caught entertaining romantic notions. The mustang mystique is suspect to many modern-day Westerners, and mustang lore is not particularly sanctioned by those Government bureaus that deal with the livestock industry.

One official in Utah wrote me that it was the general consensus in his region that the wild horses found in that district by the first Mormon settlers were not "true" wild horses lost by the Spaniards, but were more likely animals lost by ranchers in surrounding areas.

How incredible this explanation is becomes apparent when one examines the history of Utah. The Mormons, who pushed handcarts across the Plains in the late 1840's, were the first white settlers to reach the Salt Lake Basin. Their settlement predated the birth of the cattle industry by several decades. Any "ranch horses" that the Mormons might have found when they arrived in Utah would have had to travel not only across considerable space but through a good deal of time as well.

The present-day Westerner is correct in asserting that a pure-blooded Andalusian Barb is a rarity. Nevertheless, many wild horses appear to be strongly marked by a Spanish strain, proving their connection with a col-

---

* I later was able to trace this concept to a flyer published in Washington and distributed to all district offices of the Bureau of Land Management.

orful past. Not only do their bones and appearance bear testimony to Spanish ancestry, but circumstantial evidence also points to the same conclusion. Three factors in particular deserve attention:

First, there has been no break in the continuity of the wild herds since the West was opened to settlement. Though many bands have been eliminated and the total number of wild horses has dwindled drastically, the wild-horse population did not at any time vanish to re-emerge at a later date.

Secondly, where domestic horses from ranches and farms were deliberately released to breed with and to breed-up the wild horses, these were the very ones that were later recaptured. The small wild horses were ignored and grew wilder.

And finally, when domestic runaways and strays joined the wild-horse bands, it was the animal that was originally the most "Western" that survived the harsh test of the wild. The big, slow, gentle farm horses and the high-strung, grain-fed race horses were not creatures that could easily adapt to bleak habitats and rugged winters.

The type of wild horse still found in the West, though he may not qualify for pedigree papers, clearly reveals his Andalusian background and there can be little doubt that a great many of his assorted ancestors witnessed and helped to make a lot of history. No figure so symbolizes and illuminates the mosaic story of the conquest of the West as does this picturesque

The type of wild horse still found in the West, though it may not qualify for pedigree papers, clearly reveals his Andalusian background and there can be little doubt that a great many of its assorted ancestors witnessed and helped to make a lot of history. No figure so symbolizes and illuminates the mosaic story of the conquest of the West as does this picturesque animal.

26. *The Reform of the Range*

Since the American Revolution, the United States Government has acquired—by purchase, treaty, and annexation—dominion over the vast territory which is the present United States. Over the years the greater portion of that vast domain has been disposed of to states, private individuals, and companies as grants or homesteads. However, in ten Western states,* a surprising amount of land still remains in the hands of the Federal Government. Regions too dry or rocky for farming either were not claimed by homesteaders or reverted back to the Government when agriculture failed and homesteaders abandoned their claims. Excluding what Federal land in these states has been reserved for Indians, or set aside for military installations, monuments, National Forests and National Parks, 158,484,030 acres (an area larger than France) still remained in the public domain as of 1968.

Prior to the arrival of the white man, when the Indians lived in the region, many million buffaloes and several million wild horses pastured on this land, which by 1934 had grown too poor to sustain more than ten million head of cattle. Only a half-century earlier, when the West was being opened to settlement, the same land had carried more than double that number of livestock (twenty-two and a half million head).

But fifty years of exploitation had altered the region drastically. Gone forever was the palatable bluebunch wheatgrass, the ricegrass, the giant wild rye, the dropseed, and the oat grass. These fast-cycling plants had been grazed to extinction and were replaced by the unpalatable sand sage,

* Arizona, California, Colorado, Idaho, Montana, Nevada, New Mexico, Oregon, Utah, and Wyoming. Alaska is over ninety percent Federal land.

greasewood, zucca, and winter fat. But even more serious was the fact that because of insufficient ground cover, the earth's protective topsoil was no longer tied down and was blowing away.

Responsibility for this tragic deterioration could not be laid on any one group. Mismanagement, ignorance, greed, and politics had all played a part in the despoiling of the West. One underlying cause was the provincial attitudes of the Eastern legislators whose point of reference in the well-watered East had caused them to regard the early cattlemen as roving trespassers obstructing the progress of a stable agricultural society. Yet, while they promoted Land Acts that provided for the sale of the public domain to farmers, they restricted the size of these homestead allotments to 320 acres. In the dry and unpredictable Great Plains, farmers who staked their claims on such small areas were destined to fail. Though this allotment was doubled in later years, much damage had already been wrought both to the soil and to the people who had struggled to make it produce.

When it became apparent that the West was largely unsuitable for agriculture, the disillusioned farmers who had been guilty of destroying the open range by fencing their fields to protect them from the roving herds of cattle, began themselves to acquire cattle and sheep and to crowd their livestock onto the surrounding public lands. The established stockmen bitterly resented these newcomers, and competition over the dwindling grass led to range wars. Though the ruined farmers had little alternative but to turn to ranching, too many people were trying to make the best of their lives on what was left of the range.

By 1934, when Senator Edward Taylor introduced legislation to control the use of the public domain lands, twenty-five million acres of the Plains had been plowed, found unsuitable for agriculture, and abandoned in a state of erosion. Thereafter this land was not even adaptable for grazing. Moreover, according to a Forest Service Survey, the range land itself had deteriorated by sixty-seven percent. Senator Taylor told Congress: "At this time there are large areas where it is a free-for-all and general grab-and-hold-if-you-can policy with roving herds using the ranges. There is no security or safety to honest stock business."

One stockman testified at the Hearings on the Taylor Grazing Acts: "The difficulty on the public lands is that nobody has control. The only way a stockman can get grass for his stock on the public land is to get there ahead of anyone else and have his stock eat it up. The rule has been to take as you go. If you do not, somebody else will take it, and you have only invited intrusion of other stock."

Though many Western ranchers favored the measure, and even went to Washington to testify in its behalf, the Taylor Grazing Act was viewed with suspicion by others. These stockmen, though anxious to have the public domain officially sanctioned as pasture land, did not wish to pay a grazing fee for grass that heretofore had been free and they did not want to be limited in the number of cattle and sheep they could put on the public range.

Eastern conservationists also looked askance at the bill. They did not see why Government money should be spent to preserve grass. They could appreciate that the woods, the mountains, and the beauty spots of the deserts should be preserved for posterity to enjoy, but the grassland, according to their view, should be in private hands and under cultivation. Even at this late date, the vagaries of the unique American prairie were not grasped by the remainder of the country, and the stockmen who knew this region were still regarded as robbers and looters of the public domain, who were getting something for nothing.

The stockmen, however, saw the situation somewhat differently. According to their view, the homesteader was the despoiler who, after tearing up the range, had crowded onto it himself. The homesteaders, in turn, laid the blame on the Government, whose policies had lured them to waste their lives at farming such submarginal lands.

After many hearings, in June of 1934, a surprise witness appeared. Dust from a storm raging on the Plains blew all the way to Washington and landed on the desks of the Senators who were debating the issue. This graphic testimony apparently convinced Congress, for the Taylor Grazing Act was passed on June 28, 1934, and the Department of Interior was authorized to classify the public domain according to its suitability for agricultural crops, native grasses, or other valuable use, and to set up a land-management agency to administer the grazing districts. Thus the United States Grazing Service, which later became the Federal Bureau of Land Management, was born.

The bill specified that this agency, which shall henceforth be referred to as the Bureau of Land Management or the B.L.M., would have authority to regulate the occupancy and use of 143,000,000 acres (since enlarged to 453,000,000 acres including Alaska) of Federal land, to preserve it from unnecessary injury, and to provide for the orderly use, improvement, and development of the range. Range surveys were to be made, a permit system devised, nominal grazing fees would be collected, and the public lands were, in effect, given over officially to the use of the livestock industry.

But the cattlemen, perhaps the most individualistic single group in America, resented the bureaucracy about to be imposed on them almost as much as they appreciated the fact that their industry had at last received the blessing of the country. Fiercely independent and toughened by a business which at best is precarious, the small rancher in particular was angered by the additional factor that would further complicate his business. He therefore did not welcome the Bureau of Land Management employees who opened offices in the West in the late thirties, and he accused the Federal officials of being armchair naturalists who counted spears of grass with a magnifying glass.

In the beginning, the Federal employees had no easy task gaining the cooperation of these recalcitrant stock growers who were raising a clamor for local autonomy. However, since it was the cattle and sheep men who were principally affected by the Taylor Grazing Act, it is only natural that they should have wanted a hand in the organization of the regulatory agency. But the degree of power they (or an elite segment of them) obtained probably exceeded what they had imagined possible.

In an effort to establish reasonable dialogue with the people it had been established to regulate and serve, the Bureau of Land Management invited the local stockmen to participate in the drawing up of districts and to assist in determining which ranchers should have rights to what lands. The Bureau officials so depended on the knowledge of these local ranchers, that the advisory boards of stockmen, according to Phillip Foss, author of *Politics and Grass,* "quickly assumed more than an advisory role."

These eight-member advisory boards became permanent fixtures attached to each of the Bureau's fifty-two district offices throughout the West. Today, board members are elected by secret ballot cast by the permittees to serve two-year terms. From these local boards, state representatives are appointed to a National Advisory Board.

Since the Bureau of Land Management from the start has been underfunded and understaffed, it has had difficulty carrying out many of the functions it was intended to perform. As a result, it has been forced to rely much of the time on the experience and counsel of its Advisory Boards. During one period, when Congress failed to appropriate the necessary funds to cover the bare operating costs of the Bureau, the Advisory Boards paid the salaries of the Federal officials out of their own pockets. Thus the stock interests (or, as has been said, an elite segment of the stock interests) succeeded in wresting considerable authority from the hands of the Federal agency. Phillip Foss in his book, *Politics and Grass,* describes the present-day relationship between the powerful Advisory Boards and the Bureau of Land Management officials as follows: "When administrators [meaning the B.L.M.] have acted contrary to objectives of the stockmen, they have ordinarily been unsuccessful and occasionally have been subject to punitive actions."

Shortly after this compact between ranching tenant and Federal rent collector was formed, wild-horse-range clearance programs on the public lands began in earnest. The wild horses had traditionally been regarded by certain stockmen as competitors for grass, and now that the Federal Government was forcing these men to reduce their livestock inventory, they reasoned that by removing the wild horses, more cattle and sheep would be permitted to use the public range.

The fact remained, however, that the wild horses were only in rare instances found in the grazing districts desired by the cattlemen. Nevertheless, bargains were made and wild horses were arbitrarily removed from remote areas and cattle and sheep men were given licenses to carry more livestock on their ranges.

The Bureau of Land Management, in an effort to deal with its tenants, let itself be intimidated into horse-removal programs that made absolutely no sense. During the fifteen years immediately following the passage of the Taylor Grazing Act, thousands of wild horses were flushed from regions so uninhabitable that aircraft had to be used to get them out. Dr. T. L. McKnight, in a report in the *University of California Publications in Geography,* gives some indication of the extent of these programs:

"Approximately 1,000 trespass horses were shot on Sitgreaves National Forest between 1935–42. There are several reports of thousands of horses being removed from a single Montana county in the 1930's. As many as 4,000 trespass horses were taken from Oregon's Malheur County in a two-year period, and less than five percent proved to be branded animals."

Since these areas were unsuitable for grazing, it is curious that the horses should have been hunted and killed there. But it wasn't until after the Second World War that large-scale clearance operations commenced. With readily available airplanes, the wild herds were decimated. Dr. McKnight quotes a letter from a Bureau of Land Management official which clearly implicates the government agency in this horse-removal activity:

"Within a period of four years we [the Bureau of Land Management] removed over 100,000 abandoned and unclaimed horses from Nevada ranges. Branded horses were turned over to the owners for disposition by sale. Unclaimed horses were taken by the people operating the airplanes under title from the state and sold as compensation for their work. This program was carried out without cost to the government except some assistance in building holding corrals and truck trails where needed."

That the horses taken in some of these roundups were in certain cases unbranded domestic stock put out on the public lands illegally by ranchers who did not wish to pay grazing fees for them is common knowledge. The ranchers, after letting their herds build up, would strike a bargain with the Bureau of Land Management to gather and remove the so-called wild horses in exchange for an increase in the number of stock they were permitted to carry. It was a profitable game for the rancher. No forage was purchased, no grazing fees paid, and after the horses had been sold for gain, the bonus came in a license to carry more livestock in a given district.

In a personal interview with a woman rancher near Elko, Nevada, I was told: "The horses we gather are our own. We released Thoroughbred stock three years ago to breed with the wild ones, and they have proliferated so that now we have to gather them."

It is doubtful that the Bureau officials were fooled by this trick. Probably they closed their eyes to the ploy in order to win co-operation on other issues.

Unfortunately, this dishonest practice led the public to the false conclusion that wild horses multiply like rabbits and had no need of protective legislation. In fact, some people, who did not realize that their neighbors were stocking the range with unbranded horses, expressed alarm that, if wild horses were granted protection, they would overrun the range.

These people are not only unaware of the illegal ranching practices in their region, but have failed to note the very significant historical fact that in the past wild horses had recruited fresh blood from Indians' camps and ranches, and so maintained their numbers.

Even the Indians' range horses had not multiplied very rapidly, and the Comanches and Osages had often complained that they had difficulty raising colts. Had it not been for the constant traffic in stolen stock obtained from the Mexican ranches, the semiprotected herds of the Indians would have dwindled. The wild horses were even more vulnerable to the elements than were the animals belonging to the tribes. They sustained their population at the expense of the Indians' herds, and the stock belonging to ranchers who lived near their habitat.

Though no scientific study had been made of the survival rate of wild horses, one herd of 217 animals had been under observation for a number of years. Only seventeen were under two years old. Little is known about the stabilization of animal populations, but mortality among wild colts appears to be extremely high. Most of them are born in the early spring and must survive at least one severe blizzard shortly after birth. If the mare had a colt the previous year, the yearling will still be nursing in the spring, and the newborn foal will get no milk. A hunter of mountain lions in an article which appeared in *The Western Horseman,* gives some indication of the low survival rate of colts:

"The lion population of Nevada has grown to the point that lions have even hurt the deer herds. Now that their natural food supply is short, they have hit the horse herds hard. They have always had a taste for horse meat, but now more than ever.

"Two winters ago, I saw a herd of thirteen mares and a roan stallion. In the spring, I watched the same bunch, and there were ten new foals in the herd, but a month later only one foal was left. The others had apparently fallen victim of lions."

Mountain lions, disease, lightning, blizzards, snakebite, forest fires, droughts, and accidents take a high toll of young and old alike in a wild-horse herd. Stallions are frequently mortally wounded doing battle for their harems. Since a horse depends on speed to save himself from his enemies, an injury to a leg or foot can often prove fatal.

The Taylor Grazing Act, though it gave the livestock industry long-overdue recognition and sanctioned its traditional usage of the public lands, was not designed to donate the entire public domain to the exclusive purposes of less than sixteen thousand stock growers. Section 9 of the Act specifies that forage should be allocated for the use of wildlife.* The wild horse, however, was deemed feral and so did not benefit from this clause. The Taylor Grazing Act, in the long run, had an adverse effect on the wild herds, for it whetted the ranchers' traditionally keen sense of competition for range usage (once expressed in wars against sheep), and resulted in a renewed attack on the horses.

Despite the fact that much of the public land is not suitable for grazing, the agency that administers it is not set up to supervise much else. In 1964, the Multiple Use Act was passed in an attempt to modify the monopolistic control the livestock industry now has on the public domain. The Act authorizes the Bureau of Land Management to administer the

---

* Recently a ninth member has been added to the Advisory Boards to represent wildlife interests. In most districts, however, this minority member has shown little interest in species that are not target animals.

public lands for recreational purposes. As of 1968, 177 recreation sites were developed. Horse lovers hoped that the Federal Bureau, among other projects, would set up wild-horse refuges for the benefit of horse enthusiasts and Western buffs.

According to high-level official in the Department of the Interior, however, the Bureau was not committing itself to any program until it heard the report of the Public Land Law Review Commission, a committee appointed by the President, the President of the Senate and the Speaker of the House to study the question of existing laws and procedures relating to the administration of the public lands of the United States, and on its findings depended the future of the public domain and the remaining wild horses that inhabited it.

27. *Wild Horse Annie*

The charge that wild horses were without legal protection and were fair game for anyone who would exploit or harass them has been repeated throughout this book. There was one Federal law, however, the Wild Horse Annie Bill, passed by Congress in 1959, which protected feral horses from being hunted by aircraft of motorized vehicles on the public domain. This bill had considerable merit and was the type of measure that should be applied not only to horses but to all wild animals that are pursued by hunters seated in cockpits and equipped with telescopic guns. Unfortunately, however, it was very limited in scope. Only unbranded horses inhabiting Federal lands were protected by the measure. Furthermore, the law was very difficult to enforce because of a number of stratagems devised by horse runners to circumvent it.

The passage of this humane measure (PL 86–234) was the work of the late Mrs. Velma Johnston of Reno, a slight woman weighing less than a hundred pounds, familiarly known as "Wild Horse Annie." Annie, who had been zealously working for two decades to expose the cruelties inflicted on wild horses by dog-food hunters, was not a female "gun-toting" outlaw as her nickname might suggest, but a sensitive and highly feminine individual who got an enormous amount of work done in a quiet way. Aside from the tremendous drive that must have been required to translate her personal indignation into a Federal law, Annie's accomplishment was even more impressive in view of the fact that she was physically handicapped. As a child, she contracted polio and, though she was ambulatory, she nevertheless suffered bouts with pain and fatigue in a body that was not perfectly aligned.

Ironically, Mrs. Johnston was labeled "Wild Horse Annie" by opponents of her measure, who attempted to discredit her through mockery. The name, however, caught the fancy of her horse-loving followers, including a large number of the nation's children. As a result, Wild Horse Annie insisted that all horse lovers address her by her nickname.

Annie's popularity with children was a by-product of Marguerite Henry's prize-winning children's book: *Mustang: Wild Spirit of the West,* the story of Annie's struggle as a young girl to overcome her handicap and her later fight to win protection for wild horses. After the publication of this biography, Annie's daily mail invariably contained a number of letters from children, whose grasp of the plight of the wild horses was refreshingly uncomplicated. The following excerpt from a child's letter succinctly summarizes their deep concern:

"It makes me angry and I think that the horses should be allowed to run free. They will soon be like the Buffalo that used to roam the plains of America. Extinct!"

Another child wrote: "I hope people will learn to give a little respect to wild horses."

Though Annie had no difficulty reaching the sensitive, uncorrupted youngsters of America, her fierce struggle with the exploiters of the mustangs, men whose consciences regarding animal life had been dulled by years of commercial activity, was quite a different matter. As she told it, her confrontations with horse hunters and their attempts to intimidate her might have made even a grade-B Western movie seem rather tame. "There was only one thing lacking," she said. "They didn't park their sidearms out in the vestibule."

In order to make use of her files for research, I visited Wild Horse Annie in her home in Reno for a week in 1968. During that time she told me the story of her fight for protective legislation for the wild horse.

"I hadn't even seen a wild horse when I first got into this, and I'm a native-born Nevadan and a rancher. That kind of gives you an idea of how little the wild horses bother anyone," she said, as we sat in a living room filled with horse souvenirs and other objects—paintings, lamps, bookends, ceramics—fashioned after colts, stallions, and various horse accouterments.

"When I introduced my bill," she continued, "strangers from all over the state came to see me. They would say to me, 'Mrs. Johnston, we're so grateful to you 'cause all those aerial roundups are harassing our cattle, and sometimes they pick up some of our horses, too.' You see, most of the ranchers in our state had come to realize how scarce the wild horses had become and they were thrilled to catch sight of a band once in a while. But the Government land agencies operated hand in hand with the profiteers, as if the horses were still overrunning the range."

Despite the fact that the mustangs were infrequently seen, Nevada supported, and still continues to support, the largest population of wild horses of any Western state. In the decade of the fifties, when Annie went to war against the commercial horsemeat interests, five thousand wild horses were thought to exist principally on Nevada's barren deserts, and in the rough and broken country of the Sierra Nevada range. These surviving herds had retreated to regions so rugged and isolated it was impossible to approach them on horseback. The horse hunters, however, were not to be thwarted. Employing low-flying aircraft equipped with sirens, they began to rout the holdouts from their hideaways and drive them across miles of wilderness to more convenient locations, where they could be captured in corrals and trucked to dog-food packing plants.

If the horses refused to abandon the safety of their desolate retreats, they were blasted with buckshot and many were blinded. By means of buzzing, hazing, and firing on a circling herd, the terrified animals eventually could be persuaded to leave the safety of their stronghold, and once they were panicked, they would stampede. During their long flight to a makeshift corral on the flatland, many dropped dead from exhaustion. Not until the survivors came into painful contact with the actual trap did they stop. Here they would frequently begin to fight, pile up, and trample each other to death. Injured and mutilated horses were then roped and dragged into trucks, where they were packed tightly without regard to space, as though they were mere slabs of meat.

Once the truck was loaded, the door was not opened again during the long haul to the packing plant and the horses were neither watered nor offered food. A transportation regulation known as "killer-rate" exempts truckers carrying livestock to market from a law which requires that in-transit animals must be fed and watered at regular intervals. It is argued that animals en route to a packing plant are condemned cargo anyway, and the transporter need not spend time and money maintaining their physical well-being. Yet, though "killer-rate" unfortunately applies to all livestock, domestic animals do not suffer the kind of maltreatment inflicted on the wild horse during its ride to slaughter. Cattle, at least, are not injured and terrified prior to being loaded, but are watered, fed, and calmed. By contrast, the nervous mustangs have been pursued until they are exhausted and dehydrated, and are quivering with fear and pain when finally dragged into the dark vans.

I asked Annie, "Who could be capable of treating a horse so cruelly?"

"Well, not the real old-time ranchers, I'll tell you that," she replied. "We have a lot of new people out here, though. People who moved into the ranching industry for tax write-offs. Our state is particularly advantageous as far as that kind of thing is concerned. We have no state income tax, no state inheritance tax and, in addition, people who invest in the food-growing business get a special concession from the Federal Government. So a lot of people don't even live on their holdings, but send out a hired manager to run things. And those fellows aren't above getting a cut, running some wild horses by air, and picking up a few extra bucks. But most of the old-time ranchers—well, they feel differently about such things. They might try to catch a mustang to break out, but they'll run it on horseback, you can be sure, and if they catch one, they're darn proud of themselves. But chasing them by air—NO!"

This statement sounded strangely reminiscent of attitudes of a bygone time when the nineteenth-century cattle barons from Wall Street claimed and overstocked the public range, killed off the wildlife, and left the West bankrupt and in a state of deterioration. Then, as now, the small rancher and the cowboy objected to the slaughter of the wild horses, but were powerless to stop the depredations.

In view of my own difficulty in searching out wild herds to photograph, I was not surprised to hear that Annie had never seen a wild horse until one day in 1950 when she was driving along Highway 395 to Reno. Traveling ahead of her on the road, she noticed a truck carrying what appeared to be live animals on their way to market, and from what she could see, blood was leaking out of the van, leaving a trail along the road.

Annie followed the vehicle to find out what kind of transport company would handle livestock in such a manner. When at last the truck came to a halt, she was sickened to discover all the animals to be horses, packed so tightly that one colt had fallen down and was trampled to a pulp. The rest were suffering from buckshot wounds, and some had bloody stumps where their hoofs had been worn off from running over hard rocks. The stallion was blind. His eyes had been shot out. As Annie tells it: "I saw them, and they were still alive! I asked the driver, 'Where did those horses come from, and why are they in such terrible condition?'

" 'Oh,' he told me, 'they were run in by plane out here.'

"I went home that night and I knew I couldn't live with myself unless I did something about it. I decided right then that I would not rest until I had done everything humanly possible to stop such atrocities. When my husband and my dad heard about it and realized that I was determined, they agreed to help me. My dad said, 'I think you ought to try. But remember a few things. Dress like a lady, act like a lady, talk like a lady, but think like a man.' I have followed his advice all through the campaign, and I have tried to look at these things from as unemotional a point of view as a man would."

Perhaps this explains how Wild Horse Annie became such a formidable foe of the Nevada horse hunters who previously had experienced no interference with their method of gathering animals, and who considered it their right to realize gain by whatever means they employed.

Annie, though she did not look like one who could fight like a man, plotted her campaign against these entrepreneurs with cool disdain for their threats and mockery. Her first step was a visit to the district office of the Bureau of Land Management in Reno, which had been issuing permits to pilots to "run" the wild horses on the public domain. According to Annie, when she introduced herself as a rancher's wife, they couldn't tell her enough.

She explains: "You see they thought they were doing us ranchers such a big favor getting rid of the horses. The director boasted to me one day, 'Why, Mrs. Johnston, by letting these profiteers run the horses, we've been able to get those wild horses off the ranges to make more land available for your sheep and cattle without any expense to the taxpayer. Everybody profits.' "

Later, when Annie was invited to testify before the House Judiciary Committee in Washington, D.C., and described this attitude on the part of the Federal Bureau, she put the matter into quite a different perspective, as noted in the *Congressional Record,* July 21, 1959:

"What the officials have failed to take into account," said she, "is the fact that the humane aspect has been completely disregarded. The public would have much preferred to have had [any] necessary range clearance carried on at a price, providing it had been properly supervised, humanely carried out and intelligently planned."

In 1959, when Annie appeared before members of the House and the Senate, ten years of fact-finding had gone into the preparation of her testimony, and she was ready with a case that would convince not only elected officials who had never before heard of a wild horse, but also certain Western representatives who were traditionally committed to livestock interests in their underpopulated states. One representative, Walter S. Baring from Nevada, however, needed no persuading. A staunch advocate of the reform, Congressman Baring was the sponsor who introduced the so-called Wild Horse Annie Bill in the House of Representatives.

At the hearing, each of the sixteen congressmen present was given an

Motorized predators pursue wild horses to exhaustion. Gus Bundy

(OPPOSITE PAGE) *A wild mare protests capture by dog-food hunters.*

Gus Bundy

A captured mustang is dragged onto a truck
for shipment to a processing plant. Gus Bundy

album containing photographs taken on an actual aerial roundup. Annie thereupon launched into a detailed description of the practice of horse hunting. In a voice resonant with conviction, she told how the mustangs, after being pursued to exhaustion by planes, were finally captured by men on the ground. These men, operating from speeding trucks, would fling a noose over the necks of the tired animals. To each rope was attached a one-hundred-pound tire and if the first whiplash of the heavy drag did not break the horse's neck, the animal would spend all its remaining strength in rearing and fighting to free itself of the encumbrance.

While the committee members examined pictures of dead horses— animals found on the range that had not survived the ordeal, unweaned colts left to starve because they did not weigh enough to warrant space in the truck, animals wandering on the mountains whose eyes were empty sockets, animals whose hoofs had been worn off during a wild stampede across mountain boulders, and animals whose lungs had burst from exhaustion—Annie questioned the Government's indirect role in this activity. For even though the district managers of the Bureau of Land Management in Reno had confessed to her a short time prior to her appearance in Washington that the wild horses did not seem to be harming the range, Government anti-horse policy had apparently become habitual, and range clearance had continued. With the airborne horse runners pressing the Bureau for permits to operate as usual, and very little public awareness of what was taking place far out on the deserts of Nevada, the Bureau had found it difficult to reverse its own policy on horse running. As a result, through inertia and habit, permits to capture horses on the public domain continued to be issued. But Annie pointed out the following to the Judiciary Committee:

"The necessity for wide-scale range clearance operations is behind us now, and the one point upon which we [the B.L.M. officials in Reno and those behind Annie's movement] are all in agreement is that except in widely remote instances, the mustangs are no longer a threat to the ranges. [Yet] Private interests [stockgrowers, hunters and canners] have again won in their demands for the monopolistic use of the ranges to the exclusion of everything not commercially profitable. Because so few of the animals are left, it is now that we should not only pass legislation for their protection, but plan for their control as well, so that there will never be an excuse for the mass extermination programs heretofore. . . .*

* Unfortunately, Congress did not follow through and adopt a policy of management and control as suggested by Wild Horse Annie.

Annie's testimony was so impressive that it was placed in the *Congressional Record* and ran eight columns on July 21, 1959. Six weeks later due in large part to strong support from Senator Mike Mansfield, the bill passed. The bill, which is reprinted in total in the Appendix, prohibits the pursuit of wild horses or burros by aircraft on the public domain. At the time it was the only law in America which offered the wild horse a modicum of protection from abuse; still it did not prevent the herds from being hunted and captured by other means for sale to slaughterhouses. Gathering wild horses by horseback or trapping them at water corrals remained legal. Nevertheless, the victory was impressive.

28. Bootleg Roundups

Four years earlier, in 1955, Annie had presented the same findings before the Nevada law-making body and, with the help of state legislator James Slattery, had seen the measure adopted on a state level. However, her satisfaction over this achievement was short-lived. One day in 1967 the supervisor of Livestock Identification for the Nevada Department of Agriculture, Stanley Routson, called on Wild Horse Annie, introduced himself and announced, "For God's sake, Mrs. Johnston, I was just called to inspect thirty-eight horses that had been shipped out of Nevada to Newark, California. They were all taken on an aerial roundup, that was clear enough. I was called in an official capacity to check for privately owned stock. Well, they all turned out to be unbranded, but I have to tell you, Mrs. Johnston, I had to order them all slaughtered to put them out of their misery. Eyes were shot out and lips hanging down where they'd been shot off."

Had the horses been branded stock, Stan Routson would not have found himself in the dilemma which led him to seek the aid of Annie. Though he no doubt would have found the inhumane treatment of branded animals equally objectionable, privately owned horses did not come under the protection of the Wild Horse Annie law. What troubled Routson was the realization that he was in indirect witness to a violation of either a state or a Federal law. However, without having personally observed the aerial roundup, he was uncertain what to do. As a start, he had ordered the horses put out of their misery. Then he had located Annie and volunteered his services in her campaign to stop such abuses.

Routson's assertion that aerial roundups had commenced again in Nevada came as no surprise to Annie, but she was delighted to find a friend where she least expected one, in the Nevada State Department of Agriculture (the stockmen's association of Nevada). From that day, Stan Routson became a staunch defender of the cause of wild horses. In July, 1967, before the National Livestock Brand Conference, he introduced the following resolution:

"Whereas, it is the opinion of this group that the Wild Horse of the West is being endangered of extinction, and

"Whereas, Wild Horses and Burros are not a dangerous wildlife species, and

"Whereas, the Wild Horses and Burros are one of the great heritages of the West, and

"Whereas, said animals are an asset to the ranges,

"Therefore, be it resolved that the National Livestock Brand Conference beseech the Secretary of the Interior to declare the Wild Horses and Burros to be under the protection of the National Wildlife Service."

The above was a most heretical resolution to be presented at a national meeting of the state stockmen's associations, the legal owners of the wild horses. It not only proposed that the state agencies relinquish their claims on the wild horses, but it also propounded that the wild horses were in fact an asset to the poor lands in the dry West. Interestingly, many of those in attendance agreed.

As a brand inspector, Routson's conclusion that the wild horses were headed for oblivion was based on firsthand knowledge. The fate of the thirty-eight unbranded horses had opened his eyes to the wide-scale illegal activity, and he had subsequently examined and certified thousands of wild horses leaving Nevada for packing plants in California.

In a letter to Annie dated July 8, 1968, he wrote: "A few days ago you asked my opinion as to the future of the wild horse in Nevada. Frankly, Mrs. Johnston, the wild horses of Nevada have no future. That is, provided the illegal capture and the wanton killings keep pace with the past four or five years.

"Having personal knowledge and access to records pertaining to the foregoing, I can make an educated prediction that one of the great heritages of the West, the Wild Horse, will no longer be in existence within ten years, unless drastic measures towards their preservation are taken.

"I trust you will be successful in your endeavors to preserve this courageous animal for the enjoyment of future generations of Western folk."

Since it would be impossible for large consignments of horses to be gathered by horseback, and since large consignments of badly shot-up horses were constantly being shipped to packing plants out of state, there was little doubt as to the method by which they had been gathered. The question was: How had the horse hunters managed to flout a state and a Federal law and get away with it? To investigate this, Routson allowed Annie access to his department's records of brand certifications and, by reviewing these, she was able to make a shrewd guess as to what the pilots were doing to cover themselves and give their activity an air of legality.

In nearly every shipment of unbranded horses, one or two creatures bore brands. It was evident to her that the horse hunters were deliberately releasing a branded mare or two in the vicinity of a wild-horse herd and corralling them together. If accosted by a sheriff, they could then point to the branded animals and claim that they had only been gathering their private stock and couldn't be held responsible for unbranded horses mixed with them.

Unfortunately, the Federal Bureau of Land Management lent credibility to this ruse. A Bureau release stated: "The rancher may use any method he wishes . . . including driving the animals with trucks or airplanes . . . as long as they belong to him," and a later paragraph added: "They [wild horses and domestic stock] may be grazing side by side. If someone intends to round up his own animals, he may accidently take wild horses at the same time."

However, it was becoming increasingly evident that the Bureau of Land Management was overreaching its authority in interpreting a law that had never been put to a test in the courts. It seemed to Annie and to her International Society for the Protection of Mustangs and Burros, therefore, that a court case was necessary to resolve this question.

While it was apparent that the horse hunters had resumed their motorized activities (Annie frequently received anonymous complaints by phone), it was extremely difficult to gather sufficient evidence to apprehend the offenders. In the vast and largely uninhabited regions where the wild horses still existed, it was purely accidental if a witness could be found who had observed an air hunt. Such a witness would also have to have checked all the captive animals for brands to ascertain that they were indeed wild horses and not privately owned stock. Usually the people who telephoned Annie reported only that they had watched an air roundup of wild horses and could tell her who the pilots were. Understandably, they did not realize that this evidence was not substantial enough.

"If a person just saw a thing happen, it didn't mean anything," Annie told me. "We still didn't have anything to go on. Even if we knew who was doing it, it still didn't help. I examined the records of horses shipped to a packing plant in Newark, California, and out of 158 horses inspected, only 4 were certified as branded. It was obvious to everyone by the condition of the animals that they had been run and gathered by plane, and though we had the name of the consignor, we still didn't have a case. In this instance we knew the horses were unbranded, but we needed a witness who had seen the roundup taking place."

Despite these obstacles, one case did at last come to trial. In February of 1967, three men were indicted for violation of the Wild Horse Annie Law, and the evidence was heard by the United States District Court in Reno the following July.

Testifying for the prosecution were Brand Inspector S. G. Robinson and the White Pine County Sheriff Archie Robinson, who witnessed the rounding up by aircraft of five wild horses. Mr. S. G. Robinson told the court that he and the sheriff were driving in a remote mountain area on an old sheep-trail road, and they noticed a circling plane losing altitude as though it were working over some horses.

"We observed it from this position for a few minutes as it dived and circled and were unable to see the horses, so we moved on up over the summit and found a better vantage point, and from there we were able to see seven head of horses coming off the mountain. The plane kept circling and diving sharply at the horses; also during those dives and circles the plane would use a siren and we could hear reports of a gun being used when the plane was at a low altitude. We also observed a rope about 15 feet long hanging below the plane and some large object tied to the end of the rope. We believed that the siren was suspended on this rope, but later found tin cans tied to the rope and that the siren was mounted on the left wing of the plane. . . .

". . . After about 45 minutes of this constant harassing and chasing, one yearling was unable to continue running and dropped back while four other horses continued into the valley. . . . The plane stayed with the colt, but far enough back so that the colt would not give up altogether and stop on them. After the plane worked the colt far enough down into the valley so that it could not get away, it left and went after the other four horses. We observed the plane harass and turn these horses at will."

When the aircraft landed one-quarter mile from the makeshift corral (created from bulldozed cedar trees), the two occupants were served with summonses by Sheriff Robinson. The pilot of the plane was Art Cook, and riding "shotgun" was Ted Barber. Both claimed they had been hired by Julian Goicochea, a cattle rancher in White Pine County. According to the two men, Goicochea had the necessary permits from the Bureau of Land Management and the Office of the County Commissioner to run horses in the region.* This claim later was proved to be untrue. In any case, permit or not, an aerial roundup of unbranded horses would still be in violation of the law.

At the trial, the court was shown a number of photographs of the captured horses, pictures taken from many angles, several at a distance of four feet. The sheriff and deputy brand inspector verbally described the animals as follows:

1. Black stallion, no brand, and no other identifying marks or white hairs.

2. Bay mare, no brand, left hind fetlock white, same foot black and white.

3. Bay filly, no brand, left front foot and right hind foot white, white star on forehead.

4. Light bay filly, no brand, left hind foot and leg white with stocking about one foot up, white spot on outside of right front foot at top of hoof, white blaze face.

5. Steel gray mare, branded 2A, right shoulder and C on right thigh. This mare was bleeding from eight shotgun wounds, which Barber admitted having inflicted by shooting from the plane to control and turn the horses.

In concluding his testimony, the deputy brand inspector testified that on backtracking into the valley, he and the sheriff had come upon a severely injured bay horse about one hundred yards from the road.

"I observed it through binoculars and was unable to see any brands, but his shoulder was a big mass of dried blood where he had been shot from the plane with a shotgun. This horse no doubt was one of the bay horses we first observed running off the mountain but was not corralled because he had to stop from exhaustion."

Since one branded animal was found among the herd, the case was ideal from the point of view of determining the question of the legality of hunting unbranded horses in a mixed herd. Off the record, Annie was informed that the five horses which figured in the court case were part of a much

---

* A permit is required from the Bureau of Land Management to run horses on the public domain. In Nevada, the Office of the County Commissioner requires that a two-thousand-dollar bond and notice be posted prior to a wild-horse roundup as a precaution against injury to privately owned stock that might be mixed with the wild herd. Naturally, this bond is redeemable.

larger operation. During January alone, 158 horses had been shipped from the same district to a packing plant in Newark, California. Without the use of planes, these could hardly have been gathered from such rugged wild-horse country in the dead of winter.

Inasmuch as the evidence was so well documented, the trial seemed but a formality. However, Annie was concerned over the fact that the prosecuting attorney was not too well informed about horses. As a precaution, she invited him to make use of her files for study.

The third defendant, who had not participated in the actual roundup, was rancher Julian Goicochea. On the second day of the trial Goicochea told the jury that he leased seventy-two square miles of the public domain for grazing cattle, sheep, and horses. According to his testimony, in 1958, during the time the Wild Horse Annie bill was pending, he had rounded up and disposed of all the wild horses in the region, and the following year he had put on the public range one hundred of his own horses. Thereafter, said he, all the horses in the area, whether branded or not, were the progeny of his foundation stock.

However, judging from the number of horses that Goicochea had shipped over the past five years, one would have to conclude that all of his animals had given birth to quadruplets. Furthermore, despite Goicochea's claim, ranchers who do not gather and brand their colts forfeit their animals, according to state law. In Nevada, all horses over twelve months of age that do not bear brands are technically "mavericks" and as such are the property of the state. Such horses are embraced in the laws which protect wild horses from pursuit by motorized vehicles. The director of the Bureau of Land Management, Boyd Rasmussen, clarified this in a directive to all B.L.M. district managers:

"A major problem in the controversy over wild horses is one of semantics and definitions. When is a horse 'wild'? Although the unclaimed and unbranded horses and burros presently found on public lands are feral and not wild in the same sense as deer or elk are wild, from a practical view and as far as the general public is concerned, these animals *are wild.* Therefore, wild horses or burros as defined by the B.L.M. are *any unbranded and unclaimed horses or burros utilizing lands administered by the Bureau.*"

Goicochea, however, stuck to his claim that all the horses on his grazing lands, branded or not, belonged to him. The Bureau of Land Management, he told the court, had ordered him to reduce his horse herd (the Bureau of Land Management denied this) and since there was no possible way for him to gather the animals from their remote habitat without the aid of pilots, he had found it necessary to hire Cook and Barber to perform this service for him.

Next, a surprise witness for the defense was put on the stand, who like one of the witnesses for the prosecution was a deputy brand inspector for the state of Nevada. This witness told the court that in the wintertime it is not possible to determine whether a horse is branded or not without first shearing the animal.

Defendant Cook then returned to the stand and under the skillful guidance of his lawyer described how he had taken the corralled horses to Goicochea's ranch after Sheriff Robinson and Deputy Brand Inspector Robinson had finished photographing the animals and had left the scene of the alleged crime. There, he asserted, he had sheared the horses and found them all to be branded. Photographs were then produced of sheared and branded horses, and these were exhibited to the jury.

Wild Horse Annie was fiercely critical of the conduct of the trial by the prosecuting attorney. Said she: "They showed the jury these pictures of sheared horses and, sure enough, there were brands. . . . Now the next question our attorney should have put to the defendants was 'When did you take those pictures?' Because the horses were gathered in February and the case didn't come to trial until July . . . time enough for a fresh brand to heal up. So, even if they actually were the same horses, where do you think they had been all that time? In Goicochea's corral!

"Well, as I told you, our lawyer didn't know much about horses, so he didn't do anything but just sit there. The jury brought in a verdict of not guilty. Afterward our attorney said to me, 'Mrs. Johnston, I've learned so much about horses from this case.' I could have cried."

I asked Stan Routson, the supervisor of the two deputy brand inspectors who had given conflicting testimony at the trial, "Is it customary to shear horses?"

"No," he said, "you never shear unless there is a dispute over the identity of the brand. Deputy Brand Inspector Robinson was in the corral with the horses, and he certainly would be able to see if they were branded."

The most regrettable feature of the trail was that it left a confused situation with regard to the interpretation of the Wild Horse Annie Law. After that defeat, no violator was apprehended and brought to trial. Sheriffs were reluctant to make arrests, and witnesses who happened to see horses corralled illegally, not being equipped with horse trailers with which to impound the evidence, felt they could not substantiate their testimony. As a consequence, unlawful horse hunting continued throughout the West.

29. *No Room for Wild Horses*

Though many wild species have been saved from extinction through the efforts of hunters, sportsmen's organizations, with a few notable exceptions, have opposed legislation which would give the wild horse a change of status and would offer it a permanent place on the American landscape. The reasons for this opposition become obvious when one examines our wildlife laws and the structure of the government agencies in charge of wild-animal management.

In America, jurisdiction over wildlife is claimed by the individual states and controlled by each state's fish and game department.* Since these bureaus, or commissions, are funded from the sale of hunting and fishing licenses and an excise tax on ammunition and fishing tackle, it is not surprising that nontarget animals are given short shrift by their human managers. No tax money is appropriated by the state legislatures for the objective management of collective wildlife, and consequently fish- and game-department programs very often are limited to the poisoning of predators, the removal of "competing" nontarget animals from the wilderness, and the artificial buildup of "harvestable game."

In these enlightened times, as a result of modern man's management, North American animals are prevented from existing in a natural balance, one species with another. Instead, their populations are at the mercy of state officials who manipulate them primarily for the benefit of sportsmen. Though target animals have increased as a result of this type of management, other animal forms have dwindled or disappeared altogether.

Apparently, not only are ecological principles largely ignored by those who control our wildlife, but under the present laws it appears virtually

* The titles of these agencies differ from state to state, although their functions are strikingly similar.

impossible to introduce wholesome practices into the management of what wild areas remain in our Western states. Employees of state bureaus (established many years ago) today jealousy oppose reorganization of their entrenched departments and resist reforms which might cost a few jobs. Moreover, the hunters they serve are well satisfied with the preferential treatment they presently pay for and receive. And the general public, for the most part, is oblivious to what is going on.

However, when a state politician, or a bureau official, or a representative from a sportsmen's organization vociferously protests any real or imaginary Federal interference in the management of wildlife, his concern is rarely for the welfare of the animal, but more often is related to the profits gained through the sale of sports equipment, guns, ammunition, and "canned hunts," to say nothing of the revenue obtained for the state through the licensing of hunters. Hunting, a popular pastime in the West, has become big business, and the right of each state to grant preferential treatment to its target animals is regarded as sacrosanct and guaranteed by law.

There are two exceptions to state jurisdiction over American wild animals. Creatures living within the boundaries of the National Parks are held to be Federal property and, as such, come under the protection of the United States Department of the Interior. Furthermore, any species threatened with total extinction can be "claimed and managed" by the Federal Government under the Migratory Bird Treaty Act. As long as such an animal remains on the endangered-species list, it is the responsibility of the United States Fish and Wildlife Service.

The Migratory Bird Treaty Act is an international agreement that was originally negotiated to protect Canadian wild fowl that migrated across the United States. So many birds were killed en route to their summer or winter nesting sites that the Canadian Government became alarmed. Individual states admitted they were powerless to stop the depredations for, as one commissioner put it, "We knew if we didn't get the birds, the next state would take them." Finally the Federal Government was forced to step in and assume responsibility for the protection of this class of animal. Included in the act is a clause which further permits the Federal Government to manage and protect any native animal in danger of extinction.

Yet both these exceptions to state control over wildlife grant the Federal Government only limited power over very specific categories of animals, and neither exception benefits the wild horse. In the first instance, it will be recalled, the Department of the Interior, acting on a recommendation that it restrict its National Parks to native species, excluded the wild horse from these sanctuaries.

In any case, since most National Parks are heavily forested, they are not ideal habitats for wild horses. The wild horse prefers the wide-open spaces of the plains and the deserts, though at least one band of wild horses seems to have thrived in a wooded area. The Bookcliff wild horses of western Colorado successfully inhabit cedar breaks, thick with juniper and piñon. This wooded region, though it restricts the wild horses' urge to gallop, nevertheless affords them the unusual advantage of total concealment. Hidden by the thick foliage, they are no easier to spot from the air than on the ground. I had great difficulty locating and approaching the Bookcliff horses for this reason, and succeeded in getting only one photograph of that herd—the one that appears in this book. Inevitably, twigs snapped and leaves crackled as I stole through the brush, and when the horses heard me coming, they quickly vanished among the trees. Though this particular band of horses has survived well in the wooded mountains, it must be conceded that the forested National Parks are not habitats that the horses themselves seem to prefer.

Unfortunately, the Federal Government has never established a National Park on the American prairies. However, should the Department of the Interior ever decide that this unique feature of the American landscape ought to be preserved, prairie dogs, buffaloes, coyotes, and wild horses, all would make appropriate tenants of a Prairie National Park.

As for the clause attached to the Migratory Bird Treaty Act which permits the Federal Government to proclaim itself the temporary custodian of an endangered species, the wild horse, on two counts, does not fall into this category either. First, the wild horse, though likely to disappear forever as a wild, self-sufficient creature, is in no danger whatsoever of extinction as a species. Proof of this fact is evident in every barn, show ring, race track, and polo field across the country. In fact, the horse, as a species, is thriving as never before in history. Secondly, the language of the act specifies that the government shall manage "endangered *native* animals." The horse is believed to be an imported animal, although the species originated in North America. The legal terminology of the act would seem to exclude the wild horse from its auspices.

Having exhausted the possibilities of placing the wild horses under existing Federal programs, other concerned individuals have sought a means by which the wild horses could qualify for management on the state level, but with no greater success. In Colorado, Senator George

Jackson and Congressman John Fuhr cosponsored a bill which would have reclassified the wild force in their state, defining it as legitimate "wild life," thus placing it under the management of the Colorado State Game, Fish, and Parks Departments.

This measure had strong support from certain sportsmen's organizations that recognized the legitimacy of the horse lovers' demands and willingly agreed that room should be made for nontarget animals in the West. Nevertheless, despite this support, the measure died in committee in the House, after passing in the Senate. It is alleged that pressure brought to bear against the bill by the livestock industry was responsible for its defeat.

Though several hunting clubs had backed the measure in Colorado, it is not clear what position had been taken on the issue by the Colorado State Game, Fish, and Parks officials themselves. In other states fish and game commissioners have expressed opposition to the idea of managing nontarget animals.

In an interview, Frank Groves, fish and game commissioner in Nevada, explained why: "If any law was ever passed to declare the wild horses wildlife and they were put under the jurisdiction of my department, they'd better also find a way to finance the horses because once our department starts spending sportsmen's money to finance wild horse programs, the hunters will rise up in indignant wrath and say, 'We're not paying our license money for the management of anything but huntable population of wildlife only.' We're a self-supporting government organization and we don't ask for money from our taxpayers to carry on our work. It all comes from hunting licenses, you see."

To those who have become accustomed to hearing wildlife management described in glowing "scientific-ese" terms, it no doubt will come as a shock to learn what some of these programs actually are. In no case is the over-all welfare of the balance of the collective animal population ever regarded as of primary importance. Instead, each government bureau serves its own special-interest group. Often bureau officials are convinced they have bowed to the will of the public when in actual fact they have merely yielded to the clientele of another government bureau, for inter-bureau co-operation is standard procedure and agencies trade favors. The demands of an amorphous public, however, are often ignored, and many government bureaucrats view the letter-writing animal lover as a crackpot who has at stake no legitimate economic interest that need be taken into consideration.

A brief description of a few programs will serve to illustrate this point.

Predator control, which in most states is handled by a state bureau of agriculture, is set up as a service to the livestock industry primarily, but the state fish and game officials can also receive help from this department on request. Though it is understandable why sheepmen want the coyote and mountain-lion population under control in grazing districts, it is sad to think that these animals are also ruthlessly exterminated in remote mountain and desert areas where they survive by killing an occasional deer or antelope. However, fish and game commissioners are expected to show a yearly increase in their target herds prior to the opening of the hunting season. Getting rid of the predators is one method by which this can be accomplished. Hunters then enjoy the incidental satisfaction of knowing that the game they are shooting and killing would become too numerous and die of starvation were it not being hunted.

Propaganda regarding the importance of hunting in order to maintain a healthy balance between wild animals and their food supply has long been accepted as an irrefutable fact by hunters and nonhunters alike. Very likely in some areas where for long decades the game has been artificially stocked, carnivores systematically destroyed, and competing animals removed by government officials, an imbalance has become irreversible. But it is also likely that some hunters who use this rationale to justify their sport and make it more "meaningful," are unaware themselves that many game officials are fostering this condition.

In some instances, animals that are only vaguely suspected of "competing" with wild game are destroyed. Though it is questionable that the wild horse, a grazer or grass-eater, competes with the wild game, most of which are browsers or brush-eaters, nevertheless, the wild horse is viewed with suspicion by some game-department officials for the occasional nibble of leaves and twigs that it takes. With plenty of funds at their disposal for the exclusive purpose of building the target-animal population, state commissioners often request and receive permission from the state stockmen's associations, legal owners of unbranded horses, to remove the herds.

However, many fish and game commissioners are not in favor of these artificial practices and carry out such manipulative programs against their personal convictions and only under pressure from sportsmen's organizations. One commissioner privately confided to me: "Sportsmen want a deer behind every tree, but there isn't enough food for them. We lost 3,000 deer in one winter in a canyon. We tried to tell the sportsmen that would happen but they wouldn't believe us."

Nevertheless, the following year the incident was used to prove to a gullible public that the hunter's role as a predator is critically important to the over-all well-being of the game. No mention was made of reasons why the habitat was "overstocked" in the first place.

Unfortunately, parallels were drawn and dire prophesies were made regarding an imminent wild-horse population explosion by those who would have them removed. Because the horses were not "culled" by hunters, the public was told it was only a matter of time before the herds would overpopulate and starve. In the case of the wild horse, an animal that was not being "managed" for game, no such catastrophe had ever been recorded. Left to their own devices, the wild horses had not multiplied until they ate themselves out of their habitat.

The brief descriptions of wildlife management given in this chapter are a few of the programs that are hailed as "scientific and progressive," and, ironically, the public has absolute confidence in them. Any commissioner who shows an increase in a local deer herd is praised not only by hunters, but also by an unsuspecting public, unaware that enhancement of one species may be at the expense of other types of animals.

It is difficult to find a place for any nontarget animals in this picture. Laws, as they now stand, are antithetical to the protection of a multiformity of animals on an ecological basis. The wild horse, with its peculiar feral status, faced additional impediments. As one frustrated wild-horse lover put it, "If you can't eat it, or sell it, or mount its head, it just doesn't get to live!"

30. The Pryor Mountain Controversy

The Pryor Mountains are dry and bleached and covered with sage, like a dune bordering the greener ranges that crest to the northwest across the state of Montana. On the Wyoming side, the Pryor Mountains ease into red hills, and then become a plain. This is cattle country.

The Pryor Mountains and most of the surrounding area are public domain, under the jurisdiction of the United States Department of the Interior. Wyoming ranchers, in order to put livestock on its lower slopes, must take out grazing permits from the Federal Bureau of Land Management. Up to four-thousand-feet elevation, the land is suitable for cattle. Then it becomes steep and lacks water holes. Above the four-thousand-foot level, the region is stony and tufted with colorless sage plants known locally as "rabbit brush."

Here less than ten inches of rain fall annually, and no springs bring moisture to the brittle brush that struggles for existence. In the deeper crevasses between the summits and in the canyons that split the higher plateaus, single rows of trees follow the thin water routes which, in the spring, trickle to the plain below. This is the home of the Pryor Mountain wild horses.

No one knows for certain where these particular horses came from, or how long they have lived here. Old-timers, settlers, say that when they arrived in the late nineteenth century the horses were "standing up in those hills." Indians from the adjacent Crow Reservation tell of wild horses in the region before the coming of the white man. The Crows, who are reputed to have acquired more horses than any Northern tribe, used them to pursue the buffaloes, once so abundant in their territory. During the summer months, hunters camped on a high plateau that overhangs the deep gorge carved by the Bighorn River.* Their teepee rings are still in evidence. When autumn came, the Indains packed their tents, rounded up what horses they could catch, and moved to winter camp along the Wind River, where the climate was milder and easier on their horse herds.

Some hard-to-catch horses were inevitably left behind to be rounded up the following summer. But by then the horses were wiser and wilier and more determined than ever to avoid capture. No doubt, many were never enslaved again. These may have been the first wild horses in the Pryor Mountains, a nucleus which over the years attracted stray horses from many sources—expeditions, battles, and ranches.

Local people sometimes wonder if any of the wild horses' ancestors might have belonged to Custer and been survivors of the Battle of Bighorn fought only a few miles away. Though history books credit a horse by the name of Comanche as being the sole survivor of that historic battle, the fact remains that three whole days and nights passed before scouts reached the site of the massacre and found the wounded animal. Any horse able to travel would surely have fled the scene of action during the intervening time. Even while the short battle was being waged, a horse, suddenly finding itself riderless, would not wheel and face the guns again, but would most certainly gallop away. The Pryor Mountain wild-horse herd may well have acquired some cavalry stock at that time.

I have already mentioned the member of the Lewis and Clark expedition who had been detached to lead horses through the Pryor Mountains and lost the animals one night while he slept. These may have been the first wild horses to inhabit the area.

But no matter how far back the Pryor Mountain wild horses can be traced, one fact has been determined: They at least predated the white man's settlement of this region. Though ranchers' domestic horses later mixed with the wild herds, the mustangs were already on the mountains when the first white settlers began to arrive in the 1890s.

So, in 1964, when the Bureau of Land Management announced that the two hundred wild horses in the Pryor Mountains had been marked for roundup and auction, the local ranchers around Lovell, Wyoming, who had long regarded the wild herd as a symbol of the Old West, did not take the news complacently. They strongly protested the action at a series of public hearings and temporarily succeeded in blocking the government plan.

But by the spring of 1968, all their tactics for delaying the proposed

* This portion of the Bighorn River has been renamed the Yellowtail River after the family of the Crow chief.

(ABOVE) *Horses of rare colors.*
Odd shades of dun still found in the Pryor Mountain mustang herds.
(OPPOSITE) *Surefooted from birth, high-stepping wild horses rarely stumble.*

roundup seemed to have been exhausted, and the Bureau of Land Management, after surveying the horses' water holes for a trap site, announced its plans. According to a government news release, the Bureau was considering three possible courses of action: Remove all two hundred horses, remove all but fifteen of the two hundred horses, or remove all but thirty-five of the two hundred horses. The Bureau invited the public to make known its wishes in regard to these three alternatives.

It was at this point that the Wyoming ranchers organized the Pryor Mountain Wild Horse Association to fight the impending roundup altogether, and the controversy flared up again. This was where matters stood when John Walsh of the International Society for the Protection of Animals gave me the tip on the wild-horse story. The conflict between the ranchers and the Government Bureau fit well ito ABC's concept of a news feature, and I was sent to Wyoming with a television news crew to film the story.

When I arrived, the Bureau of Land Management district manager, Mr. Dean Bibles, gave me a conducted tour of the Pryor Mountains to view the doomed horses. Mr. Bibles expressed the view that the animals were being removed from the region partly for humane reasons. The horses, said he, had seriously overgrazed their habitat and inevitably would face starvation if not removed.

Bibles admitted, however, that his main objective as a manager of public lands was to conserve the soil which had begun to show signs of erosion. Without this basic resource, he pointed out, no wildlife could survive anyway.

It did not require an expert to see that the area was in poor condition. At eight-thousand-feet elevation, the scrubby mahogany brush and the dry sage seemed dwarfed and brittle, and grass was sparse on the coarse and rubbly earth. Yet, despite the paucity of plant life, the horses appeared to be thriving. I was anxious to ask the local ranchers about the general health of the herd, for during two trips into the mountains, the approximately eighty animals we photographed seemed to have great spirit and energy.

The horses were small, but well formed with compact bodies, narrow chests and small heads. Their manes and tails were full and luxurious and their colors were sensational, with many red roans, blue grullos, and buckskins. Though an occasional old, swaybacked mare was in evidence, such creatures seemed to be enjoying longevity rather than suffering from malnutrition.

*An expensive wild horse trap built by the
United States Bureau of Land Management.*

Mr. Bibles explained that the B.L.M. planned to capture the horses by
humane means, trapping them in a corral being built around their major
watering place on the Wyoming side of the mountains. An auction would
then be held on the hill beside the corral. Should the Bureau decide to
spare either fifteen or thirty-five horses,* these selected animals would then
be withheld from the auction and branded before being released.

This branding procedure was essential in order to redeem the horses
from the proprietorship of the stockmen's associations in Wyoming and
Montana, legal owners of all unbranded animals in their respective states.
Since the horses ranged back and forth across the state line, both states
now had equal claim on the animals, a technicality that no doubt had
prevented either from taking action against the horses. Moreover, because
the horses inhabited Federal property, neither state could hold a roundup
without a permit from the Bureau of Land Management. Thus, while the
B.L.M. did not own the horses, it did hold the power to permit or to
prevent them being chased and captured on the public domain.

Once branded, however, any horses that the Bureau should decide to

* According to the Bureau of Land Management, if as many as thirty-five horses
were released in the area again, no other wildlife would be managed in the region.
Since the hunting interests were insistent on maintaining a large deer herd in the
area, however, it was unlikely that more than fifteen horses would be authorized
for release.

retain on the Federal land, would no longer be considered the property of the state stockmen's associations. But the question of who would then be responsible for the animals had not been resolved. The Bureau did not want to assume the burden, nor did it have funds allocated for such a project. So, in a public statement, the B.L.M. announced that unless some organization or group declared itself willing to sponsor and manage whatever wild horses might be retained in the mountains, none would be spared. Among other duties that would devolve on such a sponsoring group would be the annual roundup of the horses for the branding of colts. Since, at most, only thirty-five horses would be involved, this task, however, did not seem to be too formidable.

I next went to Lovell, Wyoming, to talk with the Pryor Mountain Wild Horse Association, a group of a dozen citizens including ranchers Lloyd and Royce Tillett; a Lutheran minister, Pastor Floyd Schwieger; an advertising man, Charles Wagner; and a housewife, Phyllis Hill. These Lovellites denied that the herd of two hundred horses had overgrazed their habitat, and disputed the B.L.M. contention that the horses were in any danger of starvation. Only one mare had died during the previous winter, they told me, and she from old age. Besides, they added, the birth rate seemed to be quite low. Not every mare produced a colt every year. It was their opinion that nature was keeping the horses' reproductive rate low, in balance with the available forage. Moreover, the plants and soil, according to them, looked no worse now than fifty years ago. To corroborate this opinion, they had even brought in their own range expert, Mr. Patrick Church, who gave it as his judgment that the erosion so evident in the region had stabilized at least a thousand years ago.

As for the B.L.M.'s token offer to spare either fifteen or thirty-five horses, according to the Horse Association, this was nothing but a sop to horse lovers and would be tantamount to wiping out the animals by gradual stages. Such a small number would unavoidably inbreed, and the horses would soon weaken and die out. Besides, they asked, what about the 165 horses they plan to do away with?

"We're talking about the two hundred horses that are doing fine up there right now," one of the Tillett brothers explained to me. "Those are the horses we want to see stay there. Fifteen or thirty-five horses are not enough horses to make it, and the B.L.M. knows it. The B.L.M. has suggested putting stallions in to upgrade the stock in case thirty-five horses get inbred. Well, we don't want to raise domestic horses. We want our wild ones that are already up there."

The question of branding aroused equally strong reactions among the group. Objections were raised on esthetic, humane, and common-sense grounds.

"Whoever heard of gathering elk or moose every year and branding them?" they asked. "If the law requires that we brand wild horses, it's the law that's wrong."

Furthermore, they pointed out, once the horses had a brand burned on them, they would no longer qualify for protection under the Wild Horse Annie law, which prohibits the running of unbranded horses by airplane or motorized vehicle on the public domain.

Though the Pryor Mountain Wild Horse Association was interested in becoming the sponsors of the wild horses, they were fearful that in volunteering for this duty they would be acquiescing to all the stipulations set forth by the B.L.M. So, with great circumspection, they had drafted a letter in which they declared their willingness to sponsor all two hundred horses in the Pryor Mountains, to dig out water holes for them, and to drop feed for them over hard winters. In the same letter they registered their objection to the idea of branding any of the animals. Though this letter had been sent to the B.L.M. three months earlier, no reply had been received. In fact, the Lovellites had been surprised to read in a recent government news release that no group had as yet come forward and expressed a willingness to sponsor the wild horses.

But the question I was still interested in having answered was what the Bureau of Land Management intended to do with the Pryor Mountain range after they removed either 165, or 185, or all 200 wild horses. Whereas the wild horses could run the ten- or twelve-mile distances between the water holes and had no difficulty maneuvering the steep rocky inclines and rough terrain, cattle certainly could not. The Pryor Mountains, even were the range replanted and made into grassland, could not be made habitable for much other than the nimble wild horses.

The Association members listened to my question and suggested that I direct it to the Montana Fish and Game commissioners who, they said, had been talking about planting bighorn sheep in the Pryor range. They then showed me correspondence from the game officials which stated that "trespass horses" were presently using the same area which the bighorn sheep would be expected to use, and were posing an obstacle to the plan.

"The B.L.M. is just playing along with the state Fish and Game Department and getting rid of the horses so they can give the range over to the Montana hunters," the Association members said. "The trouble is, the area isn't any good for bighorn sheep. They already tried a transplant over here at Missouri Flats, and all the sheep ran away to the Rockies. These hills aren't high enough for wild sheep and, besides, the road goes right across the top. That ruins it for the bighorns. They like to be able to climb up above you and look down on you. They won't stay here, and we're going to lose our horses while the B.L.M. finds it out. We think these hills look just as well with horses on them as with nothing."

With this information I returned to the district office of the Bureau of Land Management to hear what the Federal officials had to say in response to the Horse Association's allegations. They did not deny the charge that the Montana Fish and Game officials wanted the horses removed to make room for bighorn sheep, but answered evasively. They further hinted that the Montana Fish and Game Commission had been highly critical of the overgrazed condition of the Pryor Mountain range and had complained that, as a consequence, there had been a decline in the ratio of surviving fawns to adult mule-deer population. The Fish and Game complaint was an indictment against the B.L.M., whose responsibility it was to protect the soil and plant life in this habitat, and I could understand why the B.L.M. was not immune to this type of criticism. Moving the "trespass horses" out of the region was a step toward pacifying the game officials and improving conditions for the deer herd.

But the Bureau of Land Management, according to other sources, was not only catering to the Fish and Game Commission on the wild-horse issue, but was deferring to the Montana Livestock Commission as well. The Wyoming *Eagle Tribune* published a story titled: "Montana Agency Tagged in Wild Horse Flap," in which Tom Holland, president of the National Mustang Association, was quoted as saying, "It appears the Montana Livestock Commission is dictating to the Bureau of Land Management in this matter."

The story went on to say that the Montana Livestock Commission (Montana's stockmen's association) had been carrying out a campaign to rid the state of wild horses. Holland said, "They told us they gathered 700 head (of wild horses) north of Billings last year."

Shortly thereafter, Wild Horse Annie came to a similar conclusion. In a monthly newsletter published by her organization, she wrote, "The federal Bureau is continuously pressured by special interest groups who subscribe to the theory that what is not commercially profitable to themselves in their use of the public lands must go."

The charge by Holland and by Wild Horse Annie that the B.L.M. was catering to commercial interests (behind the guise of state agencies) was never denied by the Federal officials. But since it is a common practice for one government agency to regard the interests represented by another government agency as being somehow more "legitimate" than the wishes of an amorphous public, the B.L.M. felt no compunction to conceal the alleged collusion. This habit of thinking among bureaucrats arises quite naturally from the fact that government agencies are so specialized that co-operation with one another is imperative if anything is to be accomplished. Besides, most government bureaus have been set up, in the first place, to protect economic interests, and only in theory do they represent all the people, hence government workers are quick to recognize economic values above less tangible considerations.

Therefore, in the minds of the bureaucrats, the livestock industry and the hunting interests, as represented by respected state commissions, merited more consideration than the horse-loving public that had no vested interests at stake. To the bureaucratic way of thinking, the letter writers were not making or losing any money on the public domain anyway, and had little right to dispute the valid claims of those who benefited economically from the use of the government lands.

But in defense of the B.L.M.'s attitude of ready compliance with the wishes of the state agencies, it should be pointed out that the Federal Bureau has no easy task, functioning, as it must, on a local level. In the face of traditional Western resentment against so-called Federal interference, to get along with state and local agents is not only politic, but for a B.L.M. official it is imperative. Local stockmen who sit on the B.L.M. advisory boards are very often the same individuals who are appointed to serve on the state stockmen's associations. Many of these Westerners in the livestock industry still have difficulty accepting the fact that the public lands which they have been utilizing since the days of the open range are not actually their own exclusive property, but belong to the public at large. And the B.L.M., if it is to carry out its own work effectively, and protect the public domain from excessive pressures from this group, must somehow keep peace with the individuals who use it.

Furthermore, on purely legal grounds, the B.L.M. could defend its deference to the wishes of the Montana Livestock Commission inasmuch as unbranded horses are actually the property of that state agency and do not belong to the Federal Government. Nevertheless, it was Federal money that was about to be spent to dispose of the horses.

On a strictly personal level, the B.L.M. officials seemed to be in sympathy with the wild horses. Dean Bibles, I learned, had traveled a good many miles across the state of Montana in an attempt to solicit private buyers to attend the auction and save the horses from being purchased for slaughter. Though this information helped me to understand Bibles' personal dilemma (he had inherited the issue from his predecessor), I doubted that he would have much success finding homes for wild horses. It is common knowledge in the West that there is no market for mature mustangs. According to the International Society for the Protection of Animals, ninety-two percent of those sold at auction go directly to canneries. Though Bibles was evidently aware of this fact, he was still willing to do some private legwork in an effort to mitigate the desolating statistic.

My last stop in Wyoming was a visit to a horse dealer, Andy Gifford, to obtain his opinion regarding the fate of the horses and to learn who would attend the auction. He told me that the canneries would be well represented and that the horses would bring no more than four cents a pound. Although he personally hated to see the animals removed from the Pryor Mountains, he admitted that he himself would bid on the horses.

"If I don't, someone else will," he said. "They're going to the cannery anyway. Experience has proven that there isn't any other market for them. You're not going to buy a wild horse for your kids to ride!"

He added that the Bureau of Land Management would be lucky if as many as thirty-five horses survived the corralling and were still healthy enough to be released again should the government agency decide to spare that number of horses.

"The mustangs'll just go crazy in that corral, like so many elk in a pit," said he. "Once they find themselves trapped, the stallions'll fight and the horses'll panic and trample each other to death. It'll be terrible. The Bureau of Land Management will probably have to ship them out as fast as they can, or even butcher them right there on the range. There won't be any time for an auction. You can't gather that many horses together and hold them in a pen for an auction like they plan to do. They don't know what they're doing."

A later interview with Carwin Rule, an old-time mustanger who had corralled horses in the Pryor Mountains as far back as World War I, confirmed that the roundup would be a bloody massacre. He explained: "Well, you don't want to run wild horses into a corral like the one the Bureau of Land Management has built. You want a corral that's on the level—on flat land—where you can handle the horses. You don't want to build a trap that they can commit suicide in. They will, you know. They'll just pile up in a corral on a steep hill like that. When a horse is wild, he doesn't know what anything is. He can even get hurt on a water trough. They'll jam them around and break their legs, and they'll pile up. They'll kill half of them before they catch them out for auction."

The corral under construction was large enough to hold the entire herd of two hundred wild horses. Inside, were various gates to separate the animals. However, many people feared these would only create more hazards for the horses. The sides, when completed, would measure 10 feet high and would be supported by 10-inch poles set 3 feet into the ground at 6-foot intervals. According to an estimate obtained from a lumber company in Billings, the cost of the lumber alone for this mammoth enclosure might exceed $35,000. Added to this expense would be the cost of labor and an electric-eye gate to alert the government officials when an animal entered the trap. Some estimates of the ultimate cost of the trap ran as high as $80,000. (The BLM later denied spending this amount.)

Before leaving for New York, I priced hay in Wyoming and compared the cost of feeding the horses (and thus relieving pressure on the plant life in the region) with the extravagance of rounding them up. Interestingly, it appeared that the horses could be fed for eight years, for the cost of just the lumber for the trap.* Since this period of time would certainly be sufficiently long for the Bureau of Land Management to build up its range without interference from the grazing horses, it seemed to me a more practical solution and worthy of further investigation.

With these facts and plenty of film footage of the roan, buckskin, grullo, and mouse-colored wild horses typical of the Pryor Mountain region, I put together a news feature which was aired by the Frank Reynolds Evening News on ABC on July 11, 1968, just six weeks before the scheduled roundup was to take place. For the next month and a half, both ABC and the Bureau of Land Management were deluged with mail from an outraged public.

---

* The United States Cavalry Manual recommends that a one-thousand-pound working horse be fed twelve pounds of hay a day. It is safe to say that an eight-hundred-pound nonworking horse can get along without any difficulty on ten pounds of hay a day. Therefore, it would take one ton of hay a day to feed the two hundred horses in the Pryor Mountains. The U.S. Forest Department operating in the state of Montana sells hay at twelve dollars a ton. For the price of the corral lumber alone (thirty-five thousand dollars) the horses could be fed for eight years. This figure can probably be doubled when one adds the cost of the electric eye and labor to the total cost of the trap.

31. An Aroused Public Fights

Shortly after our news feature was aired, I made a trip to Washington to register a personal protest against the removal of the horses and, in particular, against the method by which the Bureau of Land Management intended to gather them. The B.L.M. officials told me that no decision had as yet been made regarding the horses in the Pryor Mountains and, pending such a final determination, they would make no statement.

When I suggested that, in the meantime, work be stopped on the costly corral, I was told that no corral was under construction.* Since I had seen and photographed the trap myself (it appears in this book), this denial on the part of high-level Government officials did little to increase my confidence in them.

As the trap neared completion, numerous individuals and societies joined in a last effort to save the wild horses. The International Society for the Protection of Mustangs and Burros, the National Mustang Association, American Horse Protection Assoc., Animal Welfare Institute, the International Society for the Protection of Animals and the Humane Society of the United States are a few of the organizations that protested the Government plan to round up the wild horses. Many ABC viewers also called and wrote, asking what they could do to save the animals. Those who contacted the B.L.M. received, by way of reply, printed information sheets and form letters reiterating that the horses were being removed to protect the forage and to save the animals themselves from inevitable starvation. The following is typical of the high-sounding, but misleading, statements that were issued to the public by the B.L.M. officials at this time:

* In a telephone conversation with the public information officer for the Bureau of Land Management a few days later, Mrs. Pearl Twyne, president of the American Horse Protection Association, was also told that no trap was being built.

"We plan to round up all the branded horses in the herd and return them to their owners. What to do with the remaining surplus is a question we are presently exploring. Moving them to other tracts of public domain land has been suggested; but with approximately 17,000 wild horses on the public lands,* our problem is not one of a shortage of horses but rather a shortage of suitable places to put them."

The implications of the above statement would lead one unfamiliar with the facts to conclude that the West is overrun with wild horses, and that they are so numerous, in fact, that they might even become a nuisance. To the majority of American people who are unaware of the vastness of our public domain (453,000,000 acres), seventeen thousand wild horses might indeed sound like a great many animals to be accommodated on the public lands. Certainly such a number could not be contained in a single National Park without creating a great many problems. But the public domain is by no means overcrowded with wildlife. The productive sections of this immense region are presently being utilized almost exclusively by the livestock industry, and it is only in the poorer sections, such as the Pryor Mountain range, that the pitifully few wild horses that have survived the advance of civilization are presently found. Since these rugged areas are unsuited for almost all animals except the hardy wild horses, the problem would appear not to be one of "finding suitable places to put them," but rather to protect the horses that have already proved they can survive where they now exist.

The specific problem, moreover, did not involve "seventeen thousand" wild horses, but was far more limited. Time was running out for the two hundred horses in the Pryor Mountains, yet the Bureau of Land Management remained silent regarding its final decision on how many, if any, of these animals it intended to preserve. In the meantime, work steadily continued on the trap.

In July, Mrs. Pearl Twyne and Mrs. William Blue of the American Horse Protection Association of Washington, D.C., and I conferred with senators and congressmen to ask them to look into the matter and to intervene if they saw reason to do so. Congressmen Baring and Harrison, as well as Senators Mansfield, McGee, Hansen, and Byrd, all made efforts to obtain the real facts regarding the trap-corral under construction and the plan to remove the wild horses.

---

* Although no census had actually been made of the wild horse herds in the West, this arbitrary figure of 17,000 head had been bandied about by the BLM for more than a decade.

But, in reply to their queries, they too received ambiguous generalizations and printed flyers, explaining that the wild horses in the West are not the romantic mustangs you read about, but horses released by farmers during the late thirties when they made the transition from horses to tractors. An accompanying letter explained that a range study made by the Bureau of Land Management indicated that the Pryor Mountain area was seriously overgrazed and eroded, and needed immediate relief from the wild horses that had abused it.

Though many people, including several senators, requested a copy of this range study, it was never forthcoming. Eventually, it was disclosed by a high official in the Bureau of Land Management that the study was not a written report but had been made "by eye" by competent field men.

When this fact came to light, the Humane Society of the United States offered to finance an independent range study by outside scientists to determine impartially the actual conditions of the horses and their habitat. The offer, however, was ignored by the Bureau of Land Management. Their stubborn reluctance to make public either their past range study or their future plans regarding the horse roundup aroused a great deal of suspicion among the horse-loving public. Some suspected that a "deal" had been made between state agencies and the Federal Bureau which the B.L.M. was now having difficulty "weaseling out of."

On August 20 the ranchers in Lovell phoned to say that the corral trap had been completed and the horses could be rounded up and disposed of within a matter of a few hours. On the same day David Dominick, administrative assistant to Senator Clifford Hansen of Wyoming, sent a letter to the director of the Bureau of Land Management in which he said:

"I note from the very extensive file we have accumulated on this subject that you have not written a single letter of substance to Senator Hansen in reply to the many policy questions he has addressed to you and your Bureau. Since the controversy is beginning to reflect so unfavorably on your Bureau, we are sure that you will want to give it your personal attention.

"In addition, we ask that this office be provided with a written report of the range survey conducted by the B.L.M. personnel which apparently led to the conclusion that the horse numbers on this range needed to be reduced.

"Finally we ask that no action be taken with respect to unbranded horses in the Pryor Mountains until an independent range survey can be conducted and analyzed."

On August 21, I received a phone call from the ranchers who informed me that the electric eye on the trap gate had been found defective and, while it was being repaired, the B.L.M. had been delayed in trapping the wild horses. This gave the protest group a few days' grace, but it was now obvious that we could wait no longer for the Bureau of Land Management to reveal its plans.

On August 22 the Humane Society of the United States, through its general counsel, Shaw, Pittman, Ports, Trowbridge and Madden, sent a registered letter to Secretary of the Interior Stewart Udall, asking for his assurance that no action be taken with regard to the wild horses until the Bureau of Land Management had made public its management plan for all animals in that area. The letter said in part: "We do not want to discover next week that these horses have been destroyed and are already on their way to the cannery. Thus, it is not unreasonable that we must ask for your assurances by noon tomorrow, Friday, August 23, 1968. This lacking, we are presently prepared and have no alternative except to seek judicial relief."

To this explicit request, the Humane Society of the United States received no reply. So, five days later, on August 27, Murdaugh Stuart Madden, Esquire, of the Washington law firm, went before Judge George L. Hart of the United States District Court for the District of Columbia and requested that the court enjoin the United States Bureau of Land Management division of the Department of Interior from trapping and destroying the wild mustangs in the Pryor Mountains.

At the hearing photographs of the completed trap were presented as evidence of the Bureau of Land Management's unannounced intention to round up these horses, and photographs of the wild horses and the grass were also shown to demonstrate the fact that the horses were about to be destroyed under a false claim that they were in danger of starvation.

After hearing the case, Judge Hart requested that the two Bureau of Land Management officials present (represented by three United States attorneys from the Justice Department) give assurances under oath that there was no plan to trap or dispose of the animals and that any decision regarding the wild horses would be formally announced with plenty of opportunity for all to be heard and all rights to be preserved. He then denied the request for a temporary restraining order on the grounds that it was premature, but left standing the Humane Society's complaint to prohibit permanently the destruction of the mustangs. Since this ruling would enable the Humane Society to reopen the case at a moment's notice should the Bureau of Land Management announce a decision to remove the wild horses from the Pryor Mountains, the court action was deemed a complete victory by the horse lovers.

The embarrassment to the Department of the Interior caused by this court action can only be guessed. However, if rumors from inside the Department are true, Secretary Udall was extremely displeased with the Bureau of Land Management for flouting the expressed will of the horse-loving public. It is not known to what extent he had been personally informed regarding the wild-horse controversy. Though attempts had been made to reach him directly, and copies of all correspondence with the B.L.M. had been forwarded to him, replies indicated that all such mail had been diverted to the Bureau of Land Management division. Now, however, Secretary Udall took full command of the situation and publicly announced that the Pryor Mountain range would henceforth be designated a Wild Horse Refuge!

Senator Mansfield responded to this good news by publicly congratulating the Bureau of Land Management and printing the entire text of its news announcement in the *Congressional Record* (September 12, 1969). The majority of wild-horse enthusiasts, believing that the battle was won, relaxed and celebrated the victory.

But the·controversy was not to be resolved so quickly or so simply. In a Bureau of Land Management news release, Director Boyd Rasmussen said that the question of how many horses would be allowed to inhabit the new Wild Horse Refuge was still being studied. A committee would be appointed to investigate the condition of the range and the Bureau would await its recommendation.

He wrote: "It is essential that we move ahead immediately to designate these lands to provide federal protection for this national heritage, and as quickly as possible to establish long-term management for both horses and wildlife [game], including a mule deer herd. After signing this designation, Secretary Udall has authorized me to appoint a special Advisory Committee to help us study humane and practical means to operate this range and to advise use of a suitable method to arrive at a balance between the horses and deer and the food available to them. . . .

"Another factor is that forage on 8,000 acres of this area was identified years ago as important for mule deer. Thus I want the best advice possible from a wide range of interest within this committee before developing a multiple use program for the area with our State directors in Montana and Wyoming."

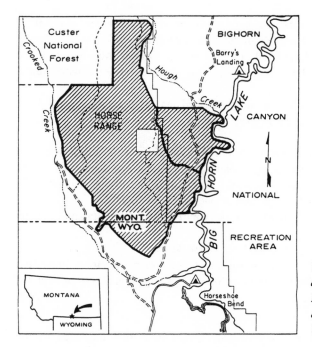

Wild Horse Range set aside in the Pryor Mountains by Secretary of the Interior Stewart Udall.

This statement rearoused apprehension in the minds of wild-horse lovers. Though it was unlikely that the Bureau would now attempt to remove all the horses from the Pryor Mountains, it still remained within their power to reduce the herd drastically to a number too low to be viable. Yet, having been taken to task by the public and, perhaps, even by "higher-ups" of the Department of the Interior, the B.L.M. officials would not be likely to make such a move themselves. Perhaps the only way out of their embarrassing position was to appoint members to the proposed Advisory Committee who would represent both sides of the controversy and let them battle among themselves. It is impossible to know what commitments, if any, the B.L.M. had previously made to state game officials and stockmen's associations, but it is obvious from the appointments made that the B.L.M. felt some obligation to these special-interest groups. The following list of appointments certainly epitomizes how an "immovable object" can be confronted by an "irresistible force":

1. Frank H. Dunkle. Montana Fish and Game Director and author of the plan to plant bighorn sheep in the Pryor Mountain range.
2. William G. Cheney, executive officer of the Montana Livestock

Commission, reported to have been responsible for the removal of hundreds of wild horses from the state of Montana.

3. Dr. Frank Craighead, an authority on wildlife who had done excellent work on bears and is regarded as an expert on environmental research.

4. Clyde Reynolds, the newly elected mayor of Lovell, who did not participate in the fight to save the horses, but turned out to be a wild-horse enthusiast.

5. Dr. Wayne Cook of Colorado State University, an authority on range management. Being a plant specialist, it was feared Dr. Cook would be more concerned about plant life in the Pryors than the wild horses, but such fears, it turned out, were groundless.

6. George L. Turcott, a representative from the Bureau of Land Management.

7. Mrs. Velma Johnston, Wild Horse Annie.

8. Mrs. Pearl Twyne, president of the American Horse Protection Assoc., who helped wage the protest in Washington, D.C., against the removal of the wild horses.

The Committee, it was announced, would hold two meetings in the Pryor Mountain region to view the horses and their habitat, one in the fall of 1968, the other in the early spring of 1969. No action would be taken to reduce the horse herds until the Bureau of Land Management received a full report from this "blue ribbon" Committee and had studied its recommendations.

Though many people viewed the Committee as "stacked," at least the horses had been given a year of grace while the group deliberated their fate. Many horse lovers feared that the two women chosen to represent the wild horses would not be able to hold their own against the professional men who represented other special interests.

But, as is often the case, the women were not to be underestimated. Nor should the integrity of any member of the Committee have been questioned regardless of his persuasion. Dr. Wayne Cook, chairman of the group, was not a man to be swayed by personal considerations or special interests, and much credit for the success of the Committee and its smooth functioning should go to him. Though it was said that some members of the group "crossed swords" at the first meeting, tension eased when it became clear that all sides of the question would be explored impartially.

The first meeting of the Advisory Committee was held in Billings, Montana. Among those in attendance were a number of members of the

Rod and Gun Club, who came to protest the designation of the Pryor Mountain range as a Wild Horse Refuge. In fact, these hunters were bitterly opposed to preserving any wild horses in the region. As one spokesman for the group told the Committee: "Our harvest of game animals has fallen off, and we want the horses *out of there.*"

Denunciations and protests of this character made it clear to the horse lovers just how difficult had been the position of the B.L.M. in the face of determined pressure from both sides!

Though the Montana hunters were given ample opportunity to be heard, significantly it was during this meeting that two facts came to light. First, it was disclosed that the study regarding the decline in surviving fawns and yearlings in ratio to the adult doe population had not even been made in the Pryor Mountains. The count had been taken elsewhere in the state of Montana and was being used as misleading evidence that the wild horses were "overcompeting" with the mule deer in the Pryor Mountain range. This fact absolved the horses from all responsibility for the decline, for even when the deer were later shown to be doing poorly in the Pryor Mountains, the situation, being general, could hardly be blamed on the horses.

At the spring meeting, Dr. Cook took exception to some of the Bureau of Land Management's assumptions regarding the wild horses' effect on the range. Though no one had actually seen the wild horses doing it, they were said to have changed from grazers into browsers, and were accused of eating the mountain mahogany shrubs, which is the deer's chief forage. As evidence of this, the Bureau of Land Management officials pointed to the stunted and unhealthy-looking mahogany brush in the mountains. But Dr. Cook countered by explaining that there are two types of mountain mahogany and the B.L.M. had mistakenly identified the Pryor Mountain plant as the larger variety and therefore believed that it had deteriorated. In actual fact, however, the mountain mahogany in the region, he pointed out, was the smaller type and could even be considered to be in relatively good condition except for an insect parasite that was visible on it. Again the horses were absolved from any responsibility for the damage.

There was no denying by any member of the Committee that the region was eroded and needed building up. Obviously, the Bureau of Land Management had been justified in its concern over the deterioration of the range. But, according to Dr. Cook, the damage had been done fifty to one hundred years earlier and appeared to be the work of domestic sheep. The horses had neither caused this condition, nor were they greatly aggravating it, except for the network of trails they had created in their long treks to

An argument against wild horses?
Hunters' harvest of mule deer declined in 1967.

water. If plastic water tanks could be put into the region to relieve the horses of the necessity of so much traveling in search of water, the trails, he felt, might even heal over.

Since no attempt had ever been made to replant the region, the success of such a positive approach to the problem was speculative. Generally speaking, dropping seeds from the air does little good unless hoofed animals are present in large numbers to trample them into the ground. Horses, it was brought out, can partially serve this function, though less effectively than a large herd of migratory buffalo. Two citizens of Lovell, as a demonstration of the feasibility of planting the region, invited the committee to view a patch of sweet clover they had grown from seeds scattered the previous summer.

When all arguments had been heard, however, the most impressive exhibit of all was the condition of the wild horses themselves. At the fall viewing, the animals appeared sleek and fat, and even in March, when wild horses look thin from wintering on scant feed, it was obvious to all on the Committee that the Pryor Mountain herd was in no danger of starvation.

The only indication that the horses might not be enjoying the best of all possible habitats was evidenced by their low reproductive rate. There were few colts.* The horses, it would seem, were curbing their own population and keeping it in balance with the available forage. It was suggested that this mysterious mechanism of nature be studied and perhaps some information of far-reaching significance might be discovered.

In June of 1969, the Committee was ready to submit its report on the wild horses to the Department of Interior. After ten months of study, it appeared to them that nature had fostered the survival of the creature best suited for this poor habitat, and man could not improve on the plant-animal relationship by substituting another species. Their unanimous recommendation was that the public lands in the Pryor Mountains be retained for the use of wild horses above all other purposes.

The wild horses, of course, did not need to be told by a committee that they were well adapted to their habitat. They'd been living in the Pryor Mountains for as long as any living person could remember.

* Later that year I visited the region and observed a few more colts born since the Committee's visit into the Pryor Mountains.

32. Refuges: The Answer?

Inasmuch as it has become increasingly apparent that no government agency was either funded for or wished to address itself to the problem of wild-horse protection, mustang lovers were coming around to the idea that wild-horse refuges, such as the one recently established in the Pryor Mountains, might provide the best solution for the animal with the peculiar status. Certainly where a wild-horse haunt was too rugged for less hardy animals, there was no reason why the horses should not continue to use it. It was a sad fact, however, that even in these rugged areas, the horses were often hunted and removed by government officials, for the Federal, state, and county bureaus that had jurisdiction over wildlife and wilderness lands were in a state of confusion regarding the wild horse, and three types of negative policies prevailed: permit-to-exist, removal-for-sale, and extermination-on-the-spot.

All three of these policies would ultimately lead to the extinction of the wild horse, for the best did not offer protection from nongovernment interference, and the worst—extermination—was not infrequently practiced by the Federal officials themselves. According to government manuals, wild horses were "in trespass" when found in National Forests or Parks and were sometimes ordered shot. In the following letter, one retired forest ranger expressed his feelings about obeying such an order:

"Controlling their numbers is a distasteful task for anyone who loves horses and has seen these magnificent and intelligent little animals in action in their native haunts. It is no easy task to do away with these last remaining remnants of these rapidly vanishing little horses from the western ranges. There was only one method of eliminating excess numbers of

Mustangs within reasonable safety and cost limits. That was with the use of highpowered rifles under a closing order issued by the Secretary of Agriculture. Describing the problem of too many Mustangs, and recommending that a closing order be issued by the Secretary, was as far as I could ever go in the elimination program. One cannot resist admiring their proudness and tenaciousness and their ability to endure the rigors of deep snows and extremely low temperatures in the high, windswept areas. It is my contention that their willingness to use areas too rough and too far from water to be used by other range animals should entitle them to protection consistent with the available forage supply in these rough areas."

Privately, many government officials had come to share the view of this forest ranger, and in areas where sympathy for the mustang ran high, sporadic attempts had been made to establish refuges for specific bands of horses. The horse-refuge idea had been tried, with varying success, not only by Federal officials, but by county and private organizations as well.

On the East Coast, a wild-horse refuge was set up during the 1930's by citizens of the island town of Chincoteague, Virginia, to protect 150 wild ponies that inhabit the neighboring island of Assateague. The Chincoteague Volunteer Fire Department legally owns, manages, and protects these animals, thought to be diminutive descendants of horses swept overboard during a storm at sea in the seventeenth century. Whether this account of their origin is legend or fact, wild ponies have been eking out a living on the sandy marshes of the Atlantic seacoast island for as long as local citizens can remember.

Since no natural enemies share the ponies' isolated habitat, to keep the herd compatible with available forage, the firemen hold a yearly roundup and sell colts. Vacationing families, many of whom have come to buy a pony for their children, attend the four-day-long festivities which take place during the last week in July. Events begin on Thursday when mounted men ride across the marshy island of Assateague, ferreting out ponies and herding them into the narrow channel that separates the sister islands of Assateague and Chincoteague. As the crowds line the shore, men in boats prod and guide the swimming horses to the opposite bank where, as if by memory from previous years, the wet and snorting animals pull out of the water, and trot down Main Street, heading for the holding pens where they are traditionally confined.

Since every horse in the herd has been handled and penned annually from the time it was a newborn foal, the horses are docile and go through the penning process in an almost perfunctory manner. In some respects,

Confined to swampy lowlands by fencing erected by the United States Fish and Wildlife Service, numbers of Chincoteague ponies were drowned during a severe storm in 1962.

Reluctant pony is forced to ford narrow channel separating two islands.

Colt making its first swim
from Assateague to Chincoteague is checked by mother.

these wild ponies, like the bears in Yellowstone and the deer in Yosemite, are "tame" in the sense that they will stand still for pictures and accept food from human hands. Except for the fact that they forage for their living and stallions battle for their harems of mares, the ponies of Assateague bear little resemblance to the intractable wild mustangs that live in the mountains and deserts of the West and keep out of sight of man.

Nevertheless, the importance of this herd of ponies to the once prosperous seafaring town of Chincoteague is obvious to any visitor during Pony-Penning Week, when motels, restaurants, and souvenir shops do a booming business. Even during the winter months, sightseers come to this off-the-beaten-track island in the hope of catching a glimpse of a wild pony, and the attraction has spared Chincoteague the economic collapse other seacoast towns experienced with the decline of the fishing industry. The refuge itself, however, is nonprofit, and proceeds realized through the sale of colts are used only to manage the herd and to purchase fire-fighting equipment.

The experience of the firemen in their role as private sponsors of a wild-pony refuge has not been one that would encourage others to assume a like burden. According to their accounts, however, trouble did not begin until 1943 when Assateague Island was designated a National Wildlife Refuge. Since that time, a conflict of interests between the private citizens group operating the Pony Refuge and the Federal Fish and Wildlife Service in charge of the island's wild fowl steadily escalated.

Though ponies and ducks had coexisted on Assateague for uncounted decades, their managers had not. To protect their government-built pools, disks, and dikes from being trampled by ponies, the Fish and Wildlife officials began to erect fencing, and thus restricted the ponies' movements and grazing to a small, low, and marshy eastern portion of the nine-thousand-acre island.

One fireman told me: "All has changed from fifteen years ago, and we have had to cope with physical changes created by the Fish and Wildlife that have caused the ponies to be pushed to approximately five percent of the total land area they once enjoyed. The good land management policies that they [the Fish and Wildlife] are always talking about seem to be accompanied by nothing but retreat for us."

The firemen lamented the fact that the fencing done by the Fish and Wildlife Service not only severely curtailed grazing, but also prevented the horses from reaching the ocean surf where they habitually had obtained relief from the swarms of mosquitoes and flies that pester them during the summer months. Moreover, since many of the island's 275 varieties of birds depend on insects for food, no spraying of the area could be done (a restriction that was agreeable to the firemen, however), and so the insect problem had become severe. In addition, the firemen told me the tourists complained that they were seldom able to see the little horses where they were now confined. But the firemen's most serious concern was over the fact that the ponies were imprisoned, so to speak, in a low region where, in the event of a storm, they would not be able to climb to safety.

In March of 1962, the firemen's dire fears were realized when a storm did blow off the Atlantic and tides inundated the lowlands of Assateague. Half of the ponies were trapped by the high water, carried to sea and drowned. Twenty dead ponies later washed up on the shore.

Immediately following this disaster, another storm, this time of letters and telegrams, poured into Chincoteague from children offering to return colts purchased during previous Pony-Penning years in a spontaneous campaign to restore the herd. Several children even parted with pet ponies that had not originated on the island.

This effort on the part of children to restock the decimated pony herd of Assateague did not sit well with the Fish and Wildlife managers. Although, theretofore, they had shown little interest in the historical significance or the economic importance of the pony herd, they now demanded that only those ponies that were genuine descendants of Chincoteague stock be readmitted to the refuge, and any outside blood be immediately removed.

In actual fact, the pony herd was in need of some outbreeding; they had grown small and had lost much of their color variation.* However, the firemen complied by rounding up the horses and removing the unrelated stock. Notwithstanding the attrition, which naturally occurred during the period when the newly introduced animals adjusted to the change from life in a stable to freedom in a rugged environment, the pony herd was soon restored to its original number.

But within six months a letter from the Fish and Wildlife Service forecast more stormy times for the ponies. It read:

"Prior to the March 1962 storm, we recognized that the ponies were causing serious damage to dikes, sand fences, and to water-fowl habitat. The maintenance of sufficient cover on the dike and dune areas is essential if we are to be successful in preserving Assateague Island for any purpose, including waterfowl, other wildlife, recreation, and for the ponies. It is almost impossible to maintain adequate cover to prevent wind erosion

* Nearly all are pintos now.

where there is heavy pony grazing. Within our freshwater impoundments, heavy grazing either seriously reduces or completely eliminates certain desirable waterfowl food plants. Since the March storm, food supplies for waterfowl are greatly reduced, and every effort must be made to restore these as quickly as possible. Unless this is done, the waterfowl population in the area will decline to the extent that hunting on areas adjacent to the refuge will be seriously affected.

"We feel, therefore, that some changes will be needed in the pony grazing program. Someone from this office will be at Chincoteague in the near future to discuss this matter with you and your committee."

In the discussions that ensued the firemen demanded to know how the wild ponies, now occupying a small and treacherous portion of not more than five percent of the island, could be held responsible for the recent damage to the Fish and Wildlife's dikes and dunes.

The Fish and Wildlife, on the other hand, argued that as public officials they had a serious responsibility in the expenditure of the public funds that had been used to build up the birds' nesting habitations, and they went on to say that in particular they felt an obligation to the nation's hunters, who had paid for the original land acquisition through the sale of Duck Stamps.

Since, however, a general appropriation from Congress had also been allotted to the Fish and Wildlife Service to maintain and manage the Refuge, the firemen objected to the preferential treatment that the Federal agency showed to the hunting industry in preserving ducks at the expense of ponies. They wanted to know why the nonhunting public was not given equal consideration.

Though concessions have been made by both the Fish and Wildlife Service and the firemen, the issue has not been resolved.

In 1965, when Congress passed the Assateague Island National Seashore bill, still another bureau of the Department of the Interior, the National Park Service, began to operate on the island and to develop portions of the Maryland section for recreation. Unlike the Fish and Wildlife Service, however, the Park Service did not object to the ponies and permitted them to range freely on the dunes in areas that were put under their jurisdiction. Human beings and ponies, according to the views of these officials, could coexist. As a result, part of the pony herd was granted relief from the crowded conditions brought about through the segregation of ponies and ducks.

Since the Chincoteague experience was an unprecedented experiment on the part of private individuals in sponsoring a wild-horse refuge, I thought it important to hear the firemen's views regarding the feasibility of such a solution for the wild horses in the West. Most thought that privately operated refuges on public lands would not succeed for the reason that special-interest groups with long-established Federal agencies to back them would quickly "best" the private citizens.

"The government can always defend their position with legal terminology," they told me. "They tell us that a wild pony cannot be considered wildlife. Well, it appears to us that the ponies are guilty of acting like wildlife, but for some peculiar reason they just can't be put in that category."

Many horse lovers, after examining all sides of the complicated problem, began to feel that the Federal Bureau of Land Management was the agency best qualified to manage and protect wild horses in refuges which might be established on the public domain lands. Interestingly, immediately after the enactment of the Multiple-Use measure which increased the Bureau's scope, and prior to the confusion and controversy that erupted over the Pryor Mountain wild horses, the B.L.M. was showing signs of a growing interest in just such a plan. In a directive to all district managers on this subject, dated September 5, 1967, Director Boyd Ramussen wrote:

"The Bureau is responsible for the protections, management and improvement of the many public land resources. Wild horses and burros have a high public value and, therefore, herds of these animals will be maintained within a balanced program that considers all other values on the range as well. In the development of multiple-use resource plans, consideration will be given to reservation of forage for wild horses or burros where-it is needed and is definitely in the public interest."

This promising statement did not, however, lead to any positive activity on the part of the Bureau. An earlier B.L.M. experience, which ultimately resulted in the creation of a Federal wild-horse refuge in southwestern Nevada, had taught the Government agency to move with caution on the subject of horses. In 1962, stockmen's organizations had violently opposed a B.L.M. plan to set up a wild-horse refuge on the public lands, and it was with great difficulty that an area was at last found which did not create resentment among the established users of the public domain. The location finally decided upon was the military withdrawal zone used by Nellis Air Force for practice bombing. In announcing its decision to the public, Secretary Udall alluded to the difficulty the Department of the Interior had experienced:

"One of the biggest problems faced by the department in its search for a suitable refuge is competition between wild horses and other stock. Since the Air Force range is already a military withdrawal where domestic animals are not permitted, wild horses and wild game have shared this area in recent years."

According to the Bureau of Land Management officials, danger to the horses by military use of the region was unlikely due to the vastness of the area—435,000 acres. Though air-to-ground bombing and gunnery training is carried out on a portion of the range, other sections are only buffer zones between the public and military activities, and it was supposed by the officials (and hoped by the horse lovers) that the horses would migrate to these regions of safety.

With the help of B.L.M. offices in Reno and Las Vegas, I obtained permission from the military to visit the refuge in 1968, and together with two B.L.M. field workers, Malcolm Charlton and Eddie Mayo, I spent twenty-four hours on the desert range which, incidentally, is sumptuous in plant life and spectacularly beautiful, encircled by red and purple mountains.

Neither of the two B.L.M. men had visited the range previously, so we had some difficulty deciding where to begin searching for horses. Nellis officials had assured us that they were not dropping any bombs between three o'clock on Friday and Monday morning. So at three o'clock sharp we passed through a gate posted: "Restricted Area: Do Not Enter," and headed for the northeast corner of the sprawling range where Charlton and Mayo had been told the horses might be found.

The distances were vast, and the road rough, so it was almost dark before we saw wild horses. Then suddenly in the fading light, three dark shapes loomed in front of us on the road, and when we turned on our headlights, a pure black stallion and a pure white mare and colt were caught in the beam and galloped ahead of the truck for about a hundred yards before veering off into the night.

Since this seemed a good omen, and as it was already almost dark, we decided to stop for the night. When we checked the area, horse droppings and tracks leading to a spring convinced us that we had by sheer luck found the ideal spot for me to hide to await horses at dawn. So we drove the truck about a half-mile beyond the spring and parked in a land depression. Then we unloaded our gear, built a fire, and after a meal of hot coffee and grilled cheese sandwiches, I took my camera equipment and a sleeping bag, said good night, and headed for the spring. With the help of the brilliant desert stars and my flashlight, I picked my way to the water hole and ensconced myself in a clump of sweet-smelling sage where I waited for daybreak.

The two men had assured me that they would be "only a holler away" should I need them, but the bright silence of the desert night was not frightening. I thought about the roving cowboys who had camped on ranges such as this when the nation was young, and I understood why they had loved the West.

After a short sleep, I awoke suddenly, sensing movements around me in the dark, and peered out of my sage screen at vague shapes of animals moving to water. In the dark, I heard a horse blow. Though a cool desert breeze was in my favor, the light was not; I couldn't get a jiggle out of my meter needle. As I lay quietly waiting for the sun and listening to the horses drink, it suddenly occurred to me that the animals were having difficulty getting water. After each slurp, they would pause for a full minute, and I guessed that they were waiting for the spring to fill up again—a drop at a time. Later in the morning when I was able to check this, my guess proved to be correct. The spring was in bad condition and needed to be dug out, but no Duck Stamp fee paid for such a service to wild horses.

When the light grew stronger, I noticed for the first time that two mares and a newborn foal were standing on the opposite bank waiting for their turn at the spring which was too small to accommodate more than the two animals whose drink was in progress. Since no stallion was in the vicinity, I wondered if the mare had left the herd to drop her foal, which appeared to be only a few hours old. The mother was accompanied by a companion mare who took great interest in the little colt.

The foal frisked about on unsteady legs, and after a few minutes of kicking up its heels, folded itself into a tired bundle, legs tucked under, and rested. The mother and "aunt" attended the creature and, from time to time, gazed suspiciously in my direction, but until I actually began to shoot pictures, they did not become alarmed. At the sound of the camera shutter, however, the horses took off over the brow of the hill and were gone—just as two kit foxes, who had been my unwitting neighbors during the night, popped their heads out of a concealed burrow to see what was going on.

All Saturday we drove about the refuge, scanning for horses. Herds were frequently visible on the horizon, but melted like mirages as we jolted across the tough brush with gears grinding, trying to get close enough to photograph them. At last I suggested that the next band sighted I approach on foot, for it began to appear that the horses, perhaps as a result of the

A wild stallion tries to "spook" author as mares (ABOVE)
await outcome on nearby ridge.
(BELOW) Stallion decides to drive mares away from threat.

One domestic horse has been released with a wild band so mustangers can claim all are strays. Note "S" brand on shoulder of far right horse.

military activities here, had learned to give motor vehicles a healthy three-to-five mile berth. The horses, we conjectured, might not be so alarmed at the sight of a two-legged creature picking her way across the desert.

So when Mayo spied a herd of six, I alighted and began circling to stay downwind and out of sight of the horses. After about an hour of walking, I climbed the last land rise that separated the herd from my viewfinder: I was within fifty feet of the six animals, and they had not seen me.

But just as I raised my camera to begin shooting, the stallion noticed me, started, and began to dance in place, all the while snorting and blowing his nostrils clear to get my scent. From his behavior, I was convinced he had never seen a human being before, and since he couldn't pick up my odor from where he was situated, he didn't know how to react.

Horse herds will tolerate the company of antelope and deer and do not automatically flee from every animal that approaches unless their nose reports it to be a dangerous species. Instinctively, however, a wild horse will run the first time he smells man. And once he has connected that odor with man's appearance, the sight of a human being will forever after cause him to flee.

After studying me and pawing the ground for a long minute, the dominant male began to collect his mares, who also were exhibiting curiosity about me, and to move them to a ridge a short distance away. Then he trotted back to a downwind position for further investigation. But when he got to within fifty feet, he stopped in his tracks, gave a low snort, and turned back. Apparently a message had been wafted to him that I was no benign species. Dust enveloped me as he charged uphill, head lowered, ready to bite any mare not quick enough in the retreat he had just commanded. A minute later, when they were already a long distance away, the stallion made one turn to stand me off. He was a beautiful red bay, short coupled, compact, and very Andalusian in appearance.

As I trudged back to where I had left Charlton and Mayo, I noticed the 120-degree heat for the first time and was glad to see the truck headed toward me. But as it approached, I saw that it was a military vehicle. Not until I found myself looking into the suspicious eyes of a Wackenhut security officer, however, did I begin to realize that I had done something wrong.

I am sure that the officer did not believe me when I explained to him that I had just been taking close-up pictures of wild horses and had no interest in military secrets.

"On foot?" was his only comment as he confiscated my film, searched me, and commanded me to open my camera. Then he walked a short distance off and spoke in low tones into a walkie-talkie to someone who blared back orders for him to bring me in.

As we drove toward where I had left Mayo and Charlton, I explained that we had been granted permission from Nellis Air Force to visit the Wild Horse Refuge over the weekend.

"Well, then why aren't you on it?" he asked. I pondered his question and then asked, "Would you please tell me where I am?"

Tight-lipped, he told me, "You're on the Sandia Atomic Testing Range."

After Charlton and Mayo had been picked up, we were taken to a building at the opposite end of the range for further questioning, then given a military escort off the installation. One glance at a map told us we were too far from where we had entered to circle around to the Nellis range for more horse watching. So we headed for Las Vegas.

I was bitterly disappointed over the loss of my film,* but more important, I was concerned over the fact that the wild horses were not only exposed to the hazards of high explosives, but also might be endangered by nuclear fallout. No fence or barrier prevented them from ranging onto the atomic testing ground, as I myself had done. Since Sandia is ringed by the restricted Nellis range, there is no danger that human beings might enter the nuclear test site, and so barricades have not been erected.

Obviously, the so-called wild-horse refuge is anything but a haven for the horses. The very fact that the region is so lovely and alive with creatures compounded the irony of the situation. Coyotes, jackrabbits, badgers, mule deer, bobcats, and ground squirrels, deceived by the absence of man, thrive on the isolated test site. The tranquility and beauty of the region are dazzling. Perennial grasses, long gone from most of the West, stand two feet tall and gleam with health. And though it is hot and dry, portions of the surrounding mountains are piney and cool.

Originally, when the Bureau of Land Management designated this unspoiled region a Wild Horse Refuge, the concept of future development was very much part of their long-range plan. If and when the military is ever withdrawn, 78,620 acres of land will be made available by the B.L.M. to that segment of the American public that is hungry for just such unmarred wilderness.

In a letter to Wild Horse Annie, director Boyd Rasmussen expressed

---

* Through the help of Wild Horse Annie and Congressman Walter Baring, who interceded with the Department of Defense in my behalf, the film was mailed to me in New York a month later.

regret that since 1962 continuing military requirements have thwarted this B.L.M. dream:

"We were well aware of the military requirements at that time," he wrote, "and felt that management of wild horses would be quite compatible since the area is so large. Optimistically, we hoped the military requirements would lessen. Unfortunately, with the world situation what it is today, the Air Force must increase its use of the area and cannot allow public access. For the time being, we must continue the Nevada Wild Horse Range in its present status."

The "present status," however, was just what the wild horse had to be rescued from. For wherever the horses had retreated—whether to desert wasteland, mountain rimrock, or ocean island—their lack of status had followed them and created problems. As a feral animal, the wild horse continued to be regarded by many as an interloper and illegitimate.

It was, therefore, the hope of many long-suffering wild-horse supporters that some responsible agency, perhaps the Bureau of Land Management, would take the curse off this unfortunate designation by granting permanent status and place to the last bands of horses living like hunted fugitives in the West they helped to build.

Since the public-domain lands where wild horses were still found had little economic value, and since this land, in any case, belongs to all of us equally, whether stockmen, hunter, or city dweller, it was the plea of the horse lovers that more refuges be quickly established for the wild horse whose long centuries of service to man had earned it the right and the privilege to return to the wild.

33. *Victory for Wild Horses*

In October of 1970, the first edition of *America's Last Wild Horses* was published and the public's response to the plight of the mustang was overwhelming. I was deluged with mail. Reporters called and wanted the story for their newspapers and magazines. *The Chicago Sun-Times* even ran an editorial on behalf of "The Last 16,000 Horses." I was invited to be a guest on numerous TV programs hosted in Washington, D.C., Boston, Philadelphia, and Providence, as well as in New York City. Many were network programs, such as "The Today Show," "The Arthur Godfrey Show," and "To Tell the Truth," and these brought a nationwide response. I also was asked to speak before such prominent conservation groups as The Sierra Club and such prestigious organizations as The Professional Horsemen's Association of America.

Amidst this flurry of activity, the cause of the wild horse was gaining momentum. But could all this enthusiasm be converted into an effective lobby? Or was the case of the vanishing horse merely a passing *cause célèbre,* a journalistic fad? Would the people, who now were saying they cared, care enough to let their congressmen and senators know their feelings?

Surely the country had awakened to the situation. On November 15, 1970, the New York *Times* carried a front page story titled, "A Devoted Few Strive to Save Wild Horses." This article brought responses from unusual quarters. The Country Art Gallery in Locust Valley, Long Island, contacted me and offered to hold an art benefit for wild horses. They raised enough money to send copies of *America's Last Wild Horses* to every senator in Washington and to one hundred representatives as well.

As a direct result of the New York *Times* article, *My Weekly Reader,* a current events magazine for primary grades, planned several wild horse reports and asked me for illustrations and information. These stories elicited an avalanche of letters from children across the nation. Many contained charming drawings and hand-printed petitions to save the wild mustangs.

As the publicity mounted, it became apparent that the press overwhelmingly supported saving the mustangs. In a few instances, however, the opposition countered. *The Elko Daily Press* in Elko, Nevada, described the movement to protect the mustangs as "a mustang cult of people who get their kicks by generating a warped enthusiasm for wild horses." The members of this cult, the article went on to say, "are led by a character who bills herself as 'Wild Horse Annie' in her press releases."

In Grand Junction, Colorado, *The Daily Sentinel,* after publishing several favorable stories on mustangs, agreed to carry an opposing opinion. The "other side" was expressed by Howard Greager, who gave the following rationale why mustangs should not be protected. He wrote:

"If you run one down and rope it and took a good look at it, this is about what you would see: a fairly small animal not over 850 pounds in weight and most of that belly A huge bulky tail draggin' the ground and so full of thistles and mud and sticks it's a real effort just for the horse to switch it. The mane is about three feet long and snarled by the wind so badly that nothing could ever straighten it out. It is also matted with cockle burrs and sticks of greasewood and shadscale."

Later, when legislation was being studied by committees in Congress, the *Casper Tribune* in Casper, Wyoming, interviewed Wyoming state representative Dean Prosser, who stated that any Federal legislation that might be enacted would be in direct conflict with existing "estray laws," which designate unbranded animals to be the property of appointed livestock commissions to dispose of as they see fit. He added:

"Besides we have gotten a lot of good rodeo horses out of this bunch and we need them."

In the same article, Bill Cheney, executive officer of the Montana Livestock Commission and appointee to the Pryor Mountain Wild Horse Advisory Committee (see description on page 262), came out against preserving any more wild horses, stating categorically that there were no specimens of the original strain of Spanish Mustangs left.

However, public sentiment and the press were clearly on the side of the wild horse, and the opening of 1971 and the convening of the 92nd Congress of the United States saw no waning of interest in this issue.

In January the *National Geographic* carried "On the Track of the West's Wild Horses." *Children's Day, The National Parks and Conservation Magazine, Colorado Magazine, The Reader's Digest* and *Time* followed suit with stories and pictures of the vanishing mustangs. Even the staid *Wall Street Journal* twice featured wild horse articles on its front page.

But were the lawmaker's listening? Letters were pouring in to me from all parts of the United States as well as from foreign countries. Many came from servicemen stationed in Vietnam. I even received a letter from a prison inmate who asked that his voice be added to the public clamor demanding protection for wild horses.

Painstakingly I answered stacks of letters and asked the writers to express their views to their representatives in Congress. I also put them in touch with the American Horse Protection Association and/or Wild Horse Annie's organization, The International Society for the Protection of Mustangs and Burros.*

As a result of all the publicity, these two organizations were also experiencing an unprecedented barrage of mail. In the West, Wild Horse Annie was meeting a full schedule of speaking engagements and in Washington, D.C., Mrs. Pearl Twyne and Mrs. William Blue were systematically calling on congressmen and senators to bring the public sentiment to their attention.

In the meantime, the wild horse population appeared to plummet. After publication of this book, the Bureau of Land Management dropped its estimate of 17,000 wild horses to 16,000. Within six months they again revised the figure to a new low of 10,000. Many horse lovers suspected this drastically lowered figure was inaccurate and that the Bureau of Land Management, fearing the passage of legislation to protect the mustangs, had reduced its count to eliminate numbers of animals from any future program.

On the state level, bills favoring the horses were introduced for yet another year in both Colorado and Nevada only to be defeated as usual. In Roseberg, Oregon, a fourth-grade class astounded everyone by getting a wild horse bill introduced into the Oregon State Legislature for the first time in the history of the state. Their teacher, Miss Joan Bolsinger, after hearing about the vanishing mustangs on the "Today Show," wrote to inform me

---

*After passage of legislation PL 92–195. Wild Horse Annie created a new non-profit organization called W.H.O.A. (Wild Horse Organized Assistance) whose purpose is to provide surveillance against infractions of state and Federal laws for the protection, management and control of wild horses.

that she had adapted her curriculum to the theme of the wild horse. Her pupils quickly proved themselves to be first-rate researchers and lobbyists. But I viewed their efforts with some concern; the children were certain to run into formidable opposition. Would the inevitable defeat of their state bill turn them into cynics?

Predictably the fish and game lobby and the livestock interests were well represented at the hearings in Salem and the Oregon measure was defeated. But the school children were not; they simply converted their energies to the task of influencing the Federal Government to pass legislation. Ultimately, a representative of this fourth-grade class, Lynn Williams, accompanied by Miss Joan Bolsinger, turned up to testify before Congressional hearings on wild horse legislation in Washington, D.C.

Concurrently, horse lovers of all ages were continuing to pressure their representatives, demanding that legislation be passed at once. Congressmen, who had never before heard of a wild horse, reported they were receiving more mail on mustangs than on any other single issue. Senator Henry Jackson counted 14,000 letters on the subject, 9,000 of them from children.

The first congressman to respond to this spontaneous public mandate by introducing legislation was Gilbert Gude of Maryland. As he dropped his bill into the hopper, he told newsmen that his son, Gregory, age twelve, had alerted him to the cause over the dinner table. Within a month, one hundred congressmen had followed suit and either were co-sponsors of the Gude bill or had introduced legislation of their own.

On the Senate side, Senator Gaylord Nelson was the first to draft legislation. Shortly thereafter, Senators Mike Mansfield, Frank Church, Frank Moss, Mark Hatfield, and Henry Jackson drew up similar measures.

Two bills, one sponsored by Congressman Walter S. Baring of Nevada in the House, the other introduced in the Senate by Senators Henry Jackson and Mark Hatfield, were particularly strong. These two closely approximated a sample bill drafted by Wild Horse Annie, the American Horse Protection Association, and myself, which we offered to interested lawmakers as an example of what we thought necessary.

This legislation called for the creation of an entirely new category for animal management. If enacted, it would designate the wild horse an *esthetic resource* and a *national heritage species*.

Since other American wildlife is managed strictly on a commercial basis (either by state managers interested in building larger target herds in order to bring in additional hunting revenue or by Federal predator control agents, who eliminate animals that conceivably might affect the income of the livestock industry),* the creation of such a nonprofit category was certainly revolutionary.

There can be no doubt that the wild horse qualified both as a symbol of our national heritage and as an esthetic resource. It was on the scene during every phase of exploration and was the major factor in the winning and settlement of the West. Its contribution as buffalo runner, warhorse, trail breaker, cow pony, pack mount, cavalry horse and pleasure animal over decades and even centuries certainly entitled it to a prominent place in our history books. This idea was obvious to one child who wrote me the following letter:

> Dear Miss Ryden,
>
> Here's what I don't understand. Long time ago when they had horses for transportation, that's the only way they could get somewhere. And now these horses are being killed. I wonder how they feel, the horses, after doing all that work and risking their own lives in battles. Now why can't they have a little peace and quiet?
>
> Your friend,
> Lisa Beatty

As an esthetic resource, the extraordinary value of a wild horse was perhaps more difficult to define in words. But another child discerned the profound truth behind the concept that beauty is its own excuse for being. She wrote:

> Dear Miss Ryden,
>
> When they ask you what good are they . . . meaning the horses . . . the horses are plenty good. They're beautiful! Consider this please.
>
> Sincerely yours,
> Kathy Burns

With such persuasive support from the American people, the wild horse issue could no longer be ignored by lawmakers. Hearings were scheduled on the various measures that had been introduced, and witnesses were invited to testify before the Senate Committee on Interior and Insular Affairs

---

* Two exceptions to this view of animals by government officials are the management of wildlife in National Parks and the protection of certain species that have become endangered. Restricted by boundaries or numbers, however, these two categories cannot exert a healthful effect on wildlife balances in general.

and before the House Subcommittee on Public Lands on April 19 and 20, 1971. Appearing before these committees were Wild Horse Annie; Mrs. Pearl Twyne; teacher, Joan Bolsinger; professor, Dr. Michael Pontrelli; veterinarian, Dr. James Naviaux; congressman's son, Gregory Gude; myself and many others. Those opposed to wild horse protection were conspicuously absent. The *Wall Street Journal* described the phenomenon in a front page story on April 19, 1971, headlined:

"Opposition vanishes as some kids gang up to save wild horses. Youngsters inundate Congress with mail. Where are the bad guys? They went thataway."

On June 29 the Senate unanimously passed the Jackson-Hatfield bill and on October 4 the House voted approval of the Walter S. Baring measure. Then on December 15, 1971, President Nixon signed PL 92-195, designating the wild horse a national heritage species and an esthetic resource, into law (printed in Appendix A).

At the original conclusion of this book in its first printings, I discussed the seeming impossibility of obtaining protection for wild horses. Greed, exploitation and insensitivity appeared to me to be too formidable an alliance for small groups of dedicated horse lovers to combat. And so I ended the book by posing a rhetorical question: "Who will do it?"

To my surprise, that question has now been answered. Unprompted and with no assets other than pen and heart, the American people heroically defeated vested interests possessing healthy budgets by which they have sought to protect their privileged status. The individuals who, one-by-one, sat down to write their congressmen could not have realized they were forming a powerful lobby. Nor could they have felt they had anything personally to gain by befriending the wild horse. Many stated that they never expected to see one, but that, nevertheless, they wanted to know that wild horses still exist out there. The idea somehow consoled them about America, they said.

Similarly, the idea that such people still exist out there consoled me about America. Through their efforts, the wild horse was given legal protection because it is beautiful, and this in itself may signify a reordering of priorities in America.

34. *A Mustang Massacre*

The wild horses did not live happily ever after. Although the opponents of mustang protection had been caught offguard when the American people steamrolled a wild-horse bill through Congress, those same opponents were not slow to challenge the new law. They quickly moved to do just that in a variety of arenas.

On site, ranchers openly defied the Federal law and conducted round-ups anyway.

In courts of law, livestock associations challenged the legality of the act, claiming that state estray laws superseded Federal authority. That question finally had to be resolved in the United States Supreme Court.

And in Congress, wild-horse opponents moved to weaken the Wild Horse and Burro Act through legislative amendment.

Even while the new law was being flouted, ignored, and undermined on every front, the horse-loving public, pleased over its victory, relaxed its vigilance. The wild horse, it was generally believed, had been saved.

A few people were less sanguine. These individuals were uneasy that the mustang had been entrusted to the care of the Bureau of Land Management. Historically, the B.L.M.'s primary function has been to protect and enhance those vast stretches of public lands leased to livestock growers. Serving in this capacity, the Bureau's range managers have traditionally regarded such grass-eaters as rabbits, wild horses, and prairie dogs to be pests and trespassers on the public domain. Now, Bureau personnel were being asked to reverse their policy toward wild horses and become their protectors. Many people wondered if they would apply themselves to this new responsibility with the same sincerity and dedication that they had devoted to other tasks.

Unfortunately, the Bureau got off to a poor start when one of its district managers orchestrated an illegal wild-horse roundup, which turned out to be one of the bloodiest mustang massacres on record. According to the B.L.M.'s own investigative report—later introduced as evidence in court —this is how it came about:

The new Federal law allowed ranchers 18 months to gather any of their own stock that might have run away and joined the wild-horse bands. B.L.M. district manager Walter Ed Jones seized upon this period of grace to get rid of some 60 unbranded and unclaimed horses that had long roamed freely on Federal land near Howe, Idaho. None of these animals were considered property of any known individual. All should have qualified for protection under the new Wild Horse and Burro Act.

But Jones wanted them removed. So he called a meeting with local ranchers to draw up plans. Rancher William Robison, who held grazing privileges for cattle on the public land where the horses roamed, attended that meeting and later reported that Jones told him to be sure every horse was removed, even if it meant shooting them all. According to others, Jones also assured the assembled men that, to make the roundup appear legal, B.L.M. would be glad to take wrist-slapping action against them for having "domestic" horses "in trespass" on the public lands.

The first two attempts to capture the Howe horses were made by helicopter, in defiance of yet another Federal law then still in effect (The Wild Horse Annie Law *), which prohibited the use of motorized vehicles in roundups. Six animals were corralled by this method. Before being sold to the Central Nebraska Packing Company, two of these were castrated to give them the appearance of being domestic.

The roundup crew then decided to complete the job on saddle horses and snowmobiles. During February of 1973 the wild herd was pursued nearly every day. And, though the mustangs were thin from wintering, 32 continued to outsmart and outrun the grain-fed domestic horses that gave them no rest. But, at last, even these holdouts were driven up a narrow canyon and trapped on a rocky shelf.

Having thus barricaded the horses, the ranchers took the next day off to attend church. On Monday morning when they returned, they discovered some of the animals had plunged over the cliff to their deaths. And

* Wild Horse Annie (Mrs. Velma Johnston) died in the summer of 1977.

those that remained were so panicked by the reappearance of their pursuers, that they began rearing and jumping about until a number had jammed their hoofs into rocks. This situation prompted one of the men to suggest sewing hog rings through the noses of the fettered horses in order to make them more manageable during transport to the cannery. This was done. In the investigative report one of the participants describes the events as follows:

"The white mare was standing there with her feet in the rocks and we thought, well, right now is a good time to put these rings in her nose . . . and we decided we better get her foot out of the rocks. . . . We worked there for up to 30 minutes on her and gave up. . . . So we went to roping these other horses, and the first one we roped was a sorrel mare. And we laid her down right there and put these rings through her nose. And while she was getting up . . . she was flying around there . . . she got her feet caught in the rocks. The next one was a black horse. And we caught him and laid him down. And in the process, we broke his leg. When we turned him up, he floundered and fell over the cliff. Well, we didn't know what to do. We disposed of them by cutting their legs off. I mean it was gruesome. It was pretty tough. We sawed that one sorrel mare's legs off with a chain saw. . . . And now that's the truth. . . . After we brought the remaining horses down from the ledge, we corralled them at Robison's ranch. . . . Then they were loaded in a truck the next morning and hauled to Rexburg and run through the chute. . . . There was a sorrel horse that fell off the cliff that was still alive when we left. We just left her."

Later, to justify their brutality, the ranchers contended that the horses were "worthless, starving to death . . . only good for dog food." Yet it had taken a crew of 18 men using relays of fresh saddle horses, snowmobiles, and even helicopters, 45 days to trap them. Moreover, had it not been for the treacherous terrain, many mustangs still might have eluded their pursuers.

The horses that survived all this were shipped to Central Nebraska Packing House and inspected by a state brand inspector. None showed brands. And since no bills of sale accompanied the shipment, three of the ranchers were asked to sign a certificate of ownership. They did. No further proof of ownership was demanded.

And so the matter might have ended, but for the fact that a number of dead and mutilated horses were discovered at the foot of that Idaho cliff. An aborted foal was among the remains. Some of the horses had hog rings sewn through their noses.

The Humane Society of the United States was called to the scene. Photographs of the carnage were taken and published widely. It was the first violation of the enthusiastically supported Wild Horse and Burro Act. The public was keenly interested to know if the new law meant anything. Would the violators be brought to justice?

The Bureau of Land Management, together with the United States Forest Service, responded to the uproar by preparing a joint investigative report on the incident. But despite the incriminating evidence it contained, the United States Attorney in Idaho declined to prosecute.

At this point the American Horse Protection Association and the Humane Society of the United States, appalled by the Government's refusal to enforce the law, got into the act. They filed suit against the Department of the Interior, the Department of Agriculture, and several Government officials, accusing them of misfeasance and failure to protect the wild horses.

The case moved slowly. At first, much time, money, and effort had to be spent obtaining the Government's own investigative report of the incident. Not until a Federal court directed it to do so would the B.L.M. turn over this damning evidence. And only then could the real issues be examined.

So began a four-year suit, which ended in February of 1977 when a United States appeals court overturned a lower court decision. But even at this late date, victory in the appeals court did not carry with it the satisfaction that the offenders would be brought to justice. It merely opened the way for further proceedings by declaring that the decision-making authority over wild horses belongs, not to the states, but to the Federal Government.

Meanwhile, only 11 victims of the brutal roundup were still alive, impounded as evidence in a stockyard corral in Idaho. Joan Blue, president of the American Horse Protection Association, had to make a hard decision. Further court action might bring the offenders to justice, but the imprisoned mustangs were in poor condition and could not be served by more delay.

Mrs. Blue decided to agree to a settlement. In exchange for custody of these pitiful creatures, the American Horse Protection Association dropped its suit. The 11 unkempt and broken-spirited horses were then turned over to Mrs. Blue for placement on private farms. Not, however, before she had consented to sign the following outrageous stipulation drawn up by someone in the United States Bureau of Land Management:

"These animals shall not be used for purpose of publicity by the assignee or by the individual having custody, or made available to any other person or organization for such purpose, including photographs, articles, exhibitions, newspapers, newsletters, congressional hearings [!], posters, or any other printed material or similar uses for fund raising, membership drives, etc., except there will be one story which may be published, to which story B.L.M. agrees."

One wonders if the Government employee who drafted this strange document knows that it violates the United States Constitution. It also makes a mockery of the independence of Congress by specifying that information be denied to committee members. One would have hoped our public servants better understood the meaning of an open society.

That the B.L.M. would want the public to forget all about the Howe massacre is not hard to understand. It is also obvious why the B.L.M. would not want the 11 survivors of that gory event to serve as reminders of the Government's role in it. Better the public remain ignorant of how truly lovely were the wild horses in that Idaho herd, wiped out at the Government's direction.

For today, after several months of pasture life, survivors of the Howe massacre are unrecognizable. Restored to health, they have lost the hangdog look they wore during their long confinement in a packing-house stockyard. Tone has returned to their muscles, defiance to their spirits. Their hides glisten. They behave like the wild horses they were born to be.

One wonders, do they remember past events on the Idaho mountain?

Some say horses' memories are mercifully short. Would that the same were true for the rest of us. It is not easy to live with the hard truth that no one received so much as a fine for breaking the Wild Horse and Burro Act and cruelly smashing one of America's finest herds of wild horses.

Even before the case of the Howe horses was resolved, another challenge to the Wild Horse and Burro Act was in the courts. It grew out of the capture of 19 unbranded and unclaimed burros near Roswell, New Mexico, in 1975. The animals were sold at public auction by the New Mexico Livestock Board.

The United States Bureau of Land Management, claiming ownership of the burros under the Wild Horse and Burro Act, demanded the animals be recovered and returned to the public lands. The New Mexico

Livestock Board refused. Instead it, too, laid claim to the animals under its own state estray law. The matter was put to a court test.

To the consternation of the mustang-loving public, a Federal district court in Albuquerque upheld New Mexico's claim. The three-judge panel declared the Federal Wild Horse and Burro Act unconstitutional!

"Wild horses and burros," the judges wrote, "do not become the property of the United States simply by being physically present on the territory and land of the United States. . . . The doctrine of common law has been that wild animals are owned by the state in its sovereign capacity."

This decision, rendered in March of 1975, put mustang supporters back on square one. Once again the wild horse was without legal status and protection.

But the implications of the decision went even beyond the question of mustang protection. If, in enacting the Wild Horse and Burro Act, the Federal Government had indeed exceeded its authority and encroached on the states' prerogative to regulate wild animals, then conceivably, all Federal regulations concerning wildlife might become invalid. Perhaps the states could force the Federal Government to open national parks and refuges to hunting. Other congressional acts, such as the Marine Mammal Act, might also be challenged.

Whatever negative attitudes the B.L.M. might still have harbored toward mustangs, too much was at stake for the Government to lose this case. The interests of the National Park Service and Fish and Wildlife Service had to be defended. Secretary Rogers C. B. Morton filed an appeal, and the Supreme Court of the United States agreed to hear the arguments. The single issue being examined was:

"Does the property clause of the United States grant Congress authority to regulate wildlife on Federal land?"

The state of New Mexico said no. At the same time it maintained that the Federal Government possessed the right—even the obligation—to protect vegetation on the public domain. To this end, New Mexico saw no inconsistency in its stand that the Federal Government possessed authority to *kill* wild animals that might be overgrazing; but *protection* of wildlife she deemed outside Federal jurisdiction.

It was at this stage that I personally became involved. As an *amicus curiae* (a friend of the court), I was given permission to present a brief of my own. With the help of a friend and constitutional lawyer, Mr. William Muir, I prepared arguments in support of the Federal Government. Several humane organizations did likewise.

On the other side, New Mexico was joined by the states of Idaho and Wyoming. Wyoming and Nevada livestock boards also presented briefs. The lines were once again drawn between the consumers and the nonconsumptive users of the public domain.

But the case boomeranged for the states. In a unanimous decision, the Supreme Court of the United States not only upheld the Federal wildhorse law, the nine judges sweepingly defined Federal authority over wildlife on public lands as being superior to that of the states. New Mexico's bold attempt to invalidate the Wild Horse and Burro Act inadvertently undermined the longstanding assumption of state ownership of wildlife.

This upset threw sportsmen into a panic. John Gottschalk, head of the International Association of Game Fish and Conservation Commissioners, darkly warned the press:

"Anything can happen! Any attempt to require Federal fish and game licenses on Federal lands would run into one hell of a fight."

Even the victorious B.L.M. in whose name the suit had been won was taken aback by the scope of the decision. B.L.M.'s George Lea tried to assuage the fears of the hunting groups:

"I hope to hell the court decision doesn't disrupt our good relationships with state wildlifers," he said. "We have made beautiful music together for a long time."

Lea went on to express hope that a provision tacked on the B.L.M. Organic Act would ride through Congress unchallenged. This provision, which passed with no difficulty, invalidated the Wild Horse Annie Act of 1959, thus permitting the B.L.M. the use of aircraft and motorized vehicles to clear the public lands of excess wild horses.

It appeared to those familiar with the issues that the wild horses' new managers were laying groundwork to cull large numbers of mustangs. The public, meanwhile, satisfied that the Wild Horse and Burro Act was still intact, was not prepared for the events that followed.

35. *Twenty Years of Mustang Mismanagement*

It was 1977 and across the West traps, corrals and holding pens pocked the desolate beauty of the wild terrain where, during the heyday of the horse-runners, mustangs established their last strongholds. Six years had passed since the United States Congress had passed legislation to protect wild and free-roaming horses and burros, and the United States Bureau of Land Management was routing the animals from their isolated retreats. Wranglers and helicopter pilots were hired to ferret out and chase them across long distances until they could be herded into holding pens. BLM plans were to cut herds in Nevada by two-thirds. In Oregon, reductions were also to be radical. And along Wyoming's Red Desert, oversized holding pens were constructed to accommodate all the horses being gathered in Colorado, as well as those caught in Wyoming. The reason given? A purported wild horse population explosion, coupled with a persistent drought in the Western states.

These roundups drew a mixed reaction from the public. Newspapers obligingly reported them, together with the Bureau's plan to put "excessed" horses up for adoption. It made good copy. According to the BLM more people were seeking to adopt animals than it was planning to gather; A waiting list of 8,000 names had been compiled.

But there were skeptics. Some accused the Government of using the 1977 drought as an excuse to rid the public lands of a nontarget, noncommercial animal. They pointed out that no one was reducing the deer population, numbering some 1.5 million head, which also inhabited the public domain. Nor did anyone suggest that drought conditions necessitated the culling of the 250,000 antelope that resided there. Yet some 65,000 wild horses and burros—the figure was the Bureau's—were viewed as too many for the thirsty land to carry.

But there was an even more fundamental reason for questioning the

BLM's drive to remove so many horses. The Bureau's counts were unreliable. Such fantastic increases as it had reported since the passage of the Wild and Free Roaming Horse and Burro Act in 1971 could not have occurred. That is if the Bureau's own base-line figures could be believed. For back in 1971 during Congressional hearings on legislation to protect horses and burros, the Bureau had insisted that only 17,000 of these animals inhabited the public domain (9,500 horses and 7,500 burros). Given that a wild mare does not give birth to more than one foal a year, and that mares do not breed until age three, and that stallions and foals and nonbreeding females under age-three comprise some eighty percent of a normal mustang population, the horse herds could not have grown to more than 29,000 head by 1977. Even that figure required one to accept an incredible premise: that every mare of breeding age had produced a live foal annually and that no horse had died of any cause whatsoever in six years time.

Obviously something was wrong. Either the BLM had grossly underestimated the 1971 wild horse and burro population or its 1977 tally was highly inflated. I had reason to suspect both figures were off and that the truth lay somewhere in the middle. It is worth noting that in 1971 at hearings on the Wild and Free-Roaming Horse and Burro Act I publicly challenged the BLM's low horse count and requested that the following statement be entered in the Congressional Record:

"I hope that this drastically lowered figure is not an attempt on the part of the Bureau to arbitrarily eliminate numbers of horses from any future program."

My statement turned out to be a prophesy. In 1977 the BLM did indeed announce its intention to cut horses and burros back to the number it had purported to be in existence in 1971 and to maintain them at that low level. This despite an earlier admission by the Bureau in 1975 that "the number of such animals using public lands is substantially greater than preliminary estimates made just prior to passage of the Wild Horse Act" (Congressional Record 12/18/75) * Moreover, nothing in the legislative history of the Wild and Free-Roaming Horse and Burro Act suggested that Congress intended to preserve only as many animals as existed when it enacted legislation to preserve them.

* In 1981 the BLM revised its estimate of how many wild equines it could accommodate in its planning process to 25,000 wild horses and 5,000 wild burros. These target numbers were as arbitrary as the 17,000 figure the Bureau had set in 1977. They were arrived at, not through environmental analysis, but pulled out-of-a-Stetson, so to speak.

Humane groups and horse-lovers asked the Bureau to present an Environmental Impact Statement to support the need for such drastic cuts. None was forthcoming. Along with others, I tried to persuade the BLM to seek alternative methods of capture. The airborne roundups that had already proceeded were creating injuries and causing pregnant mares to abort. It seemed to me that trapping horses in corrals built around watering holes would not only be less stressful on the animals, but would be a more selective method of capture. Instead of making a vast sweep of a given area and hauling away whatever number and type of horses could be herded by helicopter into huge holding pens, water trapping would provide an opportunity to gather adoptable animals on a gradual basis.

To elaborate: When a stallion would bring his harem to water, a gate would be triggered to drop behind them. A mare or two could then be singled out and removed to an adoption center and the rest turned free. The following night another harem could be trapped in the same way, a mare or two culled, and so on. This kind of slow operation offered the following advantages: (One) Because the released horses would afterwards return to their own home ranges and in fewer numbers, the distribution of animals across the land would not only be reduced but would remain even. (Two) Only those young animals most desired by would-be adopters need be removed. The old, the lame, and untamable stallions need not be brought to holding pens at all. (3) In the long run, fewer animals would have to be gathered to maintain a population at a lower level, for by skewing the sex ratio of a herd in favor of males, the BLM could slow and maybe even halt annual increase.*

The BLM, however, rejected these suggestions and continued with its roundups. Horse-lovers grew alarmed. For one thing, the Adopt-A-Horse program was not set up to deal with such a large and sudden influx of animals. The American Horse Protection Association and the Humane

---

* To see how this works, imagine a hypothetical horse herd of 100 sexually mature animals in which 10 are mares and 90 are stallions. Only 10 foals can possibly be born in a year's time, for a mare's gestation period is 11 months. Now reverse the sex ratio so that it consists of 90 mares and 10 stallions. Ninety foals can be added to the herd! The aim of a livestock grower is to produce as many animals for market as quickly as possible. He does this by maintaining herds that are almost entirely female. By reversing this strategy to favor males, the BLM could achieve the opposite effect and slow reproduction.

Society of the United States warned that the program would founder under such an inventory. Their concerns, however, fell on deaf ears.

That fall I spent three weeks in Nevada observing the wild horses, BLM's procedures for handling them, and the condition of the range. What I discovered conflicted with BLM reports. The drought, I discovered, was largely a myth. Although in certain agricultural areas water was in short supply from the unusually light snow fields in the Sierra Nevadas, plenty of rain had fallen on the open range. And the wild horses, purported by the BLM to be in poor condition, were in fine shape. Such was not the case, however, with the large number of mustangs the BLM had already rounded up.

At the Palomino Valley holding corrals near Sparks, Nevada, I observed more than 600 horses, as many as 100 to a single pen, awaiting death or adoption. The animals that had so delighted me in their wild state, were standing about in crowded, dusty corrals—their heads hanging, their eyes dull. Lacking space to run or grass to nip, they seemed to have lost their will to live.

Stallions were corraled in a pen apart from mares and their distress was agonizing to watch. Some kicked and bit each other. Others looked through the rails, whinneying and nickering in an effort to maintain long distance contact with their harems. Many were severely bruised from fighting and nearly all were so badly chewed that large patches of bare hide were exposed. In that pen of wild studs, I observed a lone frightened mare.

Females were corraled nearby in three very large pens. The sick, the lame and mares-with-foals were not segregated—a situation that created much stress at feeding time when hay was tossed over the rail onto the ground. It was a first-come, first-serve proposition, and in the crush that resulted, many mares had difficulty protecting their foals from injury. The strong animals fed well. Weaker animals ate dirt in an attempt to obtain left-over chaff. This method of feeding not only created chaos, it certainly promoted parasitical diseases, for the hay inadvertently became mixed with horse droppings. Moreover, some horses had become impacted as a result of eating dirt. I saw one such victim sorely in need of medical attention, but none was forthcoming. (Meanwhile alongside these holding facilities, near-empty pens housed horses belonging to BLM personnel. These animals were served oats in feeding troughs.)

When a torrent of rain fell, the dusty corrals turned into a slough.

Badly chewed stallion in BLM holding corral eats dirt to obtain leftover chaff.

Adult horses stood in mud up to their fetlocks: foals were sucked down to their knees. What would-be adopters had found their way to this spectacle, were not keen on taking any of the dispirited and unhealthy looking mustangs on view. I could hardly blame them. A large number of the animals had been living in these appalling conditions for nine months, during which time no attempt had been made to gentle them.

Predictably, under such conditions, some ailing horses would have to be destroyed. I was not surprised, therefore, to discover a large gravel pit containing dead mustangs of every age class, all of which had been shot by the BLM. I was unable to determine how many animals were in the pit, since gravel had been bulldozed over layers of bodies. A hoof of a small foal gave proof that young as well as old had been sacrificed in this management program. I was most disturbed, however, over information I received about a perfectly healthy, yearling filly that had been rescued from this fate only through the persistence of a determined adopter. He demanded that she be removed from a trailerload of horses headed for the pit. An eye-witness told me that once there, the filly would have had to await her turn to be shot through the trailer slats, while being present to the deaths of the other horses, packed flank by flank, in the vehicle. I was invited to see and photograph that rescued yearling. There was nothing wrong with her.

That grim trip to Nevada in the fall of 1977 produced more shocks. While there, I received a tip that a number of wild horses had been shot on the range, so I visited the site, where I succeeded in locating eight corpses of horses with bullet holes in their heads. By aging teeth, I determined that all but one had been under four-years-old and so would have qualified as adoptable mustangs. A clipping from a small town weekly carried the boastful admission by a BLM employee that he had been responsible for the act. Finally, I learned of two wild mares bearing the government's official wild horse brand at a livestock auction in Fallon, Nevada. The BLM explained that the sale of those animals had been a mistake.

Meanwhile, I was not the only one uncovering evidence that the BLM's Adopt-A-Horse program was turning into a mass liquidation of mustang populations. Investigators from the Humane Society of the United States and from the American Horse Protection Association ascertained that of the 10,000 wild horses taken from the Western range during 1977 and 1978, 35% went to "lot adopters" who had no intention of making pets of them. In January of 1978 these investigators observed 45 head of horses

(Above) Author's shadow overhangs a cluster of horses that have been shot dumped into a pit by BLM. (Below) Mustang shot on the range (discovered by the author).

This photograph of a trench full of executed mustangs, discovered by American Horse Protection Association investigator Gail Snider, is presented in court as evidence of BLM abuses.

being loaded at the Palomino Valley holding corral, ostensibly destined for a ranch in Oklahoma. They never arrived and that was the last anyone saw of them. About then, a high level BLM official, who asked to remain anonymous, told AHPA that at least 50% of the wild horses being adopted out were ending up in "killer plants."

I was sickened by all of this and so agreed to appear as an expert witness in an American Horse Protection Association lawsuit, challenging the BLM's need to conduct such massive horse removals. The judge who heard testimony in the U.S. District Court in Nevada granted only partial relief. He ordered that feeding racks be installed in the holding corrals, that horses be killed by injection only, and that no horse be killed without a veterinarian's certificate. He refused, however, to grant AHPA's request that all roundups be halted pending the preparation of an Environmental Impact Statement. As a result, AHPA appealed this part of the decision and litigation dragged on for two more years. By the time a Federal Court of Appeals reversed the lower court's decision, the horses were long gone.

Although this victory was a Pyrrhic one, nevertheless, the BLM did, as a result, correct many abuses in its Palomino Valley holding facility. It also made an effort to facilitate adoptions by shipping horses to holding corrals set up in Lewisburg, Pennsylvania, and in Cross Plains, Tennessee.

Meanwhile, a legislative event gained political support for the Bureau's drastic horse removal policy. Congressional hearings were held on the Public Rangelands Improvement Act, and United States senators and representatives, alarmed by the testimony they heard regarding the poor condition of the public domain, seized on any possible means of correcting the situation. When the BLM recommended more massive wild horse reductions, Congress again appropriated funds for that purpose without questioning what part the horses were actually playing in the depredation of the public rangelands. Over the next few years so many animals were removed that horse lovers wondered if the public range was being cleared of *all* mustangs. Certainly, the holding corrals looked that way.

Still the BLM would not slow down on roundups. Instead it argued that the overcrowded corrals could be quickly and efficiently emptied if Congress would only amend the Wild and Free Roaming Horse and Burro Act so as to grant the Bureau sales authority over the wretched creatures. Knowing that such a change would result in horses being funneled directly to canneries, I visited Washington D.C. to register my protest to

BLM director Robert Burford.

"Do you think the American public would like to see wild horses sold for dogfood?" I asked. "I thought they made their position clear on that point ten years ago."

"Well, public reaction is a problem, all right," he agreed, "but there are markets overseas."

There could be little doubt that the horse removals were politically motivated. During the early 1980s Secretary of Interior James Watt made no secret of his agenda—the transfer of public lands into private hands, calling it a "sage brush rebellion." In keeping with this philosophy, many concessions were made to Western livestock growers who wanted more public grass for their private herds. Senator James McClure of Idaho, a voice for the powerful stockmen's lobby, led the crusade.

Between 1981 and 1984, Senator McClure repeatedly introduced or supported legislation that would have effectively repealed the Wild Horse Act. When the Senate failed to take action on any of his measures, McClure made an end run around the legislative process by way of the Senate Appropriations Committee. Although the BLM had requested funding of $5 million for wild horse and burro management (to be spent during fiscal year 1985), Senator McClure saw to it that $25,000,000 was appropriated for that purpose. A joint house and senate committee did manage to reduce that sum to $17,000,000—still a staggering amount, particularly in light of the Reagan Administration's agenda to reduce government spending. When a Western newspaper questioned Senator McClure about this extraordinary budget item, he responded that the size of the appropriation ought to make the American public realize that the Wild and Free Roaming Horse and Burro Act should be repealed.

Now there was no lack of money to pay for helicopter chase planes, hired cowboys, corrals, and horse feed. The problem was how to spend the millions fast enough. Nevertheless, the BLM did not wish to be embarrassed by another lawsuit calling attention to its crowded pens, for adoptions were unable to keep pace with roundups. When the Bureau's campaign to obtain sales authority failed to gain support, it arbitrarily dropped its $125 adoption fee to anyone willing to take more than four horses at a time, and within weeks ranchers were hauling away "free" wild horses, one hundred head at a time. This despite a provision in the Wild and Free Roaming Horse and Burro Act prohibiting any individual from adopting more than four horses in a single year—a provision meant to prevent commercial interests from "adopting" horses for profit. To "legitimize" these transactions, the BLM asked ranchers to provide the names of family members, each one of whom could be listed as an adopter of four horses. According to BLM records between 1984 and 1987, 14,900 horses went to such "lot adopters."*

Clearly, the U. S. government was now party to the very activity the Wild and Free-Roaming Horse and Burro Act had been designed to end, for after a one-year waiting period, these "lot adopters" were free to dispose of their charges as they pleased, and most were sold to slaughterhouses. Meanwhile during the holding period, it was anybody's guess what kind of care the horses received, for the BLM was certainly not set up to monitor what happened to animals after they were carted away. According to a 1990 General Accounting Office Report this lack of follow-up resulted in "the inhumane treatment and death of 100s of horses during the one year period [that] . . . they were still owned by the government."

Then in 1985, after spending its $17,000,000 windfall (courtesy Senator McClure), the BLM returned to Congress to report that wild horses were again on the increase. According to its counts, numbers had again reached 60,000 head. And again the Congressional Appropriations Committee failed to question either the Bureau's tallies or its methods of control with the result that over the next five years $81,000,000 was appropriated to the BLM to round up 59,000 more wild horses.

However problematical were the BLM's horse counts, its declared inability to bring down the numbers it was reporting, despite millions of dollars spent, ought to have suggested to Congress that something was amiss. At the very least, it should have raised some questions regarding the Bureau's understanding of wildlife population dynamics.

Most BLM personnel are range managers and have little training in wildlife biology. What strategies they employ to deal with horses have been borrowed from game managers, whose aims are exactly opposite to theirs. Game managers do not try to *reduce* populations, but are in the business of manipulating environment and social factors to produce *surplus* animals for harvest. The BLM, by employing these techniques, was unwittingly creating exactly that result, namely, giving a boost to the horses' reproductive capacity. For horses, like all wild grazing animals,

---

*In 1986 I visited a holding corral in Montana which contained scores of horses· in transit to a single rancher in that state. When I questioned BLM district manager Jerry Jack about adopting out so many horses to a single party, he replied that such action was perfectly legal.

respond to cues in their environment that dictate how high or how low birth and death rates will be.

To understand how this works, it is useful to look at *un*managed, self-regulating populations, whose numbers rise and fall cyclically around a homeostatic norm. During periods of growth, these self-regulating populations become progressively more dense and, concurrently, their members experience increased social stress from crowding. At the same time, food becomes less available. At a certain critical high, these "limiting factors," together with weather cycles, trigger a rise in deaths from all causes and a slowdown in births. For some time afterward, while the animals remain at a lowered and less stressful density, vegetation has a chance to recover. Then once again the population begins to climb until it reaches the carrying capacity of the range and another sharp decline is triggered.

Game managers understand these dynamics well and indeed manipulate them to hold populations in a productive phase, thus assuring an annual surplus of animals to be hunted. Their methods are simple enough and strikingly similar to those employed by the BLM, whose aim is exactly opposite. First, they do what they can to maintain habitat in prime condition (in the case of deer, this may call for burning or cutting of forests and even the planting of rye fields). Secondly, they hold target populations at densities below that which would trigger a drop in the birth rate (accomplished easily enough by hunting them in the fall). Thus annual hunts, instead of reducing numbers as many suppose, actually produces a bumper crop of young to be hunted in the future.

It was foreseeable then that wild horse populations, which were being subjected to annual "hunts," would compensate for deep cuts in their numbers with high reproductive rates. Moreover, when range conditions appeared to be less than prime, the BLM immediately instigated horse removals. Yet Bureau personnel seemed perplexed by the fecundity of the wild horse and continued to defeat its own ends by employing these wrong strategies.

In 1986 there were 12,500 wild horses in holding corrals awaiting adoption. Of these, 1,300 (or 11%) were destroyed, suggesting the possibility that the Bureau might be overstepping its authority by killing animals that were not sick or injured or aged. That year the public began to wake up to the problem of too many penned horses. The Fund for Animals and the Animal Protection Institute took the BLM to court and succeeded in halting "lot adoptions" to ranchers. During the proceedings the BLM acknowledged that it was aware that ranchers were selling "adopted" horses for slaughter, but insisted that it had violated no law by giving them animals.

Judge Howard McKibben of the U.S. District Court in Reno, thought otherwise. In his findings he stated that such sales were "contrary to the legislative intent of the 1971 Wild and Free Roaming Horse and Burro Act," and added that the BLM "may not abdicate responsibility to place the animals with 'qualified individuals' . . . someone who will care for the animals, not someone who will exploit or destroy them."

While the BLM was appealing this decision, a television journalist from Minneapolis brought the story of "lot adoptions" into American living rooms. The public uproar that resulted caused the Bureau to rethink its policy. It suspended the horse-giveaways, at least temporarily. In the fall of 1988 the Appeals Court ruled against the BLM. Events, it seemed, were conspiring to make the Bureau accountable for the horses it was warehousing.

But what to do with all the animals? What was desperately needed was an aggressive advertising program to attract potential adopters to existing holding facilities. Also, horses needed to be showcased in more populated areas. To its credit, the BLM did take some steps toward facilitating legitimate adoptions. A new adoption center was opened in the East in London, Ohio. And a program was put in place at a Colorado prison whereby inmates worked to gentle and halter-break horses, making them more attractive to potential adopters.

As creative as this last idea was, it still attacked only the symptom of the problem (too many horses in crowded pens), not its cause (too many roundups). And because the general public failed to question the BLM's premise that too many horses were eating too much grass on public lands, public focus remained the same: how to help the BLM control or dispose of massive numbers of animals.

One idea that had been around before, fertility control*, was seized

---

*An earlier attempt was made by researchers from Eastern Montana State University to render stallions temporarily infertile. The assumption was that the possessive behavior of a wild stallion would prevent his harem mares from becoming impregnated by other males. Though the chemical prophylactics they developed were effective, it is questionable whether the scheme would reduce birth rates. My guess is that unless every stallion in a herd were to be rendered infertile, every mare in that herd would find a willing partner to impregnate her. I base this on two biological facts. Wild mares that fail to conceive will ovulate month after month and will "present" incessantly until they succeed in becoming pregnant. And stallion or no, wild mares frequently slip away from their harems to mate with young studs who are ever at-the-ready.

upon by numerous researchers looking for field studies to do. A government grant was given to a team from the University of Minnesota to conduct research on horses in Nevada, which in the end produced nothing. What's more, the study turned out to be as cruel as it was inept. Not only did it require that surgery be performed on wild mares in the field (30 out of 100 of the animals operated on died), the too-tight collars placed around the horses' necks caused infections that killed many more of them. To make matters worse, these lethal collars were printed with numbers too tiny to be read from any distance. As a result, horses were continually buzzed by low flying helicopters, which created havoc among them and caused more deaths. The final blow occurred when the researchers killed a bunch of horses by penning them without water after chasing them for fifteen miles in ninety-degree heat. Nevada's Governor Bob Miller complained to the National Academy of Science, and the BLM terminated the study.

Another approach to reducing the large numbers of horses waiting in BLM holding facilities was put forward by Dayton Hyde, an Oregon rancher. He proposed that the animals be placed in sanctuaries, which could be financed and operated by the private sector. The BLM responded positively to this idea. Not only could it solve the problem of how to dispose of the large number of horses being gathered, it could divert public attention from a more substantive issue: whether or not such drastic horse removals were warranted in the first place. Even more to the point, it could prevent examination of a question that was politically sticky: just which animals were actually responsible for the deterioration of the public range lands?

From 1981 to 1988 more than 4,350,000 domestic livestock grazed annually on the 41.5 million acres of public lands in the ten Western states where wild horses and burros are found. In addition, approximately 2,000,000 antelope, deer, elk and other large wild animals inhabited this public domain. Yet 60,000 wild horses were held to be responsible for the overgrazing of the nation's rangelands. To put these numbers into perspective, wild horses and burros did not even represent 1% of the large grazing animals on a vast public domain that, in aggregate, is equal in size to all of France. By contrast, privately-owned livestock added up to 68% of the grazing animals found there. And game animals, whose numbers were being promoted by every means known to wildlife biologists*, made up the remaining 31% of the pie.

---

* While 60,000 wild horses were being cut by more than half, 50,000 desert bighorn sheep were listed as endangered and every effort was made to bolster their numbers.

Clearly, all the land abuse occurring in the West could not have been caused by wild horses—a point that found confirmation in the National Academy of Science's Committee on Wild, Free-Roaming Horses and Burros's Final Report. That impartial committee of blue-ribbon scientists, appointed by Congress to make a thorough study of the wild horse situation, reported finding "very few (wild horse) areas with heavy vegetation impacts, although we have asked the BLM to show them to us." Moreover, the chairman of that committee, Dr. Frederick H. Wagner, in a paper presented at the North American Wildlife and Natural Resources Conference in March of 1983, questioned the need for 50% horse reductions and described the BLM's target population of 25,000 horses as being "curious, particularly since the BLM was not able to show the N.A.S. Committee any seriously impacted areas."

More recently, the General Accounting Office in its 1990 report to the Secretary of the Interior on Rangeland management found the BLM entirely lacking in information on how many wild horses the range might support. In 46 wild horse habitats visited, the committee determined that the BLM had not assessed the lands' carrying capacity in over twenty years. The Report reads: "Despite this lack of data the BLM has proceeded with horse removals based on perceived population levels dating back to 1971 and/or recommendations from BLM advisory groups comprised largely of livestock permittees."

Even had the more than $100,000,000 spent for wild horse removals during the decade of the eighties succeeded in upgrading the public lands, such benefits would have been short-lived, for in many places where wild horses were reduced or removed entirely, livestock allotments were increased by equal amounts or more. Ironically, when asked about this by the General Accounting Office investigators, the BLM responded that it lacked data on range conditions and so did not feel justified in making cattle reductions.

Undeniably, the dominant users and abusers of the public lands have long been and still are private livestock growers, but their right to cheap grazing appears to be sacrosanct. As for reducing game animals, tampering with their numbers would be political suicide. A powerful hunting lobby, backed by the National Rifleman's Association and state fish and game agencies, stands at-the-ready to make sure that that won't happen. Horses, on the other hand, have no important constituency to stand up for them. Humane organizations have never been perceived by government bureaucrats as a significant force to be reckoned with. Humane organizations are not-for-profit and so are neither producers nor consumers of wealth (unlike ranchers and hunters). For this reason, when a conflict with these interest groups arises, the humane position is viewed as being of less consequence. As for political clout, not-for-profit organizations lose their tax status if they express any opinions on candidates running for election.

Thus a proposition suggested by the American Horse Protection Association and the Humane Society of the United States that a slight percentage reduction in cattle numbers would significantly reduce pressure on the public lands and eliminate the need for massive horse roundups, met with little enthusiasm—especially among Western delegations to Congress. So once again in 1989, when the BLM presented its 1990 budget request for $13,600,000 to cover the cost of removing 8,700 more horses from the public domain, the money was appropriated. Meanwhile, the Bureau drew up policy guidelines for the establishment of privately sponsored sanctuaries into which "unadoptables" could be funneled.

At the time of this writing, two such sanctuaries have been established, one in Oklahoma and the other in South Dakota. The opening of the South Dakota sanctuary was accompanied by a good deal of journalistic fanfare. ABC TV's 20/20 carried the story, portraying the operation as the solution to the wild horse problem. It showed horses running free on private prairie land, but failed to explore the question of why such large numbers of horses had been removed from the public domain in the first place. Nor did it say anything about what the sanctuary was costing the taxpayer, leaving viewers to conclude that the rancher, whose idea it was, must be footing the bills. In actual fact, the South Dakota sanctuary has cost the government $1,479,136 for feed and veterinary care over its first two years of existence, and this subsidy will continue (at a higher rate) for one more year. After that, in accordance with BLM's Sanctuary Guidelines, the operation is expected to be self-supporting. How this will be accomplished, whether by charging admission fees or through corporate sponsorship, will be determined by the Institute of Range and the American Mustang or IRAM, the organization set up by the rancher to manage the sanctuary. According to its president, $7.5 million dollars are needed to attain self-sufficiency. At the time of this writing nothing close to that amount has been raised, nor has any corporate sponsor come forward. As a result, the GAO Report forecasts that the BLM will have to "assess the costs and benefits of continued financing of the sanctuary beyond the three years envisioned or take back the horses."

Ironically, during the very week that the GAO report was released,[20]/20 won an EMMY for its film report on IRAM's solution to the wild horse problem, and ABC rebroadcast the segment. Thus a vast viewing audience was twice lulled into believing that a complex situation had been resolved "by a lone individual stepping in to solve a problem. No one else could see the solution, but the answer was all around." Ah, television!

Nevertheless, a short term solution to BLM's self-inflicted crisis of too many penned animals, the sanctuary concept is not entirely without merit. Obviously, if properly run, private sanctuaries could provide a more humane environment than do the BLM's holding facilities. Insufficient thought, however, seems to have been given to the long range fate of sanctuary horses or to the effect that private sanctuaries might have on BLM's removal policies. Humane organizations fear the Bureau will use them as convenient places to dispose of more horses than need be removed from the range. For that matter, the sanctuary idea already seems to be relieving the Bureau of having to run an efficient adoption program. Of the first 1,300 animals delivered to South Dakota, over 600 were under seven years old and would have qualified for placement in suitable homes.

As for the future of sanctuaries once they are cut loose from government funding, one wonders how self-supporting they can be. Competition for money will become ever more fierce as more sanctuaries are established. How much and for how long will the public pay to see wild horses behind fences? For the animals on display will bear little resemblance to their wild counterparts. A placid gelding munching grass in a pasture will not call to mind the indomitable stallion he once was. The drama of real life will be absent. Moreover, after the first mares to be delivered to the sanctuaries have dropped their foals, no more leggy youngsters will be born to delight spectators. All sanctuary males must be gelded; the animals on view will be the last of their line, a kind of Shaker population, doomed to pass out of existence.

One has to wonder: Will this be the end of the trail for the tough little mount of the Conquistadors, the Indian war horse, the pack horse of Lewis and Clark, the cowpony of the first trail drivers? Or will the wild horse be allowed to exist on the range in a natural environment with a minimum of human intervention?

Perhaps there is no longer any room in our hearts for this "living symbol of our historic and pioneer spirit," as Congress so aptly defined the mustang. Perhaps these relics of the Old West no longer have value to a nation that measures the worth of a resource by how much it contributes to the gross national product. Perhaps we no longer have need for the diversity and interest that the presence of this animal contributes to our landscapes and our lives.

But I don't believe it. The 1990 investigative report from Congress's General Accounting Office is cause for hope. It asks the very question that humane organizations have been raising since 1977: Are such drastic horse removals necessary?

A spokesman for the BLM responded to this report by saying that many of the problems cited had occurred in the 1980s.

"This administration arrived in 1989," he added. "We are committed to managing the [wild horse] program and making it effective."

That is my fervent hope.

UPDATE: *Wild Horses into the Millennium*

It's good news–bad news time!

The good news is that since the previous edition of this book went to press ten years ago, the Bureau of Land Management has implemented a number of excellent changes in its Wild Horse and Burro Program. I will expand on those changes later.

But first, the bad news: What prompted many of these reforms were widespread news reports of shocking abuses and a criminal investigation of a BLM employee, James Galloway, who was charged with adopting twenty-seven wild horses with a slaughterhouse sale in mind. As an adoption facilitator, this employee had no trouble circumventing a longstanding bureau regulation that limits the number of horses an individual may adopt to four. He simply enlisted friends and family to sign papers for horses they would never receive.

Had things gone according to plan, Galloway stood to make considerable profit on his sale of these animals. Overseas, the price of horsemeat was about to skyrocket, driven by consumer fear of beef in the wake of mad-cow disease. But the scam was discovered. An informer reported seeing wild horses from New Mexico being fattened on a Texas ranch, where they had been shipped at government expense.

Thus began a four-year investigation, which ended in the rescue of the horses. Nevertheless, all charges against the wrongdoer (and those of his fellow workers who covered for him) were dropped, though not because the chief prosecutor in the case, Alia Ludlum, felt she lacked evidence to indict. In a memorandum, she wrote:

> I believe that my investigation was obstructed all along by persons within the BLM, because they didn't want to be embarrassed. There

is a terrible problem with the program and with government agents placing themselves above the law.

Her sense of frustration was echoed by Steven Sederwall—a BLM investigator who first uncovered this chicanery. Sederwall's disclosures had not been well received by his superiors. In fact, they removed him from the case and warned him not to pass any of his findings to prosecutor Ludlow.

"If you have ineffective enforcement and prosecutions," he said of the disappointing outcome, "it's as if there is no law."

Equally frustrated over the shutting down of the case was the grand-jury foreman. After sitting for months and listening to thousands of hours of testimony, he pleaded with Ludlum to indict.

"We want those charges filed and we want to be notified of what was done, regardless of who these people are. Please, ma'am," he told her.

Presumably, "these people" referred to higher-ups in the Washington BLM office who, acting out of fear that the net was widening and would soon encompass middle and upper management bureau personnel, put pressure on the U.S. Justice Department to drop the case. However it came about, in July of 1997 the U.S. District Attorney in San Antonio, bowing to a memorandum from the Justice Department, did just that.

The matter did not end there, however. In the months that followed, a reporter for the Associated Press, Martha Mendoza, set out to check adoption corrals elsewhere. In Rock Spring, Wyoming, she spoke with BLM employee Vic McDarment, whose job it was to round up excess Red Desert wild horses and facilitate their adoptions. What she learned was that McDarment had adopted sixteen horses himself—twelve more than the legal limit. Moreover, his estranged wife had adopted nine horses, his former wife had adopted one horse, his girlfriend had adopted four horses, his children had adopted six horses, and his co-workers and their families had adopted fifty-four horses.

This wholesale adoption would have cost a pretty penny had the standard fee of $125 per animal had been collected. It was not. As the person in charge, McDarment was able to waive or discount adoption fees for most of the eighty-nine horses on grounds that they were lame, old, undesirable, or for some other reason. When Ms. Mendoza asked about the horses' whereabouts, he replied: "I don't keep track."

His estranged wife, however, was more candid. She said she had never seen any of the horses adopted in her name. "I just signed the forms and Vic drove them out."

Next, Ms. Mendoza's investigation led her to slaughterhouses in Canada and the United States, where she discovered BLM freeze brands on fifty-seven horses awaiting slaughter. Such brands are put on wild horses after they have been gathered and await adoption. According to Ms. Mendoza's news story, more than three-quarters of those doomed horses were young, healthy, and quite adoptable.

It would seem, then, that what had occurred in New Mexico was no isolated incident. BLM employees in other districts appeared to be flouting their own regulations in order to make money on the horses in their charge.

When Mendoza's shocking revelations were published in papers across the country, the BLM wasted no time refuting them. The fifty-seven horses she had observed at the slaughterhouses, they said, were "titled animals," meaning they had been held for a full year following their adoption, whereupon the BLM issued ownership papers for them. Thus, they had become private property, and their fate no longer rested with the bureau.

The rationale that an individual who holds title to a wild horse has the right to sell it for slaughter, however, is open to question. The Wild Horse and Burro Act specifically forbids anyone from "processing or permitting to be processed into commercial products the remains of a wild free-roaming horse or burro." As it happened, I participated in reviewing early drafts of that act and can recall this issue being discussed. Joan Blue, Pearl Twyne, Wild Horse Annie, and I, fearful that the animals we were trying to protect might be exploited in the end, asked that language be devised to prohibit all commercial use of them. The bill's sponsors agreed and inserted the clause.

Nevertheless, the BLM was correct in arguing that it lacked statutory authority to intervene in transactions between title holders and slaughterhouses. Still, questions persist: How did it happen that the BLM assigned ownership papers to people who were planning to sell their mustangs to meatpackers? Where was the BLM's oversight in this matter?

It didn't take much probing to learn that, until recently, the bureau had little contact with most adopters once they loaded their new mustangs into trailers and drove away. This fact becomes understandable when one learns that the BLM's budget provides for only one hundred full-time employees in its Wild Horse and Burro Program and that these one hundred employees are charged with many duties beyond monitoring all 160,000 animals that have been adopted since the inception of the program in 1971. It is, in fact, remarkable that so small a staff can find time to place phone calls or make on-site visits to 450 horses a year. This sampling, however, represents only 5 percent of the 9,000 horses and burros rounded up and placed in homes each year.

And therein lies a serious weakness in the adoption program. For notwithstanding the good intentions of most adopters, even a person of good will can become overwhelmed by an animal that seems intractable, and may seek to get rid of it. New owners need moral support and a lot of help. A good many do not know how to break and train a domestic horse, much less a wild one. Yet, with guidance, a person who loves horses can learn how to do this and will likely find the experience to be thoroughly rewarding.

Unfortunately, the BLM is not staffed to offer this type of one-on-one guidance. Yet there is an answer. It should not be too time-consuming for the bureau to match up new adopters with experienced adopters who live nearby, and who have succeeded in gentling and training their own mustangs. Inasmuch as the BLM keeps computerized records containing the names and addresses of all adopters, sharing that information with those who are having trouble with their animals would be a cost-free way to boost its success rate, to say nothing of its image; inasmuch as most mustangs, when properly gentled and trained, make good press. They shine in endurance contests, roping exhibitions, and even dressage. They are a big hit in any parade. Moreover, they are especially good with children and the handicapped. Given a chance they will reflect well on their adoptive owners and on the BLM. There is no need for anyone to give up on a mustang.

The scandal resurrected yet another issue; namely, why is it necessary to excess 9,000 wild horses and burros from the public lands each year? That question has been visited elsewhere in this book, and I don't intend to raise it again except as it relates to the bureau's complaint that not enough qualified adopters exist to absorb all the horses it feels it must cull.

But is this so? Clearly, there is no lack of demand for foals and yearlings. And most mares end up being placed. It is the adult stallions that present a problem. People shy away from adopting them. As a result, they end up being corralled, sometimes for years. Better that they be left on the range to live out their lives. Yet consideration must also be given to age classes and sex balances within each wild herd. If a herd becomes top-heavy with aging males, it will die out.

And so large numbers of these once proud, harem-possessing males are gathered in roundups only to end up in holding pens for months on end. In time these unwanted are trucked back and forth across the country, from one satellite adoption site to another, in search of takers. Once heart-stoppingly beautiful, the wretched animals grow more and more dispirited and, after weeks of boredom and confinement, present a sad spectacle to prospective adopters. Some stand in one spot for hours, heads sagging, manes disheveled—perhaps mourning the loss of the harems they once protected or dreaming of the windswept mountain ridges they once inhabited.

These unwanted animals were the subject of a 1990 General Accounting Office report, which reviewed the BLM's past activities during the decade of the eighties. The report accused the bureau of removing thousands more horses and burros from the range than its adoption program could absorb; and it further noted that the bureau dealt with this problem by placing 20,000 of these animals with large-scale adopters, at least 1,000 of which were sold for slaughter.

By 1997, bruised by so much bad publicity, bureau officials sought outside advice and appointed a committee to examine all aspects of its Wild Horse and Burro Adoption Program. Twelve non-governmental experts were tapped, and in a matter of weeks, the team came up with the Culp Report—a document that contains a number of thoughtful recommendations, some of which are summarized as follows:

1. The BLM should develop a strategy with the Department of Justice, whereby egregious cases of abuse by adopters will be prosecuted under a uniform policy that ensures citations.

2. The BLM should phone or make on-site checks of 100 percent of new adopters within six months. Assistance should be offered to anyone having difficulties with their animal.

3. Outside help should be enlisted to meet the workload of on-site inspections. This might include humane officers, veterinarians, and other equine experts.

4. The BLM should prepare a Compliance Handbook for use in its district offices to provide guidelines on such things as repossession of animals, appropriate administrative actions to be taken in cases of complaints, reasons to delay giving title to an adopter, and so forth.

5. The BLM should enforce an existing regulation requiring slaughterhouses to obtain titles to all wild horses bought for killing. Moreover, these titles should be held for one year. Any animal received without a title should be identified by its freeze brand so that the BLM, upon notification, can repossess it.

6. More time, effort, and money should be spent finding good homes for older stud horses—the class of animal most likely to end up at a slaughterhouse. Efforts should be made to gentle and quick halter-break adult males prior to their adoption.

7. The BLM should respond to all complaints by making on-site inspections.

8. The BLM's computer database of animal placements should be kept up-to-date.

9. BLM employees, by virtue of their position, should not be allowed first pick of animals up for adoption.

10. BLM employees should not be allowed the fee reduction that is sometimes offered to people who adopt less desirable horses.

11. BLM employees should promote upcoming adoptions, encourage seminars and horse-training demonstrations, and publicize the mustangs' special capabilities by entering successfully trained animals in parades and horse shows.

In a foreword to this report, the Culp team looked at possible alternatives to adoption for dealing with excess wild horses. They promptly deemed euthanasia of healthy animals unacceptable to the public. Moreover, euthanasia was prohibited by a 1988 Appropriations Committee act. They judged federally funded wild-horse sanctuaries to be failures—"too expensive and not self supporting." (Those described in the previous chapter have been closed or are scheduled to be closed.) They determined that contraception was not yet ready to be used as a means of population control. Researchers do not yet have a "product that is useful beyond one breeding season."

By contrast, the team touted the adoption program as being "the best and most economical means available for providing long-term humane care for excess animals gathered from Western herd management areas."

Now the question remains: Will the recommendations by the Culp team be put in a file and forgotten, or will they be implemented?

On this score, the news is good.

By the summer of 1998, the BLM had hired more compliance officers to oversee newly adopted horses, phoned or contacted all adopters within six months of their taking horses, increased on-site visits to adopters, and made vigorous attempts to account for missing animals.

Next, the bureau revised its rules, making it impossible for any person to use power of attorney to obtain animals on behalf of other people. Acting BLM director Pat Shea commented on this change: "In the past, our investigations found that some people who obtained large numbers of animals by using power of attorney from others did so to resell the animals for slaughter. This rule removes that option."

Following that change, the bureau entered into an agreement with the Department of Agriculture's Food Safety and Inspection Service to be on the lookout for any untitled wild horses that might show up at slaughterhouses and to provide the BLM with information about the sellers.

As for generating public interest in adoption, the BLM began to make use of the Internet. Interested parties are now encouraged to log on to the bureau's Web site at http:\\www.adoptahorse.blm.gov\ and bid on the horse of their dreams from a gallery of mustang portraits. Although using this technology will not save bidders money (competing bids may run up the cost of a sought-after animal well beyond the standard adoption fee of $125) nor spare anyone travel time (winners still must drive to holding corrals to pick up their animals), it does improve a person's odds of getting the horse he or she wants. At on-site adoptions, people must draw numbers and wait their turn. Low numbers get the choice animals. High numbers get what is left.

The Internet has also generated help for the BLM in the form of grassroots mentoring groups. One such self-selected bunch of horse lovers started as a chat group. In time they became so enthusiastic about the subject of wild horses and burros that thirty of them traveled to meet one another in Antioch, California, at a 1998 wild-horse adoption event. The BLM, recognizing the potential value of these individuals, brought in three professional horse trainers to run a workshop for them.

Meanwhile, in Florida, eighteen volunteers signed up for a BLM-sponsored course to become certified inspectors at adoption facilities and to learn how to monitor adoption compliance. These individuals will be called upon to make random checks in states east of the Mississippi where 60 percent of mustangs are adopted.

More help has come from prison work programs—in existence since the 1980s. These programs make use of horse-savvy prisoners to train older, hard-to-place stallions. Gentling wild horses that have lost their freedom has proved therapeutic for men who have suffered the same loss. Both come out of this program winners.

Similarly, an experiment in South Carolina has shown that wild horses and troubled youngsters can be good for each other. The Hurricane Creek Experience, as it was called, involved four teenage boys, each assigned a mustang to feed, care for, and gentle.

"They'd never been around horses before," said Jim Hardee, the director of this family ministries program. "They were as scared of the horses as the horses were of them."

After eight weeks, however, the once defiant boys were ready to participate with their no-longer-recalcitrant horses on a 200-mile-ride along the Palmetto Trail, which spans the entire state of South Carolina. At their graduation ceremony, Hardee praised the boys and the mustangs.

"The results," he said, "were magnificent. The horses were able to reach young men who at one time could be reached by no one, and the teens transferred their positive experiences with the horses to positive experiences with other people."

Even before scandals prompted the BLM to improve its marketing of the adoption program, it had already come up with new ways to stimulate public interest in mustang ownership. In 1996 it began publishing and distributing a twenty-page newsletter, the *National Wild Horse and Burro News,* which contains informative articles on horse care, tips on training, lists of trainers, veterinary advice, schedules and locations of upcoming adoption events, reports on competitions at which mustangs have excelled, and more. It's all a good read, but most enjoyable are the letters from adopters, for these firsthand accounts are the best evidence that wild horses can and do adapt well to life under the saddle. One such letter, from the Troyer family of Mancelona, Michigan, particularly touched me. It perfectly demonstrated how love and patience can turn a so-called "unadoptable older stallion" into a first-rate, totally reliable, contented companion animal. Following are excerpts from that letter:

> We arrived at the Escanaba corral on Friday so we would have plenty of time to look over the horses and write down numbers of those we would consider—if our turn came early enough. On Saturday morning we drew a low number and chose our first pick—a beautiful, young, chestnut mare.
>
> As we waited for some friends to choose their horse, we were entertained by an eight-year-old bay stallion. He was rearing, baring his teeth, and challenging any horse that came near him. He was also scaring off any potential adopters.
>
> When the adoption came to an end, the bay stallion did not have a home, and we were approached by a BLM employee who asked us about adopting him. He pointed out that if he wasn't adopted he would be transported back to an adoption/holding facility in Cross Plains, Tennessee.
>
> We were reluctant, due to his age, but were assured that this would not be an issue. The BLM employee pointed out that despite his wild antics, the stallion had gentle soft eyes. So we decided to take a chance on him, and we named him Laredo.

For the first few weeks, we were cautious around Laredo's pen and we spent the summer just getting to know him and earn his trust. By winter we were even more skeptical about the decision we had made. We were still only brushing him and leading him around the farm.

Then one day our daughter Staci needed a horse to lead trail rides and she decided to use Laredo. We watched as she put her gift with horses to work. In no time she was riding him and pronounced him ready to go.

The following spring we opened our own riding stable and Laredo quickly became a favorite, due to his heritage and his gentle disposition. Before long, he was taking the smallest, most timid riders out on the trail and bringing them back smiling.

One day we were visited by a lady in her fifties who walked with a cane. A stroke had paralyzed her when she was twenty-eight years old and she had not been on a horse since. She asked if we thought she could ride.

We did, and we selected Laredo to be her mount. With one of her legs partially paralyzed, and one hand unable to grip, Julie and Laredo set off. Two hours later they returned to the stable. Laredo had performed beyond our expectations. He had made Julie's dream of riding again come true.

Laredo is a symbol of all the mustangs that need a home, regardless of age, gender or initial attitude. Our hope is that no wild horse will ever be unwanted again.

The Troyer family

I couldn't have said it better and I would have ended this update here except for one last piece of good news.

For years, I have asserted that the unique conformation, gait, bone structure, colors, and historical context of many wild-horse herds argue that they are descended from mounts ridden by Spanish conquistadors and, as such, they represent a unique aspect of history, as worthy of preservation as redwood forests. Some dissenters, often for self-serving reasons, have refused to give credence to this point of view. They have stubbornly insisted that the mustangs are nothing but old ranch horses that have been turned loose.

Now science has stepped into the fray with some pretty convincing evidence. In 1992, Dr. E. Gus Cothran drew blood samples from wild horses in the Pryor Mountains of Montana and compared them to the blood of thirty-seven common breeds in an effort to find genetic matches. Three variants

Laredo and friend Mandy.

were found that strongly indicated "Old Spanish" genetic influence. Additionally, seven markers of lesser importance showed up to support that evidence. Finally, one more matched variant, plus the finding of the rare Qac variant, conclusively tied the Pryor Mountain mustangs to a still extant Spanish breed, the Paso Finos of Puerto Rico. Dr Cothran summed up his findings as follows:

> The combination of evidence points to almost certain Spanish origins of the Pryor horses. If the genetic marker data is considered along with conformational and coat-color characteristics of those horses, the Pryor herd may be the most significant wild-horse herd remaining in the United States.

The Pryor horse herd is not the only one that carries genetic evidence of having descended from the conquistadors' amazing mounts. The Cerbat mustangs of Arizona have also been blood tested and their Spanish derivation has been authenticated. In addition, Dr. Phillip Sponenberg, an expert on breed conformation, has identified the Cerbat horses as being "classic Old Andalusian in type." I am happy to say that the BLM, in acknowledgment of the historic value of the Cerbat horses of Arizona, is taking great care to preserve their uniqueness.

Further testing—blood drawn from the Kiger horses in the mountains of Oregon—has turned up still another herd with a Spanish past. These stunningly beautiful mustangs come in shades of dun, red dun, and grullo, which long ago attracted the attention of breeders. In the past, Kiger horses were gathered to serve as the foundation stock for a registry. Today the BLM is managing those in the wild with a keen appreciation of their historical significance.

While these widely separated examples represent only a sampling of the wild herds still out there today, they suffice to tell us that Congress's 1971 decision to preserve wild horses as "living symbols of the historic and pioneer spirit of the West" was as astute as it was foresighted. Today, thirty years after that legislation was drafted, the Horse of the Conquest lives on.

This gives me hope, as we move forward into the new millennium, that we Americans will continue to enjoy our astonishingly colorful past and treasure the legendary horses that served it.

—Hope Ryden
Fall 1999

Notes and Sources

GENERAL

Cunninghame Graham, Robert Bontine. *Horses of the Conquest.* Norman: University of Oklahoma Press, 1949.

Dobie, J. Frank. *The Mustangs.* New York: Branhall House, 1934

Richmond, Robert W., and Mardock, Robert W. *A Nation Moving West.* Lincoln: University of Nebraska Press, 1966.

Roe, Frank Gilbert. *The Indians and the Horse.* Norman: University of Oklahoma Press, 1955.

Simpson, George Gaylord. *Horses.* Garden City, N.Y.: Doubleday & Co., 1950.

Wyman, Walker D. *The Wild Horse of the West.* Lincoln: University of Nebraska Press, 1945.

CHAPTER 2

Hestor, Jim. "Late Pleistocene Extinction and Radiocarbon Dating." *American Antiquity* 26 (1960), pp. 58–77.

Kurten, Bjorn. "Continental Drift and Evolution." *Scientific American,* March, 1969.

Leopold, A. S., Cain, S. A., Cottam, C., Gabrielson, I. N., and Kimball, T. L. "Wildlife Management in the National Parks." *Transactions of North American and National Resources Conference* 28 (1963).

Martin, Paul. "Nature of Extinction and Causes." *Pleistocene Ecology and Biography of North America in Zoogeography.* Edited by C. L. Hubbs, Washington, D.C.: American Association for the Advancement of Science Publication 51.

CHAPTERS 3 AND 4

Brislawn, Robert. "The Feral Horse." *The Spanish Mustang News,* October, November, December, 1967.

————. "Skeletal Structure of the Spanish Mustang." *The Spanish Mustang News,* April, May, June, 1968.

Cunninghame Graham, Robert Bontine. *Horses of the Conquest.* Norman: University of Oklahoma Press, 1949, pp. 118, 133.

Field, Susan. "The Spanish Mustang." *The Western Horseman,* October, 1967.

Henry, Marguerite. *Marguerite Henry's All About Horses.* New York: Random House, 1962.

Lewis, Jack. "The Modern Mustangers." *The Horse and Rider,* n.d.

Light Horses. Department of Agriculture bulletin 2127.

McMullen, Mrs. Rosemarie. "The Mustang." *The Western Horseman,* October, 1966.

Releases and literature published by the Spanish Mustang Information Headquarters, P.O.B. 26, Thompson Falls, Montana 59873.

Richards, Dr. Lawrence. "The Spanish Mustang Registry." *The Western Horseman,* October, 1958.

Smith, Joyce. "All Kinds of Horses." *The Arizona Horseman,* June and July, 1968.

Unger, Garcia. "Types of Mustangs." *The Spanish Mustang News,* April, May, June, 1967.

Western Horseman, The. All-breed issue, October, 1967.

CHAPTER 5

Bolton, Herbert Eugene. *Coronado, Knight of Pueblos and Plains.* New York: Mc-Graw-Hill, 1949.

Denhardt, Robert. Translated from the Spanish text of Bernal Diaz by Genro Garcia, 1904. "The Truth About Cortez's Horses." *Hispanic American Review* 17:525–532, 1937.

Haines, Francis. "How Did the Plains Indians Get Their Horses?" *American Anthropologist* 40, 1938.

Kroeber, A. L. *The Anthropologist.* New York: Harcourt, Brace, 1923.

Maudsley, A. P., ed. and trans. *Conquest of New Spain I.* London: pp. 180–181.

Priestly, Herbert Ingram. *The Coming of the White Man.* New York: Macmillan Co., 1950.

Von Hagen, Victor W. *The Ancient Sun Kingdoms of the Americas.* Cleveland and New York: The World Publishing Co., 1957.

Wissler, C. "Material Culture of the North American Indians." *American Anthropologist* 16, 1914.

CHAPTERS 6, 7, AND 8

Conversations with Paiute Indians near Yerington, Nevada.

Conversations with Dr. Richard Tedford, American Museum of Natural History, Department of Paleontology.

Correspondence with Kent Gregersen, vice-president of National Mustang Association.

Dobie, J. Frank, ed. *Mustangs and Cowhorses.* Austin: Texas Folklore Society, 1940.

Ewers, John C. "The Horse Complex in Plains Indian History." *The North American Indians.* Edited by Owen, Deetz, Fisher. New York: Macmillan Co., 1967.

Field, Susan, and Brislawn, Robert. "The Medicine Hat." *The Spanish Mustang News,* April, May, June, 1968.

Kellogg, Louise P., ed. *Early Narratives of the Northwest 1634–1699.* New York: Charles Scribner's Sons, 1906.

Kroeber, A. G. "Cultural & Natural Areas of Native North America." *University of California Publications in American Archeology and Ethnology* 38.

Margry, P., ed. "Memoires et documents pour servier l'histoire des origines francaises des pays d'outre mer" 1:595. Paris, 1879.

Murray, Charles. *Travels in North America During the Years 1834, 1835, and 1836.* London: Richard Bentley, 1841, pp. 277–278, 308, 351, 380.

Richardson, Rupert. *The Comanche Barrier.* Glendale, Calif.: Arthur H. Clark Company, 1933.

Tabeau, P. *Tabeau's Narrative of Liosel's Expedition to the Upper Missouri.* Edited by A. H. Abel. Norman: University of Oklahoma Press, 1939, pp. 151–153.

Tyrrell, J. B., ed. *David Thompson's Narrative of His Explorations in Western America 1784–1812.* Toronto: Champlain Society Publication, 1916, pp. 326, 334, 338.

Willey, Gordon R. "History and Evolution of American Indian Cultures." *The North American Indians.* Edited by Owen, Deetz, Fisher. New York: Macmillan Co., 1967.

Wissler, Clark. *Indians of the United States.* Garden City, N.Y.: Doubleday & Co., 1956.

CHAPTERS 9, 10, AND 11

Cox, Ross. *The Columbia River.* Edited by Edgar and Jane Stewart. Norman: University of Oklahoma Press, 1957, p. 244.

Irving, Washington. *A Tour of the Prairies.* Norman: University of Oklahoma Press, 1956.

———. *Astoria.* Portland, Ore.: Binfords and Mort Publishers, 1950.

———. *The Adventures of Captain Bonneville.* Norman: University of Oklahoma Press, 1961.

Lewis, M., and Clark, W. *History of the Expedition Under the Command of Lewis and Clark 1–3.* Edited by Elliott Coues. New York: Dover Publications, 1965, pp. 840, 955, 970–977, 979, 1125, 1148, 1171.

Tyrrell, J. B., ed. *David Thompson's Narrative of His Explorations in Western America 1784–1812.* Toronto: Champlain Society Publication, 1916, pp. 377, 378, 401.

CHAPTER 12

Carter, Major General W. H. "Story of the Horse." *National Geographic Magazine* 44: 455–566, 1923.

Comfort, Alex. *The Process of Ageing.* New York: Signet Science Library Books, 1961.

Klataske, Ron. "Wonders of Life in the Red Desert." *Wyoming Wildlife,* August, 1968.

CHAPTER 13

Correspondence with Leroy Seth, assistant secretary of the Nez Percé Tribal Executive Committee.

Cox, Ross. *The Columbia River.* Edited by Edgar and Jane Stewart. Norman: University of Oklahoma Press, 1957, p. 215.

Griffen, Jeff. *The Book of Horses and Horsemanship.* New York: Prentice Hall, Bonanza Books, n.d.

Haines, Francis. *The Nez Percés.* Norman: University of Oklahoma Press, 1955.

Interview with Chief Bobby Yellowtail of Crow Tribe, Montana.

Irving, Washington. *The Adventures of Captain Bonneville.* Norman: University of Oklahoma Press, 1961, p. 343.

Lewis, M., and Clark, W. *History of the Expedition Under the Command of Lewis and Clark* 3. Edited by Elliott Coues. New York: Dover Publications 1965, p. 1012.

Materials and correspondence from Dan Walker, editor of *Appaloosa Horse Club News,* Box 403, Moscow, Idaho 83843.

Savitt, Sam. *America's Horses.* New York: Doubleday & Co., 1966.

CHAPTERS 14, 15, AND 16

Bulletins and publications of the Canadian Wild Horse Society, 1120 Bird Road, Richmond, B.C.

Bulletins and publications of the International Society for Protection of Mustangs and Burros. Badger, Calif.: April, May, June, 1969.

Correspondence with Bureau of Land Management district offices in Oregon.

Correspondence with United States Department of Agriculture, Enterprise, Oregon.

Cushman, Don. *The Great North Trail.* New York: McGraw-Hill, 1966.

Haines, Francis. *The Nez Percés.* Norman: University of Oklahoma Press, 1961, appendix.

Hawgood, John A. *America's Western Frontiers.* New York: Alfred Knopf, 1967, p. 291.

Interviews with Joyce Smith, Mesa, Arizona; Gila River Indians on Sacatan Reservation, Arizona; George and Ann Lande, Crow Reservation, Montana; and Chief Bobby Yellowtail, Crow Reservation, Montana.

Irving, Washington. *The Adventures of Captain Bonneville.* Norman: University of Oklahoma Press, 1961, appendix.

New York *Times,* September 12, 1920, p. 11.

CHAPTERS 17 AND 18

American Turf Registry 7, 1835–1836.

Irving, Washington. *A Tour of the Prairies.* Norman: University of Oklahoma Press, 1957.

New York *Times,* June 6, 1882.

Sunder, John E., ed. *Matt Field on the Santa Fe Trail.* Collected by Clyde and Mae Reed Porter. Norman: University of Oklahoma Press, 1960, p. 98.

Webb, Walter Prescott. *The Great Frontier.* Boston: Houghton Mifflin Co., 1952.

CHAPTERS 19 AND 20

Charter, S. F. R. *Man on Earth.* Sausalito, Calif.: Contact Editions, 1962.

Cushman, Don. *The Great North Trail.* New York: McGraw-Hill, 1966.

Dobie, J. Frank. *Cow People.* Boston: Little, Brown and Co., 1964.

James, Will. *The American Cowboy.* New York: Charles Scribner's Sons, 1942.

Kraenzel, Carl. *Great Plains in Transition.* Norman: University of Oklahoma Press, 1955.

McCoy, Joseph G. *Historical Sketches of the Cattle Trade of the West and Southwest.* Kansas City, Mo.: Ramsey, Millett and Hudson, 1874, pp. 50–53.

McWilliams, Carey. *North From Mexico.* Philadelphia: J. B. Lippincott Co., 1949.

New York *Times,* December 26, 1884.

Osgood, E. S. *Day of the Cattleman*. Minneapolis: University of Minnesota Press, 1929, pp. 105, 193.

Sandoz, Mari. *The Cattlemen*. New York: Hastings House, 1958.

Santee, Ross. *Cowboy*. New York: Hastings House, 1964.

Siberts, Bruce. *Nothing but Prairie and Sky*. Edited by Walker D. Wyman. Norman: University of Oklahoma Press, 1954.

Chapters 21 and 22

Cody, William. *Buffalo Bill's Life Story*. London: Hodder and Stoughton Limited, 1928.

Cushman, Don. *The Great North Trail*. New York: McGraw-Hill, 1966.

Interview with Chief Bobby Yellowtail, Crow Reservation, Montana.

New York *Times*. August 8, 1876; July 4, 1879; October 4, 1887; April 6, 1887; September 10, 1886; December 29, 1876 (reprinted from Saint Paul *Pioneer Press*).

Romspert, George W. *The Western Echo: A Description of the Western States and Territories*. Dayton: United Brethren Publishing House, 1881.

Sandoz, Mari. *The Buffalo Hunters*. New York: Hastings House, 1954.

Webb, William E. *Buffalo Land*. Cincinnati and Chicago: E. Hannaford and Company, 1872, pp. 312–314.

Chapter 23

Interview with brand inspectors in Wyoming and Nevada.

James, Will. "Piñon and the Wild Ones." *The Saturday Evening Post*, May 19, 1923.

Osgood, E. S. *Day of the Cattleman*. Minneapolis: University of Minnesota Press, 1929.

Reprints of Estray Laws from Montana, Colorado, Nevada, Wyoming.

Wellman, Paul I. *The Trampling Herd*. Garden City, N.Y.: Doubleday & Co., 1950.

Chapter 24

Barnes, Will. "Wild Horses." *McClure's Magazine* 32, November, 1908–1909.

Interviews with Lloyd and Royce Tillett, Lovell, Wyoming; Carwin Rule, Bridger, Montana; anonymous sources in and around Rock Springs, Wyoming; Joyce Smith, Mesa, Arizona; Bill and Steve Pelligrini, Yerington, Nevada.

James, Will. "Piñon and the Wild Ones." *The Saturday Evening Post*, May 19, 1923.

Siberts, Bruce. *Nothing but Prairie and Sky*. Edited by Walker D. Wyman. Norman: University of Oklahoma Press, 1954.

Wellman, Paul I. *The Trampling Herd*. Garden City, N.Y.: Doubleday and Co., 1950.

Wyman, Walker D. *The Wild Horses of the West*. Lincoln: University of Nebraska Press, 1945, pp. 175–176.

Chapter 25

Anderson, Loren D. Paper, "A History of the Winter Flats Wild Horses." March 1, 1967.

Correspondence from Roy Hungerford, Carbondale, Colorado; and Mrs. Bertha Boies McPeek, Grand Junction, Colorado.

Interviews and file material from Bureau of Land Management offices in ten Western States.

Interviews with people in and around the Bookcliff Mountains, including Ken Weimer, Howard Caudle, Ross Latham, John Armstrong, brand inspector Earl Haller and others.

Interviews with people in and around the Pryor Mountains, including Carwin Rule; Lloyd, Royce and Bessie Tillett; George and Ann Lande; Charles Wagner; Reverend Floyd Schweiger; and others.

CHAPTER 26

Chesson, Ray. "Battle to Preserve the Mustang Continues." *The* (Las Vegas) *Nevadan,* Sunday, August 20, 1967.

Foss, Phillip O. *Politics and Grass: The Administration of Grazing on the Public Domain.* Seattle: University of Washington Press, 1960, pp. 200–201.

McKnight, T. L. "Feral Livestock in Anglo-America." *University of California Publications in Geography,* Vol. XVI. Berkeley and Los Angeles: University of California Press, 1964.

Moore, Ron. "Mustangs." *The Western Horseman,* May, 1969, p. 232.

Taylor Grazing Act and Hearings, June, 1934.

CHAPTER 27

Congressional Record. July 21, 1959.

Henry, Marguerite. *Mustang: Wild Spirit of the West.* Chicago: Rand McNally, 1967.

Personal interviews, letters and information from Mrs. Velma Johnston (Wild Horse Annie).

CHAPTER 28

Bureau of Land Management Fact Sheet.

Chesson, Ray. "Mustangs Blinded by Shotguns." *The* (Las Vegas) *Nevadan,* August 13, 1967.

Court Record.

"Father and Son Collide in Mid Air." Casper *Star Tribune,* September 17, 1968.

Interviews and correspondence with Mrs. Velma Johnston (Wild Horse Annie), and newsletters from International Society for the Protection of Mustangs and Burros, Badger, California, regarding illegal roundups.

Interviews with people in and around Rock Springs, Wyoming.

Interviews with Stan Routson, July, 1968; letter from Routson to Velma Johnston, July 8, 1969; tape of interview with Routson made by Velma Johnston, July 12, 1967.

Records from Trial in the United States District Court, Reno, Nevada, July 5 and 6, 1967.

Resolution presented before National Livestock Brand Conference, New Orleans, Louisiana, July 15, 1968.

Tumbleson, Jack. "Midwest Mustangers in Wyoming." Rock Island *Argus,* September 20, 1969.

CHAPTER 29

Correspondence with Keith Miller, district manager of Bureau of Land Management, Grand Junction, Colorado; Senator George Jackson and Congressman John Fuhr, Colorado Legislature.

Interviews with brand inspectors in Nevada and Wyoming; fish and game commissioners in Wyoming and Nevada; Bureau of Land Management officials in Colorado, Wyoming, Montana, and Nevada; Department of the Interior officials in Washington, D.C.; and members of the Public Land Law Review Commission, Washington, D.C.

Literature published by the International Society for the Protection of Mustangs and Burros, Badger, California.

Literature published by the National Mustang Association, Salt Lake City, Utah.

CHAPTER 30

Billings *Gazette,* August 18, 1968.

Department of the Interior news release, March 14, 1968.

Montana Fish and Game Department release, March 27, 1966.

Research done by author for ABC Newscast televised July 11, 1968.

Wyoming *Eagle Tribune,* Cheyenne, June 6 and 20, 1968.

CHAPTER 31

Complaint for Restraining Order and Civil Action of *Humane Society of the United States* v. *Stewart Udall, Department of the Interior.*

Congressional Record, September 12, 1968.

Correspondence from Senators Harry F. Byrd, Mike Mansfield, Gale W. McGee, Clifford Hansen, Congressmen Walter S. Baring and William Henry Harrison, and copies of correspondence between the above legislators and the Bureau of Land Management.

Department of the Interior releases, June 20, 1969.

Interviews with Velma Johnston, Pearl Twyne, Chuck Wagner, Reverend Floyd Schwieger, and Clyde Reynolds.

Quote from Bureau of Land Management letter to Senator Edward W. Brooke, July 19, 1969.

CHAPTER 32

Assateague Island. Washington, D.C.: United States Department of the Interior, National Park Service.

Correspondence between the United States Department of the Interior, Fish and Wildlife Service, and the Pony Committee of the Chincoteague Volunteer Fire Department, May 16, 1962; May 30, 1962; June 7, 1962; September 11, 1962; September 18, 1962; November 15, 1962; November 21, 1962; November 30, 1962; December 3, 1962; December 20, 1962; August 22, 1963; August 29, 1963; September 20, 1963.

County Ordinance, Millard County #76, regarding management, control, -capture, and harvest of wild horses, published in Millard County *Chronicle,* April 25, 1968.

Henry, Marguerite. *Misty of Chincoteague.* Chicago: Rand McNally, 1947.

Interview with Tom Holland, president of the National Mustang Association, January 27, 1969.

Interviews with Bureau of Land Management officials in Reno and Las Vegas.

Letter from Bureau of Land Management director Boyd Rasmussen to Mrs. Velma Johnston, November 30, 1967.

Letter from forest ranger A. E. Briggs, published in National Mustang Association's Organization and Objectives.

Millard County Mustang Refuge Management Plan, written April 1, 1968, signed December 4, 1968.

Notes from meeting held in Chincoteague, Virginia, April 28, 1963. Attended by mayor, town council, bridge authority, Kiwanis, chamber of commerce, and volunteer firemen.

Pamphlet on Chincoteague National Wildlife Refuge, published by United States Department of the Interior, Fish and Wildlife, Bureau of Sports Fisheries and Wildlife, January, 1967.

Personal visit to Nevada Wild Horse Refuge.

CHAPTER 33

Casper Tribune. Casper, Wyoming, April 20, 1971.

Chicago Sun-Times. November 24, 1970.

Colorado Magazine. May/June, 1971.

Congressional Record. January 30, 1970; March 3, 1971; March 10, 1971; May 3, 1971; May 14, 1971.

Daily Sentinel. Grand Junction, Colorado, January 15, 1971.

Elko Daily Press. Elko, Nevada, September 30, 1970.

My Weekly Reader. Middletown, Connecticut: American Education Publications, April 7, 1971.

New York *Times.* November 15, 1970.

Ryden, Hope. "Good-by to the Wild Horse?" *Reader's Digest,* May, 1971.

————. "On the Track of the West's Wild Horses." *National Geographic,* January, 1971.

————. "The Last Wild Horses." *Children's Day,* June, 1971.

————. "The Return of the Native." *National Parks and Conservation Magazine,* October, 1971.

Scholastic News Ranger. New York: Scholastic Magazine, February 1, 1971.

Science News. Columbus, Ohio: American Education Publication, January 20, 1970.

Senior Weekly Reader. Middletown, Connecticut: American Education Publication, February 3, 1971.

Time. July 12, 1971.

Wall Street Journal. June 25, 1970; April 19, 1971.

CHAPTER 34

Bureau of Land Management and American Horse Protection Association agreement, Washington, D.C., February, 1977.

Bureau of Land Management and Forest Service *Joint Investigative Report into the Unlawful Wild Horse Roundup near Howe, Idaho, in January, February and March,* 1973.

Judgment of Federal District Court, New Mexican Livestock Board *v.* United States Department of Interior, *Albuquerque, New Mexico, March* 1, 1975.

Judgment of United States Supreme Court, *Rogers C. B. Morton* v. *State of New Mexico, et al.,* Washington, D.C., June, 1976.

Monberg, Helene C. *Western Resources Wrap Up,* Series XII, no. 29, Washington, D.C., July 15, 1976.

CHAPTER 35

ABC TV's 20/20, November 24, 1989.

American Horse Protection Association, Humane Society of the United States, letter to BLM division chief John S. Boyles, May 22, 1987.

American Horse Protection Association and Humane Society of the United States, Reply to the BLM's Wild Horse and Burros Program Policy, April 1989.

American Horse Protection Association, Humane Society of the U.S., and American Humane Association. Comments on BLM's Wild Horse and Burro Sanctuary Guidelines/Adoption Compliance Procedures. Memorandum to Subcommittee on Interior Appropriations, April 20, 1989.

American Horse Protection Association News, "20/20 Program on Wild Horse Sanctuaries Paints a Pretty Picture."

Animal Welfare Institute, "Research Harassment of Wild Horses Canceled," Spring 1990.

Bureau of Land Management Appropriations Requests to Congress 1977 to 1990.

Bureau of Land Management Wild Horse and Burro Inventory Data Estimates of Population and Claims, 1973 to 1990.

Bureau of Land Management Wild Horse and Burro Program Policy, April 1987.

Bureau of Land Management's Sanctuary Guidelines/Adoption Compliance Procedures, February 2, 1989.

Cole, Glen. "An Ecological Rationale for the Natural or Artificial Regulation of Native Ungulates in Parks," *Transactions of North American Wildlife Conference* 36: 417–425, 1971.

————"Natural versus Man Caused Deaths of Wild Animals in National Parks," National Park Service Information Paper # 26, 1975.

Congressional Record, pp. S 22747–22748, December 18, 1975.

Congressional Record, May 14, 1971.

Congressional Appropriations for Wild Horse Roundups, 1977 to 1990.

Conversations with Lorraine Baegle, Hardscrabble Ranch, Sutcliffe, Nevada, regarding adoption of yearling mustang.

Judgment of the U.S. District Court, Reno, Nevada, AHPA vs. Andrus, September 15, 1978.

Judgment of U.S. Court of Appeals in 9th Circuit, AHPA vs. Andrus, Nov 23, 1979.

Judgment of U.S. District Court, Reno, Nevada, Animal Protection Institute vs. Hodel, 1987.

Judgment U.S. Court of Appeals in 9th Circuit, Animal Protection Institute vs. Hodel, Oct 31, 1988.

Los Angeles Times, Sunday, August 30, 1987.

National Academy of Science Committee on Wild and Free Roaming Horses and Burros, Report to Congress, January 1983.

Public Rangelands Improvement Act of 1978.

Rasmussen, Boyd L., Statement made to the Subcommittee on Public Lands, U.S. House of Representatives, May 1971.

Turner, John W. and Kirkpatrick, Jay. F., "Hormones and Reproduction in Feral Horses," Journal of Equine Veterinary Medicine, Vol. 6 #5, 1986.

United States General Accounting Office, "Rangeland Management: Improvements Needed in Federal Wild Horse Program," Report to the Secretary of Interior, August 1990.

Wagner, Frederic H., "Status of Wild Horse and Burro Management on Public Rangelands," *Transactions of North American Wildlife Conference,* March 1983.

Wild Horses and Burros Advisory Board, Report to Secretaries of Interior and Agriculture, December 5, 1986.

UPDATE

"BLM Responds to Associated Press Series on Wild Horses." Powell *Tribune,* Powell, Wyo., July 16, 1997.

"Case Closed, Wild Horses Still Killed." Associated Press release, March 23, 1997.

Cothran, E. Gus. "Genetic Analysis of Horses From the Pryor Mountain Wild Horse Reserve." University of Kentucky Department of Veterinary Medicine, Lexington, Ky., 1991.

Hillenbrand, Laura. "What's Best for America's Mustangs?" *Equus,* August 1998.

"Horse Adoption Story False Asserts BLM Program Chief, Tom Pogacnik." Arizona *Republic,* January 31, 1997.

"Meat Sources, Symbol of West Clash in Wild Horse Debate." Powell *Tribune,* Powell, Wyo., January 9, 1997.

National Wild Horse and Burro News, Washington, D.C.: Dept. of the Interior, Fall 1996, Fall 1997, Spring 1998, Fall 1998, Winter 1998, Winter 1999.

"Program to Protect Horses Sends Them to Slaughter." Associated Press release, January 5, 1997.

"Rangeland Management: Improvements Needed in Federal Wild Horse Program." Report to the Secretary of the Interior, U.S. General Accounting Office, August 1990.

"Report Acknowledges Wild Horses Being Slaughtered." New York *Times,* January 29, 1997.

Sponenberg, D. Phillip. "Evaluation of Sulphur Herd Management Area BLM Horses," August 1993.

———. "North American Colonial Spanish Horse Update," Blacksburg, Va: University of Virginia Veterinary College, August 1992.

"Wild Horse and Burro Adoption Program Policy Analysis." Culp Report to BLM, April 18, 1997.

Appendices

APPENDIX A

Public Law 92-195
92nd Congress, S. 1116
December 15, 1971

An Act

85 STAT. 649

To require the protection, management, and control of wild free-roaming horses
and burros on public lands.

*Be it enacted by the Senate and House of Representatives of the
United States of America in Congress assembled,* That Congress finds
and declares that wild free-roaming horses and burros are living symbols of the historic and pioneer spirit of the West; that they contribute
to the diversity of life forms within the Nation and enrich the lives of
the American people; and that these horses and burros are fast disappearing from the American scene. It is the policy of Congress that
wild free-roaming horses and burros shall be protected from capture,
branding, harassment, or death; and to accomplish this they are to be
considered in the area where presently found, as an integral part of
the natural system of the public lands.

Wild horses
and burros.
Protection.

Sec. 2. As used in this Act—

Definitions.

(a) "Secretary" means the Secretary of the Interior when used
in connection with public lands administered by him through the
Bureau of Land Management and the Secretary of Agriculture
in connection with public lands administered by him through the
Forest Service;

(b) "wild free-roaming horses and burros" means all unbranded
and unclaimed horses and burros on public lands of the United
States;

(c) "range" means the amount of land necessary to sustain an
existing herd or herds of wild free-roaming horses and burros,
which does not exceed their known territorial limits, and which is
devoted principally but not necessarily exclusively to their welfare in keeping with the multiple-use management concept for the
public lands;

(d) "herd" means one or more stallions and his mares; and

(e) "public lands" means any lands administered by the Secretary of the Interior through the Bureau of Land Management or
by the Secretary of Agriculture through the Forest Service.

Sec. 3. (a) All wild free-roaming horses and burros are hereby
declared to be under the jurisdiction of the Secretary for the purpose of
management and protection in accordance with the provisions of this
Act. The Secretary is authorized and directed to protect and manage
wild free-roaming horses and burros as components of the public
lands, and he may designate and maintain specific ranges on public
lands as sanctuaries for their protection and preservation, where the
Secretary after consultation with the wildlife agency of the State
wherein any such range is proposed and with the Advisory Board
established in section 7 of this Act deems such action desirable. The
Secretary shall manage wild free-roaming horses and burros in a
manner that is designed to achieve and maintain a thriving natural ecological balance on the public lands. He shall consider the recommendations of qualified scientists in the field of biology and ecology, some of
whom shall be independent of both Federal and State agencies and
may include members of the Advisory Board established in section 7
of this Act. All management activities shall be at the minimal feasible level and shall be carried out in consultation with the wildlife
agency of the State wherein such lands are located in order to protect
the natural ecological balance of all wildlife species which inhabit
such lands, particularly endangered wildlife species. Any adjustments
in forage allocations on any such lands shall take into consideration
the needs of other wildlife species which inhabit such lands.

Jurisdiction;
management.

Pub. Law 92-195   - 2 -   December 15, 1971

85 STAT. 650

Destruction
or removal,
authority.

(b) Where an area is found to be overpopulated, the Secretary, after consulting with the Advisory Board, may order old, sick, or lame animals to be destroyed in the most humane manner possible, and he may cause additional excess wild free-roaming horses and burros to be captured and removed for private maintenance under humane conditions and care.

(c) The Secretary may order wild free-roaming horses or burros to be destroyed in the most humane manner possible when he deems such action to be an act of mercy or when in his judgment such action is necessary to preserve and maintain the habitat in a suitable condition for continued use. No wild free-roaming horse or burro shall be ordered to be destroyed because of overpopulation unless in the judgment of the Secretary such action is the only practical way to remove excess animals from the area.

(d) Nothing in this Act shall preclude the customary disposal of the remains of a deceased wild free-roaming horse or burro, including those in the authorized possession of private parties, but in no event shall such remains, or any part thereof, be sold for any consideration, directly or indirectly.

Private
maintenance.

SEC. 4. If wild free-roaming horses or burros stray from public lands onto privately owned land, the owners of such land may inform the nearest Federal marshall or agent of the Secretary, who shall arrange to have the animals removed. In no event shall such wild free-roaming horses and burros be destroyed except by the agents of the Secretary. Nothing in this section shall be construed to prohibit a private landowner from maintaining wild free-roaming horses or burros on his private lands, or lands leased from the Government, if he does so in a manner that protects them from harassment, and if the animals were not willfully removed or enticed from the public lands. Any individuals who maintain such wild free-roaming horses or burros on their private lands or lands leased from the Government shall notify the appropriate agent of the Secretary and supply him with a reasonable approximation of the number of animals so maintained.

Recovery
rights.

SEC. 5. A person claiming ownership of a horse or burro on the public lands shall be entitled to recover it only if recovery is permissible under the branding and estray laws of the State in which the animal is found.

Agreements
and regula-
tions.

SEC. 6. The Secretary is authorized to enter into cooperative agreements with other landowners and with the State and local governmental agencies and may issue such regulations as he deems necessary for the furtherance of the purposes of this Act.

Joint advisory
board.

SEC. 7. The Secretary of the Interior and the Secretary of Agriculture are authorized and directed to appoint a joint advisory board of not more than nine members to advise them on any matter relating to wild free-roaming horses and burros and their management and protection. They shall select as advisers persons who are not employees of the Federal or State Governments and whom they deem to have special knowledge about protection of horses and burros, management of wildlife, animal husbandry, or natural resources management. Members of the board shall not receive reimbursement except for travel and other expenditures necessary in connection with their services.

Penalty.

SEC. 8. Any person who—

(1) willfully removes or attempts to remove a wild free-roaming horse or burro from the public lands, without authority from the Secretary, or

(2) converts a wild free-roaming horse or burro to private use, without authority from the Secretary, or

(3) maliciously causes the death or harassment of any wild free-roaming horse or burro, or

December 15, 1971   - 3 -   Pub. Law 92-195

(4) processes or permits to be processed into commercial products the remains of a wild free-roaming horse or burro, or

(5) sells, directly or indirectly, a wild free-roaming horse or burro maintained on private or leased land pursuant to section 4 of this Act, or the remains thereof, or

(6) willfully violates a regulation issued pursuant to this Act, shall be subject to a fine of not more than $2,000, or imprisonment for not more than one year, or both. Any person so charged with such violation by the Secretary may be tried and sentenced by any United States commissioner or magistrate designated for that purpose by the court by which he was appointed, in the same manner and subject to the same conditions as provided for in section 3401, title 18, United States Code.

(b) Any employee designated by the Secretary of the Interior or the Secretary of Agriculture shall have power, without warrant, to arrest any person committing in the presence of such employee a violation of this Act or any regulation made pursuant thereto, and to take such person immediately for examination or trial before an officer or court of competent jurisdiction, and shall have power to execute any warrant or other process issued by an officer or court of competent jurisdiction to enforce the provisions of this Act or regulations made pursuant thereto. Any judge of a court established under the laws of the United States, or any United States magistrate may, within his respective jurisdiction, upon proper oath or affirmation showing probable cause, issue warrants in all such cases. *Power of arrest.*

Sec. 9. Nothing in this Act shall be construed to authorize the Secretary to relocate wild free-roaming horses or burros to areas of the public lands where they do not presently exist. *Limitation.*

Sec. 10. After the expiration of thirty calendar months following the date of enactment of this Act, and every twenty-four calendar months thereafter, the Secretaries of the Interior and Agriculture will submit to Congress a joint report on the administration of this Act, including a summary of enforcement and/or other actions taken thereunder, costs, and such recommendations for legislative or other actions as he might deem appropriate. *Report to Congress.*

The Secretary of the Interior and the Secretary of Agriculture shall consult with respect to the implementation and enforcement of this Act and to the maximum feasible extent coordinate the activities of their respective departments and in the implementation and enforcement of this Act. The Secretaries are authorized and directed to undertake those studies of the habits of wild free-roaming horses and burros that they may deem necessary in order to carry out the provisions of this Act. *Studies.*

Approved December 15, 1971.

LEGISLATIVE HISTORY:

HOUSE REPORTS: No. 92-480 accompanying H.R. 9890 (Comm. on Interior and Insular Affairs) and No. 92-681 (Comm. of Conference).
SENATE REPORT No. 92-242 (Comm. on Interior and Insular Affairs).
CONGRESSIONAL RECORD, Vol. 117 (1971):
    June 29, considered and passed Senate.
    Oct. 4, considered and passed House, amended, in lieu of H.R. 9890.
    Dec. 2, House agreed to conference report.
    Dec. 3, Senate agreed to conference report.
WEEKLY COMPILATION OF PRESIDENTIAL DOCUMENTS, Vol. 7, No. 51:
    Dec. 17, Presidential statement.

APPENDIX B

The Wild Horse Annie Bill

Public Law 86-234
86th Congress, H. R. 2725
September 8, 1959

AN ACT

73 STAT. 470.

To amend chapter 3 of title 18, United States Code, so as to prohibit the use of aircraft or motor vehicles to hunt certain wild horses or burros on land belonging to the United States, and for other purposes.

Be it enacted by the Senate and House of Representatives of the United States of America in Congress assembled, That (a) chapter 3 of title 18, United States Code, is amended by adding at the end thereof the following new section:

"§ 47. Use of aircraft or motor vehicles to hunt certain wild horses or burros; pollution of watering holes

"(a) Whoever uses an aircraft or a motor vehicle to hunt, for the purpose of capturing or killing, any wild unbranded horse, mare, colt, or burro running at large on any of the public land or ranges shall be fined not more than $500, or imprisoned not more than six months, or both.

"(b) Whoever pollutes or causes the pollution of any watering hole on any of the public land or ranges for the purpose of trapping, killing, wounding, or maiming any of the animals referred to in subsection (a) of this section shall be fined not more than $500, or imprisoned not more than six months, or both.

"(c) As used in subsection (a) of this section—

"(1) The term 'aircraft' means any contrivance used for flight in the air; and

"(2) The term 'motor vehicle' includes an automobile, automobile truck, automobile wagon, motorcycle, or any other self-propelled vehicle designed for running on land."

(b) The analysis of such chapter 3, immediately preceding section 41, is amended by adding at the end thereof the following new item:

"47. Use of aircraft or motor vehicles to hunt certain wild horses or burros."

Approved September 8, 1959.

Horses and burros on public lands. Methods of hunting. 18 USC 41-46.

334

Bureau of Land Management
National Wild Horse and Burro Program

National Toll-Free Number: 800-417-9647

The following offices can provide you more information about the Wild Horse and Burro Adoption Program. Call, write, or e-mail the office serving your area. They are prepared to answer your questions and mail you applications, brochures, and other information.

ALASKA

Alaska State Office
222 West 7th Avenue #13
Anchorage, AK 99513-7599
907-271-5555

ARIZONA

Phoenix Field Office
2015 West Deer Valley Road
Phoenix, AZ 85027
602-580-5500

Kingman Resource Area
520-757-3161

CALIFORNIA

California State Office
2135 Butano Drive
Sacramento, CA 95825-1889
916-979-2800

Bakersfield District Office
805-391-6049

Ridgecrest Resource Area
619-446-6064

Eagle Lake Resource Area (Susanville)
530-257-5381

Clear Lake Resource Area (Ukiah)
707-468-4055

COLORADO

Canon City District Office
3170 East Main Street
Canon City, CO 81212
719-269-8500

IDAHO

Boise District Office
3948 Development Avenue
Boise, ID 83705-5389
208-384-3300

MONTANA, NORTH DAKOTA, AND SOUTH DAKOTA

Billings Resource Area
810 East Main Street
Billings, MT 59105-3395
406-238-1540

NEVADA

National WHB Center
at Palomino Valley
P.O. Box 3270
Sparks, NV 89432
702-475-2222

NEW MEXICO, KANSAS,
OKLAHOMA, AND TEXAS

Oklahoma Resource Area
221 North Service Road
Moore, OK 73160-4946
800-237-3642

OREGON AND WASHINGTON

Burns District Office
HC 74-12533 Highway 20 West
Hines, OR 97738
541-573-4400

UTAH

Salt Lake City District Office
2370 South 2300 West
Salt Lake City, UT 84119
801-977-4300

WYOMING AND NEBRASKA

Rock Springs District Office
280 Highway 191 North
Rock Springs, WY 82901
307-382-5350

Elm Creek Facility
P.O. Box 160
Elm Creek, Nebraska 68836
308-856-4498

ALABAMA, ARKANSAS, FLORID
GEORGIA, KENTUCKY,
LOUISIANA, MISSISSIPPI, NORTH
CAROLINA, SOUTH CAROLINA,
TENNESSEE, AND VIRGINIA

Jackson District Office
411 Briarwood Drive, Suite 404
Jackson, MS 39206
601-977-5430

Cross Plains, Tennessee
800-376-6009

CONNECTICUT, DELAWARE,
DISTRICT OF COLUMBIA,
ILLINOIS, INDIANA, IOWA, MAIN
MARYLAND, MASSACHUSETTS,
MICHIGAN, MINNESOTA,
MISSOURI, NEW HAMPSHIRE,
NEW JERSEY, NEW YORK, OHIO,
PENNSYLVANIA, RHODE ISLAND
VERMONT, WEST VIRGINIA,
AND WISCONSIN

Milwaukee District Office
310 West Wisconsin Avenue
Suite 450
Milwaukee, WI 53203
800-293-1781

Index

List of Photographs